Triumphant Return

The Coming Kingdom of God

Dr. Grant R. Jeffrey

Frontier Research Publications, Inc.

Triumphant Return

ISBN 0-7394-2272-3

Unless otherwise indicated, Scripture quotations are from the Authorized King James Version.

Cover design: The Riordon Design Group
Printed in Canada: Harmony Printing Limited

Table of Contents

Acknowledgments

Triumphant Return – The Coming Kingdom of God is an exploration of the tremendous prophecies about the Second Coming of Jesus Christ that form a large portion of the Scriptures. This book also explores how these prophecies were first understood by the early Christians who lived closest to the time of Christ and His apostles.

This book is the result of over thirty-eight years of research involving literally thousands of books, Bible commentaries, and the detailed study of the Scriptures. As this book demonstrates, our faith and hope for the future is grounded upon a strong conviction in the promise of Jesus Christ: "And when these things begin to come to pass, then look up, and lift up your heads; for your redemption draweth nigh" (Luke 21:28).

My parents, Lyle and Florence Jeffrey, have inspired me through their lifelong commitment to the prophecies of His Second Coming and a profound love for Jesus Christ and the prophetic truth of the Scriptures. Special thanks to my editorial assistant, Adrienne Jeffrey Tigchelaar, whose excellent editorial services have provided invaluable assistance.

I dedicate *Triumphant Return* to my loving wife Kaye. She continues to inspire my research and writing as well as being my faithful partner in the ministry of Frontier Research Publications,

Inc. Without her encouragement and constant assistance this book would never have been completed.

I trust that the research revealed in the following pages will inform, inspire, and encourage you to personally study the Bible's prophecies about the triumphant return of Jesus Christ to set up His eternal kingdom. A proper appreciation of the prophecies about the coming Kingdom of God will transform your understanding of the age in which we live as well as the extraordinary events which will soon usher in the triumphant return of Christ as the King of Kings and Lord of Lords.

Dr. Grant R. Jeffrey
Toronto, Ontario
July, 2001

Introduction

Will Jesus Christ literally return to earth in the last days? Will Christ defeat evil and set up His kingdom? Does the Bible prophesy that Jesus will establish a thousand-year millennial kingdom? After waiting for almost two thousand years, why should we believe that our generation may live to see the fulfillment of these prophecies? How should we answer critics who claim that these prophecies were actually fulfilled almost two thousand years ago when Jerusalem was destroyed in A.D. 70? What did the early Church believe about the Second Coming, the Millennium, and the Antichrist? The ultimate question to be answered is this: What does the Bible teach about the time of Christ's Second Coming? Will He return before the Millennium to defeat Satan and establish the Kingdom of God as premillennialists believe? Or will the Church gradually create the Kingdom of God on earth in preparation for Christ's Second Coming a thousand years from now? The question about when and how Christ will return is vital to everyone who longs for the day when the Lord shall victoriously appear to usher in the righteous kingdom of God.

The answers to these important questions are revealed in the fascinating research presented in this book. *Triumphant Return* provides compelling proof that the Scriptures clearly teach that Jesus will return at the end of this age to set up His dominon on earth. Remarkable evidence reveals that the early Christians who lived closest to the apostles longed for His imminent return and almost universally believed in the millennial kingdom. Finally, this book will explore the astonishing prophecies being fulfilled in our generation that point to the nearness of Christ's return.

A vital struggle is now taking place regarding the Bible's teaching about the Second Coming and the establishment of the kingdom of God. This battle is now being waged in seminaries, pulpits, Christian bookstores, and within the hearts and minds of millions of faithful Christians. The questions about the Second Coming and the kingdom have tremendous implications for all those who love Jesus Christ and who long for the prophesied dominion of God. Over a long period the Catholic, Orthodox, and the mainline Protestant denominations have gradually de-emphasized their teaching and belief in the literal return of Christ. In contrast, the Evangelical, Pentecostal, and Charismatic churches created during the last two centuries have strongly affirmed the biblical truth of the return of Christ and the Millennium. This fundamental core belief in Christ's triumphant return motivated hundreds of millions of believers in these churches to walk in personal holiness as well as launch the greatest wave of evangelism and missions the world has ever known.

However, a powerful new attack upon this fundamental biblical doctrine of Christ's coming Kingdom is beginning to influence the minds and spirits of many Christians in our day precisely as the New Testament warns us. The apostle Peter prophesied that in the last days critics would arise within the Church denying the truth of the premillennial Second Coming. Peter warned that many critics would say, "Where is the promise of His coming? For since the fathers fell asleep, all things continue as they were from the beginning of the creation" (2 Peter 3:4). Those who believe that the prophecies of the Word of God should be understood literally are now engaged in an unprecedented battle for the defense of the truth about Christ's Second Coming. This doctrine of the Second Advent is critical to the effectiveness of our evangelism, as well as to our daily walk in the faith. Jude, the brother of Jesus, wrote, "It was needful for me to write unto you, and exhort you that ye should earnestly contend for the faith which was once delivered unto the saints" (Jude 3).

Does it really matter whether Christ will return before or after the Millennium? This book will demonstrate that the answer to this question is YES. It is vitally important to both individual believers as well as to the Church to clearly understand the truth about our Lord's premillennial return and His coming dominon.

Evangelical and Pentecostal Christianity stands today at a critical crossroads concerning one of the most vital doctrines of our faith—the belief in the literal Second Coming and the establishment of His coming kingdom. The Second Coming of the Lord is taught throughout the Word of God from Genesis to Revelation. The apostolic Church powerfully affirmed this important doctrine during the first few centuries following the birth of the Church.

Whether or not most Christians are aware of this present doctrinal conflict, a powerful attack has been launched against the orthodox Christian belief in the literal Second Coming as well as the future millennial kingdom of God. This book provides compelling evidence in defense of the biblical doctrine concerning Christ's triumphant appearance as "the King of kings and Lord of lords." The prophecies clearly teach that Jesus will return from heaven to announce His glorious kingdom when He will redeem humanity and this world forever. *Triumphant Return* will demonstrate the overwhelming evidence the early Church almost universally taught this doctrine during the first three centuries following His resurrection.

The apostolic Church was clearly premillennial in its hope; Christians during the first few centuries waited expectantly for the imminent return of their Messiah. Despite the claim by critics that modern prophetic beliefs were not taught by the early Church, my research confirms that the great teachers in the early Church taught the premillennial and literal return of Christ. To my knowledge, this historical evidence has seldom, if ever, been presented in a popular format to the Church in our generation.

It is obvious that those Christians who lived and taught nearest to the time of the apostles would naturally possess an accurate memory and understanding of the true teachings of Jesus and the apostolic Church regarding the end times. Many readers will be surprised and thrilled to see the overwhelming evidence that those who lived in the generation immediately following the life of Jesus and His apostles held the same prophetic beliefs that are taught today by many Evangelical students of prophecy.

During the early centuries, faithful Christians throughout the Roman Empire often greeted each other with the ancient Greek phrase "Maranatha!" ("The Lord cometh!"). Their deeply held faith in the literal and imminent return of the Lord to set up His dominon was a foundational Christian belief. It remains an important doctrine that has tremendous implications for our daily walk, our witnessing to a lost world, and our optimistic hope for the future. Jesus Christ commanded His disciples to be watchful and ready for the moment when He would triumphantly return, regardless of how long He might tarry. Despite the many centuries that have passed since He first gave the Church His promise, the prophecy of Christ's return remains absolutely certain and unshakable.

Throughout history, millions of Christians have longed for the blessed hope. This deeply held belief transformed their worship and their daily walk with God. Their convictions motivated them to risk death as martyrs for their coming King rather than deny their faith in His deity and His coming reign.

It is almost impossible to correctly understand the Lord's plan to redeem the earth and humanity from the curse of sin unless we study the biblical doctrine of the Second Coming. Our understanding of this critical doctrine will deepen our faith in the inspiration of the Scriptures and God's unfolding purpose as revealed in both the prophecies as well as in the life and ministry of Christ. The promised rule of Christ is the focus of the various covenants that God has made with humanity. The German theologian, Dr. Christian Kling, emphasized the centrality of the kingdom of God to the Lord's plan of redemption: "The idea of the kingdom of God is the central idea of the entire dispensation of revelation; the kingdom of God is the end and motive of all heavenly revelation and institutions of the old and new covenants; yea, of the creation and promise from the beginning. The general foundation of this idea is the all-inclusive power and dominion of God."[1]

A careful analysis of the entire Bible shows that numerous prophecies concerning the kingdom of God reveal that this is the most prominent doctrine taught in the Word of God. A number of respected biblical scholars, including Dr. Pye Smith and Johann Peter Lange, have calculated that there are more scriptural passages that teach about "the kingdom of God" than all other separate doctrines combined. This discovery provides powerful evidence of the importance of the coming kingdom to the plan of God. Johann Peter Lange (1802–1884) acknowledged the fundamental importance of Christ's coming millennial kingdom in his *Commentary* on the Scriptures: "The kingdom of heaven must form the central point of all theological learning."[2]

The preaching of John the Baptist, Jesus of Nazareth, as well as His disciples and apostles, often dealt with the coming dominion of God. This topic also formed a major part of the teachings of the early Church during the first few centuries of the Christian era. The disciples continually questioned Jesus about the meaning of His parables regarding the coming kingdom. They wanted to know when "the kingdom of God" would appear on earth and what their future role would be in it. Significantly, the New Testament affirms that the message of Jesus is "the gospel of the kingdom." Matthew wrote that Jesus began His ministry teaching about "the gospel of the kingdom": "And Jesus went about all Galilee, teaching in their synagogues, and preaching the gospel of the kingdom, and healing all manner of sickness and all manner of disease among the people" (Matthew 4:23). Jesus foretold that this kingdom doctrine will be preached by the tribulation witnesses to an unbelieving world during the Great Tribulation, just before the return of the Messiah. "And this gospel of the kingdom shall be preached in all the world for a witness unto all nations; and then shall the end come" (Matthew 24:14).

The life, ministry, trial, and death of Jesus Christ are deeply connected to His promised millennial kingdom. Jesus declared that He is the promised King and that He will return to set up His prophesied dominion. Jesus taught His followers to pray the Lord's Prayer, which specifically focuses on the coming kingdom of God: "Our Father which art in heaven, Hallowed be thy name. *Thy kingdom come. Thy will be done in earth, as it is in heaven. . . . For thine is the kingdom, and the power, and the glory, for ever. Amen"* (Matthew 6:9–13). The prophecy of our eternal home in the heavenly New Jerusalem is the glorious promise of God to all those who place their faith and trust in Him. However, Jesus also prophesied that the Christian saints will rule and reign with Him on earth forever as priests and kings. The coming kingdom on God will someday encompass the entire universe including the redeemed earth, the New Jerusalem, and heaven itself.

These facts should encourage Christians to carefully and prudently examine those prophecies concerning the Second Coming that clearly relate to our generation and to the role that Christ has assigned us in His future government. The Lord commanded His disciples to watch diligently for the fulfillment of those specific prophetic signs that would indicate His soon coming. The Lord declared, "And when these things begin to come to pass, then look up, and lift up your heads; for your redemption draweth nigh" (Luke 21:28). The prophetic message about the Lord's return is not a pessimistic message of "doom and gloom" to those who love Him. Rather, Christ's message is a prophecy of hope and redemption for all those who place their faith and trust in Him and look for His approaching divine rule of peace and righteousness. The return of Christ will usher in the long-awaited kingdom of God where humanity will finally experience the peace, justice, prosperity, and joy that we have always longed for.

Notes

1. Christian F. Kling, "Kingdom of God," *Herzog's Religious Encyclopedia*, 1891.
2. Johann Peter Lange, *Commentary*, 1:254.

1

Importance of the Second Coming and the Kingdom of God

When any vital doctrine of the Word of God has been neglected in discussion and in preaching from the pulpit or has suffered serious and sustained attack by its critics, it is the profound responsibility of those Christians who uphold such a biblical doctrine to reaffirm this truth as strongly as possible. In addition, those who affirm a fundamental doctrine should do all within their power and gifts to motivate the Church to return to the faith "once delivered to the saints."

One of the greatest of the foundational doctrines of Christianity—the prophecy about the literal Second Coming of Christ to establish His kingdom—has unfortunately been neglected by many within the body of believers in our generation. However, the prophecy about Christ's return is presented throughout the Word of God. The *Parousia*, "the coming of the Lord," is taught as a personal, literal, and imminent event that the Church should hope for every day. Furthermore, the New Testament teaches us that Christ's promise of His Second Coming is a powerful motive to put on the "whole armor of God," to excel in victorious holiness, and to be watchful for His soon return. The triumphant return is constantly presented in the Scriptures as the basis of our spiritual confidence despite the evil we confront in our present world. Specifically, the New Testament teaches that Christ's return will end the reign of unrestrained evil, defeat Satan by casting him into the bottomless pit, and then establish Christ's kingdom. The truth of the parousia is so prominent and central to the teaching of the early Church that the open repudiation of the parousia in the last days was prophesied as one of the last great signs of the end times' apostasy pointing to the imminent return of Christ.

Tragically, there is a tremendous spiritual apostasy in our generation that is marked by a turning away from the clear teaching of the New Testament and early Church's beliefs regarding the literal Second Coming. Many in the western Church have succumbed to the false teaching that Christ's Second Coming refers to the gradual spread of Christianity throughout the nations of the earth. The truth is that many believers are quite content and satisfied with their position in our present world. Consequently, they possess no discernible desire to see the dramatic return of Jesus Christ from heaven to establish His messianic dominion here. The Word of God presents Jesus Christ as the Bridegroom of His bride, His beloved Church, composed of the living and departed saints throughout the ages from the Day of Pentecost until the future Rapture resurrection. The strongest reason why many in the western Church are now acting as an unfaithful "bride" in their spiritual accommodations to both materialism and the pagan New Age spiritual teachings is because many of their leaders have abandoned any serious expectation of their Bridegroom, Jesus Christ, quickly returning in our generation.

This "falling away" from the historic and prophetic "faith of our fathers" regarding the promised return of Christ naturally causes great concern among all those believers who still hold to the orthodox and apostolic teaching of the New Testament. However, those who believe the Scriptures and the words of the prophets also recognize that this situation of apostasy is precisely what the Bible warned would occur in the final days leading up to Christ's dramatic return from heaven. More important, at the same time we are witnessing an astonishing revival of the biblical doctrine of the soon return of Christ within Christians in many other nations. This book will demonstrate the scriptural truth of this vital teaching of our Lord and will document that the Second Advent is a doctrine that awakens the true Church to her important role in the events of the last days, leading to the establishment of the kingdom of God that will transform this planet and its inhabitants forever.

In the late 1880s, the well-known anti-millennial critic J. Stuart Russell, who rejected the literal return of Christ, acknowledged in the Preface to his book *Parousia* that the medieval and modern Church have lost sight of the critical importance of the vital doctrine of the Second Coming of Christ that had motivated the early Church to turn their world upside down.

> No attentive reader of the New Testament can fail to be struck with the prominence given by the evangelists and apostles to the Parousia, or "Coming of the Lord." That event is the great theme of New Testament Prophecy. There is scarcely a single book, from the Gospel of St. Matthew to the Apocalypse of St. John, in which it is not set forth as the glorious promise of God, and the Blessed Hope of the Church. It was frequently and solemnly predicted by our Lord; it was incessantly kept before the eyes of the early Christians by the Apostles; and it was firmly believed and eagerly expected by the churches of the primitive age. It can not be denied that there is a remarkable difference between the attitude of the first Christians, in relation to the Parousia, and that of Christians now. That glorious hope, to which all eyes and hearts in the apostolic age were eagerly turned, has almost disappeared from the view of modern believers.

Whatever may be the theoretical opinions, expressed in symbols and creeds, it must, in candor, be admitted that the "Second Coming of Christ" has all but ceased to be a living and practical belief.[1]

Those who reject the literal Second Coming of Christ to establish His future kingdom suggest that all of the numerous scriptural passages that refer directly to this event should be interpreted in an allegorical or spiritual manner that robs these passages of any literal reality. However, the clear and consistent teaching of the Bible reveals that the world will be in a desperate spiritual crisis under the wicked rule of the Antichrist during the last days when Jesus Christ will return to earth to defeat Satan's opposition and establish His own righteous rule.

Some writers, who call themselves preterists (meaning "past"), believe that the prophecies of Matthew 24 and the book of Revelation concerning the Second Coming and Christ's kingdom were actually fulfilled spiritually in A.D. 70 when the Romans destroyed Jerusalem and the Jewish Temple. This preterist interpretation obviously depends on treating the specific prophecies as mere allegories or symbols without any literal meaning. We shall prove in a later chapter that the doctrine of preterism is false, as demonstrated by both Scripture and early Church history.

While the preterists and numerous postmillennial and amillennial scholars deny the truth about the literal return of Christ, they suggest that the Christian Church will progressively defeat the forces of evil in our world and will triumph over Satan to establish the kingdom of God for a thousand years before Christ will return. However, the Scriptures clearly teach that the world's population will never be totally converted to Christianity through the efforts of the Church before the time of the end. Despite the best efforts of ministers, missions, evangelists, Christian media, and the hundreds of thousands of faithful churches, the Scriptures teach that the spiritual "wheat and tares" (believers and unrepentant sinners) will grow together until the arrival of the final harvest. In other words, we should not be surprised that we are witnessing unprecedented growth of the body of Christ even as evil abounds more and more in these days leading to Christ's return. Jesus prophesied, "And this gospel of the kingdom shall be preached in all the world for a witness unto all nations; and then shall the end come" (Matthew 24:14). Christ also said, "Let both grow together until the harvest: and in the time of harvest I will say to the reapers, Gather ye together first the tares, and bind them in bundles to burn them: but gather the wheat into my barn" (Matthew 13:30).

Unfortunately, millions in the Church have neglected the literal sense of the Old and New Testament prophecies during the last century due to the erroneous interpretive system of spiritualizing and allegorizing the language of the Scriptures. Tragically, this rejection of the literal Second Coming has caused millions of Christians in numerous denominations to miss the meaning of the coming kingdom of God.

Some writers have mistakenly taught that the return of Christ occurs to each believer at their moment of death. However, the clear and repeated statements of the Scriptures repudiate any such interpretation. For example, Jesus spoke to the apostles Peter and John and prophesied that Peter would die as a martyr to the faith. Then Christ made a clear distinction between death and His Second Coming in His statement to Peter about John: "Jesus saith unto him, If I will that he tarry till I come, what is that to thee? follow thou me" (John 21:22). It is obvious from this passage that death and Christ's coming are two different events. Furthermore, death is described repeatedly in the Bible as our enemy. "The last enemy that shall be destroyed is death" (1 Corinthians 15:26). In contrast, the Second Advent is based on the triumphant victory of Christ over sin and death that will be demonstrated by His resurrection of all of the saints who lived and died in faith. It is significant that Christ continually admonishes us to be watchful and ready for His imminent return but He never commanded believers to watch for or prepare for death.

The Lord's great purpose in this present Church "Age of Grace" is to gather out of the earth's population a remnant group of the "elect" who will repent and turn to God to ask forgiveness for their sins. God's purpose in this age was never stated to be the total conversion to Christ of the entire population of humanity. The Scriptures reveal that the gospel will be preached "for a witness unto all nations; and then shall the end come" (Matthew 24:14). You can search the Scriptures from Genesis to Revelation and you will not find any support for the theory that God will save all of humanity. To do so would require God to override the sovereign free will of all humans and force them to accept His salvation as if they were spiritual robots. However, the Bible affirms that God created each of us to be free to either obey Him by asking for His forgiveness for our sinful rebellion or to freely reject His offer of salvation. The Age of Grace is manifestly the time of spiritual election, but it is not the time of universal conversion. Luke wrote about God's purpose, "Simeon hath declared how God at the first did visit the Gentiles, to take out of them a people for his name" (Acts 15:14).

The Second Advent is the most important doctrine in the Bible after the resurrection of Jesus Christ. Both of these doctrines are based on events that occur historically on a single day. However, both events are profoundly transformational in their impact on humanity. Both the resurrection and the Second Coming of Christ to set up His kingdom, will transform all of human history forever after. It is obvious to Christians that the resurrection of Jesus broke forever the chains of death and fear for all those who place their faith and trust in Christ's power to resurrect all those who trust in Him.

The return of Christ will close the Church Age of Grace, and usher in the eternal kingdom of God. For two thousand years, faithful Christians have obediently prayed the Lord's Prayer, which expresses our longing and prayer for the coming kingdom of God. The Lord's Prayer exhortation "thy kingdom come" and the expression at the end of Revelation, "come, Lord Jesus," should be the daily prayer of all true believers in Christ. As faithful believers, we look back in time to the sacrificial death of Jesus Christ on the Cross. To be faithful to the Word of God, we also should obediently look forward hopefully to Christ's return. Jesus promised, "And if I go and prepare a place for you,

I will come again, and receive you unto myself; that where I am, there ye may be also" (John 14:3).

The apostle Paul promised Christians that Christ would return with a special reward for all faithful disciples who longed for His return, "Henceforth there is laid up for me a crown of righteousness, which the Lord, the righteous judge, shall give me at that day: and not to me only, but unto all them also that love his appearing" (2 Timothy 4:8). The apostle Peter encouraged believers to be "looking for and hasting unto the coming of the day of God, wherein the heavens being on fire shall be dissolved, and the elements shall melt with fervent heat" (2 Peter 3:12).

Jesus Christ's return will be both literal and personal; He will appear in the same literal manner as He departed when He physically ascended into the clouds of heaven in the sight of His disciples: "Ye men of Galilee, why stand ye gazing up into heaven? This same Jesus, which is taken up from you into heaven, shall so come in like manner as ye have seen him go into heaven" (Acts 1:11). The truth of the literal return of Christ in the sight of men is affirmed also in the Apocalypse: "Behold, he cometh with clouds; and every eye shall see him, and they also which pierced him: and all kindreds of the earth shall wail because of him. Even so, Amen" (Revelation 1:7).

When Jesus Christ returns, the earth shall be renewed and the curse of sin will be removed, Satan shall be bound in chains in the lake of fire for one thousand years, God will reward the righteous saints, and the wicked unrepentant souls will be punished. The establishment of the millennial kingdom of Christ will immediately follow the Second Coming. After He returns the prophet wrote, "the earth shall be filled with the knowledge of the glory of the Lord, as the waters cover the sea" (Habakkuk 2:14).

Note

1. J. Stuart Russell, *The Parousia* (T. Fisher Unwin, 1887) v–vi.

2

How Should We Understand Prophecy?

The study of prophecy is known as eschatology, the study of last things. This is not simply another branch of theology that is an optional area of study for a mature Christian. The prophecy scholar, J. Barton Payne, calculated that 8,352 verses out of a total of 31,124 (27 percent) verses in the Bible contain prophetic themes.[1] The fact that one quarter of the whole Bible is prophetic indicates the level of importance that God places on this subject. This provides a powerful and compelling indication of the importance of prophecy in teaching and understanding the "whole counsel of God."

The prophecies reveal God's sovereign plan for the redemption of Israel, the Gentiles, and His Church. The message of the prophets encompass two major themes: God's approaching final judgment of unrepentant sinners, and His promise of Christ's Second Coming to establish the kingdom of God, the ultimate triumph of God's purpose for humanity. The past, the present, and the future are entwined together in the inspired message of the prophet. The Scriptures reveal that God is guiding humanity toward the culmination of history at that future Battle of Armageddon when the kingdoms of this world will truly become the kingdom of Christ, the "King of Kings and Lord of Lords."

Prophetic Interpretation

The principles we use to interpret the prophetic portions of Scripture are obviously linked to the principles we use to interpret the rest of the Bible. Several fundamental principles of interpretation, which have been proven sound through centuries of biblical studies as well as during my own thirty-five years of Bible study and teaching, are reflected in this book. The critical principles of interpretation of prophecy that have guided this study are:

(1) We should interpret the language of Scripture, including the prophetic portions, in its ordinary, usual, and natural grammatical meaning, unless the context of the particular prophecy makes it obvious that the statement is purely symbolic.

(2) The symbols found in the prophecies are almost always interpreted by other scriptural passages.

(3) The inspired message of the prophet was intended to be understood by those readers living in the time of the prophet as well as by the generations of believers that would follow. The purpose of prophecy is not simply to provide factual information about the future, but rather to challenge the spiritual behavior and choices of everyone who reads the prophecy in every generation.

(4) God will never abandon His eternal covenant with Israel. Jesus Christ promised He would return at the appointed time to defeat the Antichrist, save Israel from destruction, and usher in the long-awaited messianic kingdom of God.

During the last two thousand years, many in the Christian Church, beginning in the fourth century, have dismissed Israel's role as a vital part of the plan of God to redeem humanity. Many forgot the eternal covenant that God made to Israel's ancient patriarchs. They believe that God has rejected and abandoned

Israel forever because most of the Jews rejected Jesus Christ as their promised Messiah. However, the apostle Paul warned the Church against this terrible spiritual error: "For I would not, brethren, that ye should be ignorant of this mystery, lest ye should be wise in your own conceits; that blindness in part is happened to Israel, until the fullness of the Gentiles be come in. And so all Israel shall be saved: as it is written, There shall come out of Sion the Deliverer, and shall turn away ungodliness from Jacob" (Romans 11:25–26). God will still fulfill all of His promises, including that He will "give thee for a covenant of the people, for a light of the Gentiles" (Isaiah 42:6) during the coming Tribulation. Tragically, many in the Church during the last two thousand years as well as many today have falsely assumed that God rejected Israel as His Chosen People and that He has substituted the Church as a replacement for Israel in His plan of redemption. However, the apostle Paul declared that Israel's spiritual blindness was only "in part" and that it would last only "until the fulness of the Gentiles be come in." After this, "all Israel shall be saved" when Jesus Christ returns in glory and power to set up His kingdom.

Why Prophecy Is Vital Today

There are four major reasons why prophecy is vital to Christians in this generation:

(1) The evidence of the fulfillment of past prophecies authenticates the Bible as the supernaturally inspired Word of God.

(2) The message of the prophets calls the Church to live in purity and holiness in the midst of an unholy generation awaiting Christ's soon return.

(3) The prophetic message of the imminent return of Jesus Christ should motivate Christians to witness with enthusiasm to those around us who do not yet know Him as their Lord and Savior.

(4) The message of prophecy is unquestionably one of the most effective tools for evangelism we have to reach those who have not yet accepted faith in Christ. Many nonreligious people are quite fascinated by prophecy and will consider

the salvation claims of the Gospel for the first time once they are convinced that the Bible is the supernaturally inspired word of God.

The Lord declares repeatedly that He is the only one who can accurately prophesy future events in detail and bring them to pass, regardless of the plans of humanity. Isaiah wrote, "Remember the former things of old: for I am God, and there is none else; I am God, and there is none like me, declaring the end from the beginning, and from ancient times things that are not yet done, saying, My counsel shall stand, and I will do all my pleasure" (Isaiah 46:9–10). In other words, the Lord declares that He alone correctly predicts the nature of future events and will bring them to pass as evidence of His sovereign control of the universe.

The Reasons We Should Study Prophecy Seriously

While it is certainly true that many of the details in the unfolding plan of God will never be fully understood until they come to pass, four factors encourage us to carefully examine those prophecies in detail that point to the events leading to Christ's return to establish His dominion.

First, we must consider the importance that God places on His prophecies. It is certainly significant that over one quarter of the Bible is prophetic. Furthermore, the Lord directs us as His disciples to study the prophecies. The apostle Peter declared, "We have also a more sure word of prophecy; whereunto ye do well that ye take heed, as unto a light that shineth in a dark place, until the day dawn, and the day star arise in your hearts" (2 Peter 1:19).

Second, the literal fulfillment of all past prophecies leads us to the conclusion that the prophecies that describe future events will also be fulfilled in a similar literal manner. The Lord assures us that He will continue to fulfill His ancient prophecies in the same manner as He did in past centuries. The Lord Himself declares, "For I am the Lord, I change not" (Malichi 3:6).

Third, Jesus Christ severely criticized the Jewish religious leaders for failing to pay serious attention to the messianic prophecies being fulfilled in their lifetime, and failing to "discern the signs of the times" (Matthew 16:3).

Fourth, the apostle Paul specifically reminds Christians that while it is true that "the Day of the Lord so cometh as a thief in the night" to unbelievers, he immediately declares: "But ye, brethren, are not in darkness, that that day should overtake you as a thief. Ye are all the children of light, and the children of the day: we are not of the night, nor of darkness. Therefore let us not sleep, as do others: but let us watch and be sober" (1 Thessalonians 5:4–6). Paul commands us to consider the prophetic signs and to watch for "that day" that will usher in the kingdom of God. In other words, the Lord has revealed that Christians are to watch for the fulfillment of the prophetic signs of His soon return and that we should govern our lives and priorities accordingly.

How Should We Interpret the Prophecies?

How should we interpret the thousands of prophecies found in the Word of God? Since over one quarter of the verses found in the Bible deal with prophecy, it is vital that we properly understand God's prophetic message to His Church. There are two basic interpretative methods that students of the Word have applied in their attempt to understand the Bible's prophecies during the last two thousand years—the literal method and the allegorical method.

The Literal or Normal Method

The first method of interpretation is the literal or normal language method. This approach assumes that the biblical writer wrote his prophecy with the expectation that he would be understood in a natural manner exactly as in any other portion of his writing. In other words, the literal approach assumes that the reader would interpret the language of the prophet in the same manner that they would apply when reading any newspaper account or a nonfiction book. The literal method naturally acknowledges that prophetic language often contains figures of speech and prophetic symbols. However, these prophetic symbols always point toward something that is itself literal. This natural method avoids subjective interpretation and wild speculation.

It is important to note that Jesus Christ and the apostles who wrote the New Testament always interpreted the prophecies of the Old Testament prophets in this literal and normal manner. For example, Matthew recorded that the soldiers gambled for Christ's garments and pointed out that this was predicted literally, quoting the original prophecy as given in Psalm 22:18, "They part my garments among them, and cast lots upon my vesture."

A comprehensive analysis of hundreds of fulfilled Old and New Testament prophecies reveals that all of these were fulfilled in a literal and precise manner. For example, there are forty-eight distinct and separate messianic predictions found in the pages of the Old Testament, written centuries before Jesus was born, that reveal precise details about the life, death, and resurrection of Christ. None of these four dozen predictions were fulfilled in an allegorical or "spiritual" manner. As we examine the literal method in which every one of these prophecies were fulfilled, we have confidence that the prophecies that remain to be fulfilled in the last days will be fulfilled in exactly the same literal manner. In the second century of the early Church, the respected Christian writer, Justin Martyr, wrote about the certainty of prophetic fulfillment:

> Since, then, we prove that all things which have already happened had been predicted by the prophets before they came to pass, as we must necessarily believe also that those things which are in like manner predicted, but are yet to come to pass, shall certainly happen. For as the things which have already taken place came to pass when foretold, and even though unknown, so shall the things that remain, even though they be unknown and disbelieved, yet come to pass. For the prophets have proclaimed two advents of His: the one which is already past, when He came as a dishonoured and suffering Man; but the second, when according to prophecy, He shall come from Heaven with glory.[2]

I have spent thousands of hours during the last thirty-eight years in detailed study of the prophecies of the Bible and their precise fulfillment. As a result of my analysis, I have concluded together with most of the prophecy teachers of the past two centuries that the Scripture's prophecies should be interpreted literally and in a natural manner. Significantly, the writers of the primitive Church during the first few centuries following the life of Christ also understood the prophecies about the pre-millennial return of Christ in the same literal manner. In a later chapter we will explore the fascinating prophetic beliefs of the apostolic Church.

Powerful evidence in favor of such a consistent literal interpretation is found in the following passage of the Scriptures. In Luke 1:31–33 we read the following prophecy of the angel Gabriel, "And, behold, thou shalt conceive in thy womb, and bring forth a son, and shalt call his name JESUS. He shall be great, and shall be called the Son of the Highest: and the Lord God shall give unto him the throne of his father David: And he shall reign over the house of Jacob for ever; and of his kingdom there shall be no end." Virtually all Christians accept the literal reality of the first verse of this great prophecy. The consistent principles of interpretation demand that we interpret the last two of the three verses of this prophecy in the same literal manner. Luke prophesied the literal truth about the birth of the promised Messiah. However, the prophetic words of Luke also declare with equal authority that "he shall reign over the house of Jacob for ever; and of his kingdom there shall be no end." It would be illogical and inconsistent to accept the literal reality of the first verse in this passage about Christ's first coming and then to reject the literal truth of the final verse that describes Jesus' Second Coming. Thus, we must conclude that the Scriptures teach that Jesus Christ will ultimately rule over "the house of Jacob" forever in His messianic kingdom.

There are two fundamental principles that should govern our approach to the interpretation of all Scripture and especially those prophecies related to the return of Jesus Christ. First, the authority and teaching of the Scriptures are the basis of all of our knowledge concerning the fact that Jesus Christ will return from heaven to set up His millennial rule. The overwhelming importance of the Second Coming to the writers of the Scriptures is demonstrated conclusively by the fact that up to one verse in every twenty-five verses in the New Testament (over three hundred verses in all) deal with the return of Christ. Second, the language used in the Bible provides our sole source of knowledge about the time and manner of Christ's prophesied return to set up His divine government. The method to determine the meaning of the text of the scriptural prophecies regarding Christ's return depends on the established laws of grammar and language. The vital issue of whether the language of the prophets should be interpreted literally or allegorically is examined in this chapter.

As the Protestant Reformers rediscovered the fundamental importance of a literal interpretation of the Holy Scriptures, they pursued their study of the major doctrines of the Bible. Eventually, they began to focus on the area of eschatology, the study of last things. Bishop Richard Hooker (1554–1600), a key writer during the Reformation, taught that if given a choice between a literal and an allegorical interpretation, the literal was closest and the allegorical the furthest from the biblical truth. Hooker wrote, "I hold for a most infallible rule in expositions of the Sacred Scriptures, that where a literal construction will stand, the furthest from the letter is commonly the worst. There is nothing more dangerous than this licentious and deluding art, which changes the meaning of words, as alchemy doth, or would do, the substance of metals, making of anything what it pleases, and bringing in the end all truth to nothing."[3]

The great scientist and Christian writer Sir Isaac Newton was fascinated with prophecy. Newton wrote of his belief that in the last days God would raise up men who would devote their efforts to the study of the prophetic portions of Scripture and "insist upon their literal interpretation in the midst of much clamour and opposition." Both the teachers of the early Church during the first few centuries of the Christian era and the writers on prophecy during the last few centuries believed firmly in the literal prophecies that announced the premillennial return of Christ. The theologian Johann August Ernesti (1707–1781) acknowledged the fundamental law of biblical interpretation is to utilize the same rule we apply to the interpretation of classical or secular writing. Ernesti wrote, "Theologians are right when they affirm the literal sense to be the only true one."[4]

In the early 1800s, the recovery of a literal method of biblical interpretation of prophecy and the truth of the premillennial return of Christ transformed the Church, reawakening its zeal for missions and evangelism. The spiritual fruits of the Church's earnest longing for the Lord's return have been revealed in the explosion of modern evangelism, the enormous missionary efforts to reach the world with the gospel and a renewed commitment to "occupy till I come" (Luke 19:13) expressed in numerous missions to provide humanitarian aid to the most needy throughout the world.

Some have criticized premillennialism, claiming that those who truly believe that Christ could return at any moment will therefore ignore the ills of society and abandon both social assistance and evangelism. However, experience shows that this fear is misplaced. The truth is apparent for all who will examine the record of evangelism during the last three hundred years. For the last two centuries, churches that enthusiastically taught the literal premillennial and pretribulation return of Christ have been at the forefront of the worldwide medical missions as well as missionary efforts to reach the lost. Church leaders who held the premillennial doctrine led the tremendous social reforms that ended child labor and created a strong universal educational system. For example, the Methodists, led by John Wesley (1703–1791) and Charles Wesley (1707–1788), strongly affirmed the literal truth of the Second Coming and wrote over 5000 hymns, most of which focused on the triumphant return of Christ. Significantly, the Weslyian revival produced a social revolution in Britain as well as North America with the introduction of universal education, the Sunday School movement, charitable hospitals, and strong support for social reform in labor laws to protect women and children. The religious movement to abolish slavery throughout the British Empire as well as in America was led by evangelical premillennial Christians such as the Wesley brothers, John

Newton (1725–1807), and William Wilberforce (1759–1833). The Church Missionary Force and the British and Foreign Bible Society were assisted in their formation by Wilberforce. Far from leading to spiritual escapism, the earnest hope of the return of Christ at any moment motivates Christians to live in spiritual purity and to witness with urgency to their world while there is still time.

The Allegorical or Spiritual Approach

The second method of interpreting the prophecies is to treat them as mere allegories, or symbolic pictures of some spiritual truth. This allegorizing approach to interpreting the Scriptures was adopted for the first time in the Church by Origen (A.D.185–254), a teacher in Alexandria, Egypt. His teaching was so spiritually unbalanced that he taught reincarnation and actually sexually mutilated his body to help him reject carnal temptations.[5] Origen was the first major Christian theologian to adopt the allegorical principles of the Gnostics. The Gnostics were a heretical group that rejected almost all fundamental biblical doctrines held by the orthodox Church. Tragically, the great theologian St. Augustine followed this allegorical approach of Origen and gradually influenced most teachers in the Western Empire over the following centuries to reject any literal teaching of the prophecies about the Second Coming and the millennial kingdom that would follow.

Since the time of St. Augustine, many Christian writers have interpreted the prophecies of the book of Revelation idealistically as simply a symbolic description of the ultimate spiritual war between good and evil, promising that good will finally triumph. To hold this idealist position, they interpret the visions and prophecies of Revelation as mere allegories and figures of speech. In other words, they do not expect any of Revelation's detailed prophecies of the Antichrist, false prophet, and the Battle of Armageddon to be literally fulfilled in the future. Many postmillennial and amillennial writers in both of the Catholic Church and Protestant mainline denominations interpret Revelation's prophecies in this purely allegorical or spiritual manner to avoid the clear predictions of Christ coming to defeat Satan's Antichrist before the Millennium to set up His earthly rule from the Throne of David.

The allegorical method of interpretation first became popular with mystical Jewish rabbis who ignored the obvious literal sense of the Old Testament passages in the centuries following the Babylonian Captivity (606–536 B.C.). This method of interpretation became the pattern followed by the Jewish religious and intellectual leaders who gathered in Alexandria, Egypt. As mentioned earlier, Origen was influenced by these allegorical approaches. He adopted a threefold sense of interpretation that dismissed the literal approach. Origen's voluminous writings began to influence other writers in the following years, including Ambrose (A.D. 339–397) and Bishop Augustine of Hippo (A.D. 354–430). Augustine became the most influential theologian in the Church with his book *The City of God*. He gradually adopted the allegorical interpretation teaching that there was a threefold or fourfold non-literal sense to every passage. He dismissed the literal teaching of prophecy including the thousand-year millennial reign of Christ as taught in Revelation 20:1–5. The medieval Church gradually dismissed the literal truths of Scripture. This process was facilitated by the fact that the fall of the Roman Empire produced a massive loss of literacy as Europe entered a thousand years of intellectual and spiritual darkness known as the Dark Ages. The fact that the Bible was only available in Latin made the Scriptures a virtually closed and mysterious book to the vast majority of Christians, and even to a large number of the priests who could not read Latin. The impossibility of open access to the Scriptures for many people made it difficult for most Christians to recognize and reject the gradual introduction of theological errors and heresies that developed over the medieval period before the Reformation made the Bible widely available to believers throughout Western Europe.

An example of this allegorical method of interpretation is illustrated in the theologian Emanuel Swedenborg's book *The Apocalypse Revealed*, in which he interpreted the natural and literal sense of biblical language as being of little importance and meaning. For example, Swedenborg interpreted that cows in Scripture symbolize "good natural relations" while a horse represents "the understanding of the Word of God."[6]

Church historian Joseph Milner describes the theological confusion that developed when the theologians abandoned the fundamental principle of literal interpretation during the long medieval period: "A thick mist for ages pervaded the Christian world, supported and strengthened by his [Origen's] allegorical manner of interpretation. The learned alone were considered for ages implicitly to be followed; and the vulgar, when the literal was hissed off the stage, had nothing to do but to follow their authority wherever it led them."[7] The tragedy is that this "mist" has still not been completely swept away from the teachings of many Christian denominations in our generations.

For almost a thousand years the most fundamental biblical doctrines as taught in the Scriptures were lost to the true Church until a few brave souls such as John Wycliffe, John Huss, William Tyndale, John Calvin, and Martin Luther risked their lives and livelihoods to translate the Holy Scriptures into the common European languages of their day to enable Christians to read the Bible for themselves. The placing of the sacred Scriptures in a readable format into the hands of millions of believers produced the greatest spiritual and intellectual transformation the world had ever witnessed. The great reformer Martin Luther wrote the following comment in *On God's Word*, "I have grounded my preaching upon the literal word; he that pleases may follow me, he that will not may stay."[8] In his commentary on the book of Deuteronomy, Martin Luther defended the literal sense of interpretation as follows:

> I here once more repeat, what I have so often insisted on, that the Christian should direct his efforts toward understanding the so-called literal sense of Scripture, which alone is the substance of faith and of Christian theology, which alone will sustain him in the hour of trouble and temptation, and which will triumph over sin, death, and the gates of hell, to the praise and glory of God. The allegorical sense is usually uncertain, and by no means safe to build our faith upon; for it depends for the

most part on human opinion only, on which if a man lean he will find it no better than the Egyptian reed.[9]

Another great leader of the Reformation, the Swiss reformer John Calvin, confronted the allegorical interpretations by his critics such as Quinten who wrote, "We are not subject to the letter which killeth, but to the Spirit which giveth life. . . . The Bible contains allegories, myths which the Holy Spirit explains to us." However, Calvin rejected this argument with this response: "You make your Scriptures a nose of wax, and play with it, as if it were a ball."[10]

The Protestant Reformation was based on the unshakable principle "Sola Scripture" (only Scripture). The clear teachings of the Bible refuted the accumulated errors and traditions of almost a thousand years. The Reformation unleashed the greatest outpouring of creative intellectual and spiritual energy that transformed the rest of history. One of the greatest effects of the Protestant Reformation's return to a literal principle of interpretation was the unlocking of the mind and spirit of humanity to discover the literal truth of prophecy. As the literal teachings of prophecy were taught in the West for the first time in many centuries, millions of believers began to understand the great plan of God to redeem humanity and the earth from the curse of sin when Christ would establish His rule forever.

Unfortunately, many modern theologians reject the literal and normal interpretation of the prophecies. They insist that almost all of the biblical prophecies should be interpreted allegorically, metaphorically, or symbolically. This allegorical method of interpretation rejects the clear literal meaning of the prophecies that point to the return of Christ in the last days.

Preterist theologians who espouse the Kingdom Now, Covenant Theology, and Dominion Theology positions often use this allegorical approach. They sometime identify themselves as Reconstructionists because they hope to reconstruct society upon the basis of their theology. For example, preterists interpret Jesus Christ's prophetic message recorded in Matthew 24—and in Daniel and Revelation—in an allegorical manner, suggesting all these prophecies were fulfilled only thirty-eight years later in the burning of Jerusalem and its Temple in A.D. 70. This allegorical method allows the interpreter to reject the teaching of the literal premillennial return of Christ, the last days' role of Israel, the rebuilt Temple, a personal Antichrist, and the final Battle of Armageddon to establish Christ's kingdom by denying that the words are to be interpreted in their normal literal, and grammatical sense.

The apostle Peter declared his confidence in the absolute certainty of the prophetic message of the Scriptures: "We have also a more sure word of prophecy; whereunto ye do well that ye take heed, as unto a light that shineth in a dark place, until the day dawn, and the day star arise in your hearts. Knowing this first, that no prophecy of the scripture is of any private interpretation. For the prophecy came not in old time by the will of man: but holy men of God spake as they were moved by the Holy Ghost" (2 Peter 1:19–21).

In this key passage Peter explained that prophecy was given by God to His Church to be a spiritual light to Christians to enable them to understand God's purpose during their spiritually dark times. Furthermore, prophecy was intended to motivate believers to walk in holiness and to witness with urgency in light of the Second Coming. In addition, Peter warned that prophecy did not come "by the will of man," nor is it "of any private interpretation." The message of prophecy is a divinely inspired message from the Holy Spirit to the Church in every generation to live expectantly and walk in personal holiness as we witness to those around us in light of His imminent return.

The Specific Language of Prophecy

The Bible's prophecies were written in a distinct form of religious literature, which is called "apocalyptic" or "apocalypse" relating to the revelation of truth that has been previously hidden. While the Bible often uses symbolic language and figures, the Scriptures contain interpretations of these prophetic symbols so we are not left in darkness to guess at their correct meaning. For example, in Revelation 12:7 we read the symbolic language that

"Michael and his angels fought against the dragon." Rather than being left to wonder about what the dragon symbol represents, the prophet John reveals a few verses later that the symbolic dragon is "the Devil, and Satan" (Revelation 12:9).

Another clear example of the Bible interpreting its own prophetic symbols is found in the same chapter of Revelation, when John prophesied: "And there appeared a great wonder in heaven; a woman clothed with the sun, and the moon under her feet, and upon her head a crown of twelve stars" (Revelation 12:1). What does this remarkable symbol of a woman clothed with the sun, moon, and twelve stars represent? While hundreds of biblical commentaries have creatively speculated on the possible meaning of this symbol, any religious Jew, such as John or any of Christ's disciples, would have instantly known the true meaning of this prophetic symbol. Every Jew had grown up attending synagogue every Sabbath, and the rabbis would sequentially read and discuss every portion of the first five books of the Bible every year. As a consequence of this annual course of sabbatical study, every Jew was as familiar with every portion of the Torah, as modern Christians are familiar with the details of the Christmas and Easter story concerning Jesus Christ. As a consequence of this annual, lifelong study of the Torah, every Jewish Christian would have immediately remembered the similar symbol used in Genesis when Joseph declared to his brothers, "Behold, I have dreamed a dream more; and, behold, the sun and the moon and the eleven stars made obeisance to me" (Genesis 37:9). Joseph's remarkable dream was understood by the Jews as a prophetic symbol of Israel and her twelve tribes (Joseph plus his eleven brothers), as we should understand the vision in Revelation 12:1. This symbolic picture of the woman with the sun, moon, and the twelve stars definitely prophesied about the faithful remnant of Israel that will be persecuted by the Antichrist during the Tribulation.

A "Generation"

The word *generation* appears in the Scriptures in reference to several distinct time periods. The most common use of the word is found in the Bible as a reference to the average length of life of most healthy humans—usually seventy or eighty years. For example, Moses wrote: "The days of our years are threescore years and ten; and if by reason of strength they be four score years, yet is their strength labour and sorrow; for it is soon cut off, and we fly away" (Psalms 90:10). Another use of the word *generation* often appears in the Bible in reference to a distinct period of spiritual judgment or a time of God's governing of His people. The scriptural use of the word *generation* often referred to a distinct period of forty years, including thirteen separate forty-year periods of judgment in connection with the rules of Joshua, Gideon, King Saul, King David, King Solomon, et cetera.

However, in this book the word generation will be used as it often appears in the Scriptures in the sense of the lifetime of a group of people living at a particular time with a duration equal to the natural lifetime of most people—seventy or eighty years.

The Major Views of Prophetic Interpretation

There are four major interpretive approaches to the prophecies such as the book of Revelation that have developed during the last two thousand years.

The Futurist View

The first method of interpretation, the futurist, teaches that most of the biblical prophecies will be fulfilled literally in the last days, culminating in the physical return of Jesus Christ to establish His thousand-year dominion and the New Earth to follow forever. The futurist view was taught by virtually all of the early teachers of the apostolic Church during the first three centuries following Christ's resurrection. The futurist interpretation will be followed throughout this book's study of the extraordinary Old and New Testament prophecies about the Second Coming and the establishment of His kingdom.

Futurists interpret the visions of Revelation and Daniel to refer primarily to the future prophetic events that will culminate in Christ's return at the end of this era and His establishing His kingdom on earth forever. Jesus and the apostles prophesied the coming of Christ at the end of this age. This futurist view was clearly believed and taught universally throughout the early New Testament Church, as we will see in the next chapter. Unfortunately, as the Church gradually departed from the evangelical and biblically based faith in Christ's return in the fifth and sixth centuries, it slowly abandoned the teaching of prophecy. The literal and futurist view was replaced by the allegorical method of interpretation, popularized throughout Western Europe by Ambrose (A.D. 339–397) and the famous theologian Augustine of Hippo (A.D. 354–430). During the centuries that followed and throughout the medieval age, very little was actually written about prophecy. In the dark years that followed the fall of the Roman Empire, general literacy died and very few laypeople even had access to a Bible in a language they could read.

Compounding the problem, very few priests had access to the Scriptures or could read Latin. Consequently, the study and teaching of prophecy almost disappeared and most laypeople and priests had no clear understanding of the Bible's teachings about other central issues, such as justification by faith (Romans 1:17). After the Protestant Reformation in 1520 and the rediscovery of the literal view of biblical interpretation, the futurist prophetic view increasingly came into favor. The Reformers progressively recovered many of the key doctrines of the faith that had been lost during many centuries of spiritual darkness. After 1800, the literal and futurist method of interpretation became the dominant Protestant approach to interpreting Bible prophecy. This literal method motivated the Reformers to re-adopt the premillennial view that was virtually universally taught by the early Church.

The Historical View

The historical method interprets the Bible's prophecies, especially Revelation's visions, as referring primarily to historical events that have already impacted the Church from the first century throughout the centuries until the end of this era. A fundamental part of this view is the "year equals a day principle," which interpreted the 1,260 days of Daniel and

Revelation as referring to 1,260 actual years (Daniel 12 and Revelation 11:3). As an example, this theory interprets the 1,260 days of Revelation, not as literal future days during the last three-and-a-half-year global rule of a personal Antichrist during the Great Tribulation, but rather as a 1,260-year period of anti-Christian tyranny from the rise of papal Rome (approximately A.D. 666) until the defeat of papal troops by the French emperor Napoleon around 1800.

This historical view was tentatively developed for the first time in the twelfth century by medieval theologians who were concerned about the growing abuses in the Church. Since many of these Reformation writers had lost family and friends as martyrs to the Inquisition, they naturally tended to see their religious opponents in the prophecies of the book of Revelation. This theory mistakenly interpreted the papacy as both the Antichrist and Babylon. However, Revelation 17 clearly foretells that the future Antichrist and the ten nations will destroy the Great Whore of Babylon, the ecumenical false church of the last days. Therefore, the Antichrist cannot possibly be the Papacy. This historical view became very popular with the early Reformation writers and prevailed up until approximately 1820. When all possible termination periods for the 1,260 years expired without any historical fulfillment, most Christians abandoned this method of interpretation as an obviously erroneous theory. Only a few small groups strongly endorse the historical view of prophecy in our day.

The Preterist View

The preterist view—sometimes called Covenant Theology, Dominion Theology, or Kingdom Now—interprets John's apocalyptic visions in Revelation about devastating worldwide war, famine, earthquakes, pestilence killing one-third of humanity, et cetera, as poetic or prophetic symbols that were totally fulfilled in the burning of Jerusalem by the Romans in A.D. 70. The word *preterist* is derived from the Latin word *praeter*, which means "past." An obvious contradiction to this theory is that the internal textual evidence in Revelation and the overwhelming historical evidence of the early Church confirms that John's prophecy was written in A.D. 96, some twenty-six years *after* the fall of Jerusalem. Since the book of Revelation contains detailed prophecies about the future global events affecting all of humanity during the last days when Christ returns to earth, these predictions cannot possibly refer to past events concerning the destruction of a single city. This obvious contradiction is the reason preterist Kingdom Now and Dominion theologians vehemently reject the A.D. 96 date for John's writing of Revelation. They are forced by needs of their theory to try and establish the date for John's writing of Revelation to A.D. 68, during the reign of Emperor Nero just a few years before Jerusalem was destroyed. Later we will examine the critical historical evidence that Revelation was written by the apostle John in 96, not 68, confirming that the preterist and Kingdom Now position is logically untenable.

Post-millennialist and amillennialist writers admit that their preterist system is false and will utterly fail if it can be proven that the book of Revelation was written at any time after the A.D. 70 burning of Jerusalem. The preterists admit that if John wrote his book after Jerusalem fell then Revelation's prophecies must logically point to the future coming of Christ to set up His millennial kingdom. Kenneth L. Gentry, in his enthusiastic review of the preterist David Chilton's Dominion Theology textbook, *Days of Vengeance*, wrote: "If it could be demonstrated that Revelation was written twenty-five years after the fall of Jerusalem, Chilton's entire labor would go up in smoke."[11]

Those who are committed to a post-millennial or amillennial position reject the future return of Christ to defeat the Antichrist and set up His kingdom. Preterist theology rejects the biblical hope of an imminent Second Coming of Christ despite the fact that this doctrine was taught by most orthodox Christians during the last two thousand years. However, the historical evidence presented in this book will prove that Revelation was written after A.D. 70. The preterists will be forced to come to terms with the Bible's clear pre-millennial teaching that Christ will come at some point in the future to defeat Satan's Antichrist and establish His millennial kingdom.

The Idealist View

Lastly, some writers believe the Bible's prophecies are simply a symbolic description of the ultimate war between good and evil, promising that good will finally triumph. To hold this idealist position, they interpret the visions and prophecies of Daniel and Revelation as mere allegories and figures of speech. In other words, they do not expect any of Daniel's, Matthew's, Thessalonians', or Revelation's prophecies about the coming Antichrist, False Prophet, and the Battle of Armageddon to be fulfilled in the future. Many postmillennial and amillennial writers interpret Revelation's prophecies in this purely allegorical manner to avoid the clear predictions of Christ coming to earth to defeat Satan's Antichrist before the Millennium to set up His rule from the throne of David. A multitude of prophecies reveal that Jesus will return in the same physical manner in which He ascended to heaven. The prophecies declare that He will defeat Satan and set up the promised kingdom.

The Premillennial Hope of the Early Church

During the first two and a half centuries following Christ's resurrection, the Early Church universally held a firm belief in the premillennial coming of Jesus Christ to defeat Satan's Antichrist and establish His glorious reign. They expected an apostasy would occur during the last days, followed by the rise to power of a personal Antichrist and the False Prophet, a Great Tribulation of terror, and then the cataclysmic Battle of Armageddon, when Christ will destroy His enemies and set up His kingdom.

Premillennialism is a system of prophetic interpretation that teaches the doctrine that the Second Coming of Christ will precede and establish the Millennium. The first century Christians interpreted the Bible literally, exactly as the New Testament demonstrates that Christ and His apostles interpreted the Old Testament prophecies. The well-established literal and futurist method of interpretation is the foundation of the premillennial view of prophecy. Some complain that a literal view destroys the true spiritual understanding of the prophecies. However, this is not true. The New Testament interprets the Old Testament prophetic passages literally, revealing God's stamp of approval on this literal interpretive system. In fact, every single prophecy that has been fulfilled throughout history has been fulfilled literally. There are no examples of a purely allegorical fulfillment of biblical prophecy. The literal method is biblical, practical, and logically valid as we seek to understand God's prophetic message to the Church. However, this method is also spiritual in that we must always seek to understand the spiritual implications of these vital biblical prophecies.

The evidence presented in this book provides incontrovertible historical evidence that the primitive Church almost universally believed (during the first three centuries) in the doctrine of a literal return of Christ setting the stage for a one thousand-year millennial reign of Christ's saints. Following the conversion of the Roman Emperor Constantine, the issuing of the Edict of Toleration by co-emperor Galerius in A.D. 311 set the stage for freedom of worship for the Christian Church throughout the Roman Empire. From that moment on, political considerations and power politics gradually entered into the highest councils of the Church during the following centuries. The premillennial teaching about Christ coming to defeat the evil government of this world naturally became unpopular with the civil rulers once Roman emperors and their successor kings entered into a mutually profitable and unholy alliance with church leaders. It is not surprising that the emperors of Rome did not want to hear that Jesus Christ would someday return to overthrow their governments and ultimately replace them with His eternal kingdom.

Amillennialism, the Allegorical Method of Interpretation

Origen, a third-century theologian in Alexandria, Egypt, popularized an allegorical method of teaching borrowed from the Greek pagan writers and the discredited heretical Gnostics. He was brilliant but rather unbalanced—at one point, he castrated himself to help him live a pure life. Among other false doctrines, Origen taught the reincarnation of men into animals and he rejected a literal belief in the scriptural statements. Unfortunately Origen's writing influenced many, including Augustine, Bishop of Hippo, an influential church writer from North Africa. Augustine of Hippo wrote his pivotal book *The City of God* in the beginning of the fifth century. This work rejected the literal interpretation of Scripture and denied the premillennial return of Christ and instead espoused an allegorical method of scriptural interpretation. With the allegorical method, there are no fixed standards or rules for interpreting Scripture; everything is symbolic or allegorical and can therefore be interpreted according to the theological preconceptions of the interpreter without reference to the normal sense of the prophecies.

Augustine adopted an amillennial view that rejected any literal period of a thousand-year kingdom of God before or after Christ's return. This amillennial position gradually became the dominant view of the medieval Church from the fourth century on and has remained so until today. The study of prophecy was virtually abandoned in Western Europe except for the occasional mention in writings that the Antichrist would someday appear. Following the Protestant Reformation in 1520, the Reformers examined doctrine in light of the Scriptures and consequently rejected the theological heresies that had developed during the medieval period. Unfortunately, most of the Reformers did not seriously study the area of prophetic truth, except to identify the papacy and the popes as the Antichrist and the Great Whore of Babylon. Most of the early reformers continued with an amillennial view.

Irenaeus, a respected Church leader who taught in the late second century, wrote *Against Heresies* as a rebuttal of the Gnostic heretical teaching that was beginning to corrupt the Church's hope of the Second Coming. He held to a literal, common-sense interpretation of the prophecies of both the Old and New Testament. "If, however, any shall endeavor to allegorize (prophecies) of this kind, they shall not be found consistent with themselves in all points, and shall be confuted by the teaching of the very expressions." Allegorical interpretation produces confusion because each teacher will supply his own interpretation according to his preconceptions, imagination, and personal feelings, rather than the normal sense of language. Amillennialism denies the supernatural and visible return of Christ to establish His millennial rule. Rather, amillennialism replaces the Church's confident and biblically based hope for the Second Coming with a vague idealism in which the kingdom of God becomes little more than a symbol or an intellectual abstraction.

The Postmillennial View
(including the Preterism Theory)

An English pastor named Rev. Daniel Whitby created a "New Hypotheses" called postmillennialism in 1800. This theological theory suggested for the first time in history that the Lord would not return to establish His kingdom on the earth until after the completion of a one thousand year Millennium. This theory suggested that the Millennium would be established by the Church through the successful Christianizing of the world by believers during this Age of Grace. The postmillennial view also depends upon allegorizing the scriptural prophecies which literally describe Christ's return to set up His kingdom when He defeats Satan's Antichrist. Rev. Whitby acknowledged that this postmillennial theory was something totally new, by calling it a "New Hypothesis." This postmillennial view teaches that the Church will gradually expand throughout the globe until the population of the earth will someday worship Christ without the need for the personal return of Jesus Christ from heaven to destroy Satan's Antichrist and establish His righteous rule.

This postmillennial view rejects the premillennial teaching of the Scriptures that points to Christ's return at the end of the Tribulation to defeat Satan's Antichrist and establish His righteous kingdom on earth forever. Postmillennialists often adopt an allegorical interpretation of the scriptural prophecies about the Second Coming to avoid the obvious conclusion that Jesus will physically return to destroy the armies of Satan and will then set up His holy kingdom on earth to be ruled by the saints under the Messiah. Many postmillennialists have adopted the preterist theory that suggests that all of the

The Three Millennial Views

The Premillennial View
(Christ will return to set up His Millennial Kingdom)

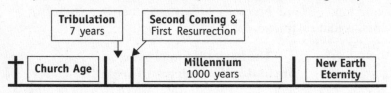

The Amillennial View
(no millennium)
Christ Reigns with His Saints from Heaven

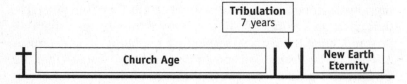

The Post Millennial View
(Christ will return after the Millennium)

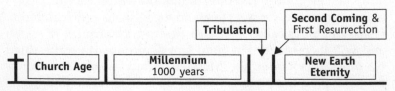

prophecies of Matthew 24 and the book of Revelation were actually fulfilled when the Roman army destroyed Jerusalem in A.D. 70. Overwhelming historical and scriptural evidence proves that this preterist theory is totally false as documented in a following chapter.

Literal Prophecies about Christ's First Coming

The strongest argument in favor of the literal interpretation of the many scriptural prophecies about the Second Advent and the kingdom in the future is the overwhelming evidence that all of the detailed prophecies about Christ's first coming were fulfilled literally. The evidence demonstrates that Jesus Christ was born, lived, and died exactly as prophesied, fulfilling the numerous predictions about Israel's suffering Messiah as found in Psalm 22 and Isaiah 53. The following list demonstrates just a small portion of the many specific predictions fulfilled during the first coming of Christ:

Consider just seventeen of the forty-eight specific and detailed prophecies fulfilled in the first coming of Jesus Christ. Note that every one of these specific predictions was recorded in the Old Testament over five centuries earlier and every one was fulfilled literally.

- "Therefore the Lord himself shall give you a sign; Behold, a virgin shall conceive, and bear a son, and shall call his name Immanuel" (Isaiah 7:14): *Jesus was born to a young virgin.*
- "But thou, Bethlehem Ephratah, though thou be little among the thousands of Judah, yet out of thee shall he come forth unto me that is to be ruler in Israel; whose goings forth have been from of old, from everlasting" (Micah 5:2): *The Messiah was born in Bethlehem, the city of David.*
- "Thus saith the Lord; A voice was heard in Ramah, lamentation, and bitter weeping; Rachel weeping for her children refused to be comforted for her children, because they were not" (Jeremiah 31:15): *King Herod slaughtered the Jewish children.*
- "When Israel was a child, then I loved him, and called my son out of Egypt" (Hosea 11:1): *Jesus' family was called out of Egypt.*

- "And the spirit of the Lord shall rest upon him, the spirit of wisdom and understanding, the spirit of counsel and might, the spirit of knowledge and of the fear of the Lord" (Isaiah 11:2): *The Messiah was anointed with the Holy Spirit.*
- "Rejoice greatly, O daughter of Zion; shout, O daughter of Jerusalem: behold, thy King cometh unto thee: he is just, and having salvation; lowly, and riding upon an ass, and upon a colt the foal of an ass"(Zechariah 9:9): *Jesus entered Jerusalem as the Messiah riding a colt.*
- "Yea, mine own familiar friend, in whom I trusted, which did eat of my bread, hath lifted up his heel against me" (Psalms 41:9): *He was betrayed by Judas, a friend, after the Last Supper.*
- "And the Lord said unto me, Cast it unto the potter: a goodly price that I was prised at of them. And I took the thirty pieces of silver, and cast them to the potter in the house of the Lord." (Zechariah 11:13): *A potter's field will be bought for thirty pieces of silver, the betrayal money, which Judas had thrown into the Temple.*
- "Awake, O sword, against my shepherd, and against the man that is my fellow, saith the Lord of hosts: smite the shepherd, and the sheep shall be scattered: and I will turn mine hand upon the little ones" (Zechariah 13:7): *The disciples deserted Jesus upon his arrest.*
- "I gave my back to the smiters, and my cheeks to them that plucked off the hair: I hid not my face from shame and spitting" (Isaiah 50:6): *The Messiah was spit upon and scourged.*
- "He keepeth all his bones: not one of them is broken" (Psalms 34:20): *Jesus' bones were not broken at the crucifixion.*
- "They gave me also gall for my meat; and in my thirst they gave me vinegar to drink" (Psalms 69:21): *They gave Jesus wine vinegar to drink on the cross.*
- "For dogs have compassed me: the assembly of the wicked have inclosed me: they pierced my hands and my feet" (Psalms 22:16): *Jesus' hands and feet were nailed to the cross.*
- "They part my garments among them, and cast lots upon

my vesture" (Psalms 22:18): *The soldiers at the cross gambled for Jesus' garments.*

- "And he made his grave with the wicked, and with the rich in his death; because he had done no violence, neither was any deceit in his mouth" (Isaiah 53:9): *He was buried in the tomb of a rich man, Joseph of Arimathea.*
- "For thou wilt not leave my soul in hell; neither wilt thou suffer thine Holy One to see corruption" (Psalms 16:10): *The Messiah was resurrected and His body did not decay.*

A careful and unbiased analysis of the dozens of Old Testament predictions about the coming Messiah will conclude that they were historically fulfilled during the life, death, and resurrection of Jesus of Nazareth. A thoughtful review of these remarkable prophecies will also conclude that every one of these predictions was fulfilled literally in a manner consistent with a normal interpretation of the original prophecy.

Many of the most important Old Testament prophecies about the first coming of the Christ were part of larger prophetic passages that also contained predictions of events that would occur in the "last days" when the Messiah would return to establish His rule. One of the specific prophecies about the coming Messiah foretold that He would be descended from King David, who was the son of Jesse. The New Testament specifically recorded the genealogy of Jesus of Nazareth to demonstrate that He truly was descended from King David, the son of Jesse, as prophesied by the ancient seers of Israel.

And there shall come forth a rod out of the stem of Jesse, and a Branch shall grow out of his roots: And the spirit of the Lord shall rest upon him, the spirit of wisdom and understanding, the spirit of counsel and might, the spirit of knowledge and of the fear of the Lord; And shall make him of quick understanding in the fear of the Lord: and he shall not judge after the sight of his eyes, neither reprove after the hearing of his ears: But with righteousness shall he judge the poor, and reprove with equity for the meek of the earth: and he shall smite the earth with the rod of his mouth, and with the breath of his lips shall he slay the wicked. And righteousness shall be the girdle of his loins, and faithfulness the girdle of his reins. The wolf also shall dwell with the lamb, and the leopard shall lie down with the kid; and the calf and the young lion and the fatling together; and a little child shall lead them. (Isaiah 11:1–6)

The prophet Isaiah predicted that the Messiah would "come forth" "of Jesse" and would "grow out of his roots." His predictions were literally fulfilled by the birth of Jesus from Mary who was descended from Jesse (see Matthew 1). However, Isaiah also prophesied that the Messiah will ultimately become the supreme ruler of the earth when He would "judge the poor" and "smite the earth with the rod." Christ will transform all life on earth when His supernatural power will transform even the animal kingdom until death will be eliminated from nature. In light of the fact that Isaiah's initial predictions were fulfilled literally, it logically follows that his prophecies concerning the Messiah's return will also be fulfilled literally at Christ's return.

Notes

1. J. Barton Payne, *Encyclopedia of Biblical Prophecy* (New York: Harper & Row, Publishers, 1973).

2. Justin Martyr, "First Apology," *Ante-Nicene Library*, 10 vols. (Grand Rapids: Wm. B. Eerdmans Publishing Co., 1987).

3. Richard Hooker, *Laws of Ecclesiastical Polity*, (1593) vol 2.

4. Johann August Ernesti, *Institutio Interpretis Novi Testamenti* (1761).

5. J. D. Douglas, ed., *The New International Dictionary of the Christian Church* (Grand Rapids: Zondervan Publishing House, 1978).

6. Emanuel Swedenborg, *The Apocalypse Revealed* (1760).

7. Joseph Milner, *Ecclesiastical History* (Cambridge: Cambridge University, 1800) 1: 469.

8. Martin Luther, "*Table Talk*," Weimar Ausgabe (1957).

9. Joseph Seiss, *Last Times* (Baltimore: T. Newton Kurtz, 1856) 253.

10. George Peters, *The Theocratic Kingdom* (Grand Rapids: Kregel Publications, 1957) 54.

11. Kenneth L. Gentry, *The Council Chalcedon*, 11:11.

3

What Did the Early Church Believe about the Second Coming?

Some who reject the futurist, literal interpretation of Bible prophecy as taught by those of us who hold to the apostolic and premillennial doctrine of Christ's Second Coming often claim that our beliefs were basically unknown to the early Church. In this chapter I hope to demonstrate to any fair-minded inquirer that the historical evidence is overwhelming that the apostolic Church generally adopted a literal and futurist interpretation of the prophecies, especially regarding the Second Advent and the premillennial return of Christ to set up His kingdom. We will examine the specific prophetic beliefs that are commonly held by modern prophecy teachers such as Hal Lindsey, Tim LaHaye, John Walvoord, and myself. Examples of these particular prophetic beliefs include acceptance of a literal and future Antichrist, False Prophet, Second Coming, the resumption of sacrifice in the rebuilt Temple in Jerusalem, and the establishment of the millennial kingdom of God by Christ at His coming.

We will compare these modern prophetic views with quotations of the early Church theologians and teachers as documented by the authoritative collection of ancient manuscripts called the *Ante-Nicene Fathers*. Years ago, I embarked on a systematic study of the writings of the early Christian theologians who taught prior to the Council of Nicea in 325. These informative writings were translated from Greek and Latin into English and assembled in a ten-volume set called the *Ante-Nicene Fathers* in Edinburgh, Scotland, in the 1890s. There is ample evidence that our modern views regarding the fulfillment of the prophecies are remarkably similar to those held by the Christians during the first three centuries following Christ. A later chapter in this book will examine the specific millennial kingdom beliefs of the early Church and will demonstrate conclusively that these early Church teachers almost universally taught the premillennial return of Christ. An examination of several key prophetic teachings of the apostolic church will provide powerful evidence that current prophecy beliefs are consistent with the earliest teachings of the apostles and the early Church.

Should Prophecy Be Interpreted as Literal or Allegorical?

One of the most fundamental issues facing those who consider the prophecies of the Bible is the question of the correct method of interpretation—literally or allegorically—as indicated in the previous chapter. However, one of the most significant considerations is to examine the question of the method of interpretation used by the Church Fathers, some of whom personally knew the disciples of Jesus. The quotations listed in this chapter provide compelling evidence that the primitive Church writers interpreted the prophecies in a quite literal manner.

Several writers from the first few centuries specifically addressed the issue of how we should interpret the prophecies. As noted the second-century writer Irenaeus declared that the literal method was correct: "If, however, any shall endeavor to allegorize (prophecies) of this kind, they shall not be found consistent with themselves in all points, and shall be confuted by the teaching of the very expressions."[1] Another second-century writer, Justin Martyr, also confirmed that we should expect those prophecies about the events in the last days to be fulfilled in the same manner as those predictions fulfilled in the past. Justin wrote, "Since, then, we prove that all things which have already happened had been predicted by the prophets before they came to pass, we must necessarily believe also that those things which are in like manner predicted, but are yet to come to pass, shall certainly happen. For as the things which have already taken place came to pass when foretold, and even though unknown, so shall the things that remain, even though they be unknown and disbelieved, yet come to pass."[2]

The Early Church's Prophetic Beliefs

Virtually all serious scholars of Church history, regardless of their personal views regarding the Millennium, acknowledge that the early apostolic Church believed in an imminent Second Coming. For example: Professor Richard Rothe states: "The apostles unanimously expected the return of Christ, to enter upon this Kingdom (Chiliastic) on earth."[3] Professor James Donaldson, the respected editor of the Ante-Nicene Library, in his *History of Catholic Doctrine and Literature*, wrote about the belief of Justin Martyr in support of the premillennial doctrine: "The opinion just adduced is one in which the whole Church shared. All expected Christ to appear on earth, to raise His saints, to grant them the possession of the earth, and to bless them with uninterrupted happiness."[4] Philip Schaff declared in his *History of the Apostolic Church*, "The expectation of the speedy return of Christ in glory, as probably one of Paul's favorite themes; that he exhorts the Thessalonians 'to be always ready to meet the Lord, who shall come unexpectedly, like a thief in the night, and warns them, for this very reason, among other errors, against presuming to calculate the day and hour of His appearing.'"[5]

The French historian Professor Joseph Renan (1823–1892)

stated, "The two Syriac words *Maran-atha* (the Lord is about to come) became the watchword of the Christians among themselves; the short, animated expression, which they passed from one to another to encourage themselves in their hoping."[6] After surveying the overwhelming evidence that the premillennial doctrine was strongly held by all of the key leaders of the early Church, Karl A. Auberlen wrote that in his view, Jesus, the Prophets, and the Apostles were all "Chiliasts" [premillennial].[7]

The anti-millennial scholar Johann A. W. Neander (1789–1850) admitted in his history of the primitive Church that the apostles were not looking for the immediate conversion of the world but for the speedy return of Christ. He wrote, "Every unprejudiced reader of the New Testament cannot fail to perceive that such an expectation filled the souls of the apostles." Neander wrote about how this expectation influenced their concept regarding the purpose of the church. "It was not the idea of a renovated time that Christianity first attempted to realize, but everything appeared only as a point of transition to a new, heavenly, eternal order of things which would commence at the Second Advent."[8]

The Last Days

The first issue is the question regarding the time when the prophecies will be fulfilled—immediately in A.D. 70 or in the final "last days" that include Armageddon and the ushering in of the promised millennial rule. Irenaeus (A.D. 120–202), who died as a martyr to his faith, wrote *Against Heresies*, one of the most important prophetic writings of the primitive Church. Irenaeus was a disciple of Polycarp (A.D. 69–155), who was personally taught by the apostle John. Therefore, he knew that John's prophecies in Revelation were not fulfilled decades earlier during the destruction of Jerusalem in A.D. 70. Irenaeus writes, "In a still clearer light has John, in the Apocalypse, indicated to the Lord's disciples what shall happen in the last times, and concerning the ten kings who shall then arise, among whom the empire [Rome] which now rules (the earth) shall be partitioned. . . . It is manifest, therefore that of these (potentates), he who is to come shall slay three, and subject the remainder to his power, and that he shall be himself the eighth among them. And they shall lay Babylon waste, and burn her with fire, and shall give their kingdom to the beast, and put the Church to flight. After that, they shall be destroyed by the coming of the Lord."[9]

Irenaeus obviously expected the fulfillment of this prophecy to occur at some point in the future, although he knew the Roman army had destroyed the city of Jerusalem eighty-five years before he wrote his book *Against Heresies*. He also understood that the apostle John taught about a final future apostasy of the Church that would lead to its prophetic and symbolic designation as "Mystery Babylon" and the ultimate destruction of this false church by the Antichrist's tenfold kingdom at the midpoint of the seven-year Tribulation (Revelation 17:16–18).

Toward the end of the second century, the theologian Hippolytus (A.D. 170–236) wrote about the fact that the prophecies all pointed to a final fulfillment during the "last days" during the final generation of this age: "These words then being thus presented, let us observe somewhat in detail what Daniel says in his visions. For in distinguishing the kingdoms that are to rise after these things, he showed also the coming of Antichrist in the last times, and the consummation of the whole world."[10] It is significant that every one of the early Christian writers taught that the prophecies of Daniel, Revelation, and Matthew 24 would be fulfilled in the last days at the end of this age until the publications of Origen (A.D. 185–254). The respected Church historian John Mosheim wrote, "The prevailing opinion that Christ was to come and reign a thousand years among men before the final dissolution of the world, had met with no opposition previous to the time of Origen."[11]

The Hope of the Imminent Second Coming

The *Didache* (also known as the *Testimony of the Twelve Apostles*) is an important Church document from the first few years of the second century (approximately A.D. 110) that gives us vital insights into beliefs that were dominant in the primitive Church. The following statement in an early Christian document, *Didache*

16:17, indicates the strongly held belief in the Second Coming: "Then shall the world see the Lord coming upon the clouds of heaven."[12] A primitive Christian manuscript known as *The Reliques of the Elders* was fortunately copied and preserved in the writings of Irenaeus. This valuable document preserves powerful evidence of the widespread popularity of the doctrine of the return of Christ in the primitive Church. The manuscript declares, "Afterwards he chanted the psalm of confession, waiting for the coming of the Lord, who washes and cleanses the man who had been bound in sin . . . and was speaking his three thousand parables on the coming of the Lord, and his five thousand songs, by way of hymn to God."[13] This remarkable statement indicates that there were thousands of statements or parables related to "the coming of the Lord" that were known during the time of the post-apostolic Church.

Another document from the primitive Church encourages all Christians to imitate those who sacrificed everything to their faith in Christ and went about "preaching the coming of Christ." Clement of Rome, an important Church leader who is reported to have become an early bishop of Rome, wrote an epistle to the Church at Corinth in which he encouraged the believers to follow the example of those who first taught the coming of Christ. Clement wrote, "Let us be imitators also of them which went about in goat skins and sheepskins, preaching the coming of Christ."[14]

The brilliant Church historian Hippolytus (A.D. 200) wrote about the Christian belief in the two advents of Christ:

> For through the Scriptures we are instructed in two advents of the Christ and Saviour. And the first after the flesh was in humiliation, because He was manifested in lowly estate. So then His second advent is declared to be in glory; for He comes from heaven with power, and angels, and the glory of His Father. His first advent had John the Baptist as its forerunner; and His second, in which He is to come in glory, will exhibit Enoch, and Elias, and John the Divine.[15]

The British historian Edward Gibbon wrote in his book

The Decline and Fall of the Roman Empire about the universal belief of the early Church in the doctrine of the literal and imminent return of Christ.

> It was universally believed that the end of the world, and the kingdom of heaven, were at hand. The near approach of this wonderful event had been predicted by the apostles; the tradition of it was preserved by their earliest disciples, and those who understood in their literal sense the discourses of Christ himself were obliged to expect the second and glorious coming of the Son of Man in the clouds, before that generation was totally extinguished which had beheld his humble condition upon earth.[16]

While Gibbon acknowledged the historical truth that the first Christians longed for the speedy return of Christ, he is quite wrong in his conclusion that the primitive Church believed, or was obligated to believe, that the Bible's prophecies *demanded* that Christ would return in the generation that first heard His prophecies. We will examine the subject of the imminent Second Coming in depth in Chapter 10. However, in brief, the prophecies taught that Christ *could* come at any moment but they did not place any time limit on how long the Lord would tarry until He returned. In fact, many prophecies warned that some critics in the last days would deny His Second Advent because of the long delay in time. The apostle Peter warned about the danger of losing faith but instructed us that the reason for the apparent delay was God's compassion to sinners. "But, beloved, be not ignorant of this one thing, that one day is with the Lord as a thousand years, and a thousand years as one day. The Lord is not slack concerning his promise, as some men count slackness; but is longsuffering to us-ward, not willing that any should perish, but that all should come to repentance. But the day of the Lord will come as a thief in the night" (2 Peter 3:8–10).

The French theologian Jean Baptiste Massillon (1663–1742) acknowledged that "in the days of primitive Christianity it would have been deemed a kind of apostasy not to sigh for the return of the Lord."[17] However, the abandonment of the foundational doctrines of the Word of God together with the continued growth of apostasy within the ranks of Christian pastors has produced the lamentable situation where those "who love His appearing" and powerfully teach the scriptural doctrine of the soon return of Christ and His millennial kingdom are often criticized as "prophecy speculators" and considered to be eccentric in their teaching. Tragically, many who lead in the Church today consider those who state "Even so, come Lord Jesus" to be on the theological fringe and unbalanced when they teach the historic doctrine of the return of Christ. This rejection of the biblical prophecies regarding the Second Coming and the kingdom of God is clearly a fulfillment of the New Testament prophecies of the last days, in which the apostle Peter warned "there shall come . . . scoffers, walking after their own lusts, And saying, Where is the promise of his coming? for since the fathers fell asleep, all things continue as they were from the beginning of the creation" (2 Peter 3:3–4).

The Antichrist

The primitive Church was fascinated by the prophecies about the future world dictator known as the Antichrist and his horrific and bloody rule over Israel and the nations during the last days. One of the most interesting of the early Christian writers, Hippolytus (A.D. 160–236), wrote that the Antichrist would arise from among the Jews to deceive them: "For in every respect that deceiver seeks to make himself appear like the Son of God. Christ is a lion, and Antichrist is a lion. . . . The Saviour was circumcised, and he in like manner will appear in circumcision . . . he in like manner will gather together the dispersed people of the Hebrews. . . . Christ arose from among the Hebrews, and he will spring from among the Jews."[18] Another key writer, Lactantius, wrote in A.D. 313 that the Antichrist will imitate and seek to replace God in the worship of humanity in the last days. "Now this is he who is called Antichrist; but he shall falsely call himself Christ, and shall fight against the truth, and being overcome shall flee."[19] Lactantius also wrote that Satan will attempt to set himself up as God in this final conflict. "But that king will not only be most disgraceful in himself, but he will also be a prophet of lies; and he will constitute and call himself God, and will order himself to be worshipped as the Son of God."[20]

Irenaeus wrote about the career of the Antichrist in relation to Christ's return. "For he [Antichrist] being endued [empowered] with all the power of the devil, shall come, not as a righteous king, nor as a legitimate king, [one] in subjection to God, but an impious, unjust, and lawless one; as an apostate, iniquitous and murderous; as a robber, concentrating in himself (all) satanic apostasy, and setting aside idols to persuade (men) that he himself is God, raising up himself as the only idol, having in himself the multifarious errors of the other idols."[21]

The False Prophet

The Scriptures indicate that the False Prophet, the partner of the Antichrist, will perform supernatural acts to deceive people. Possibly he will falsely claim to be the prophet Elijah as foretold by Malachi 4:5. It is fascinating to note that Lactantius (A.D. 260–330) confirmed this interpretation regarding the False Prophet in his book *Divine Institutes* in the third century:

> He will also be a prophet of lies; and he will constitute and call himself God, and will order himself to be worshipped as the Son of God; and power will be given him to do signs and wonders, by the sight of which he may entice men to adore him. He will command fire to come down from heaven, and the sun to stand and leave his course, and an image to speak; and these things shall be done at his word—by which miracles many even of the wise shall be enticed by him. Then he will attempt to destroy the temple of God, and persecute the righteous people; and there will be distress and tribulation such as there never has been from the beginning of the world.[22]

Another Christian writer, Victorinus, wrote a fascinating commentary on the Apocalypse in A.D. 280. In it, he declared that the False Prophet will set up an image of the Antichrist in the rebuilt Temple in the Holy City. Victorinus wrote, "He shall cause also that a golden image of Antichrist shall be placed in the temple at Jerusalem." He also noted that the False Prophet will counterfeit the supernatural signs of the genuine prophet Elijah, who will minister as one of the two witnesses during the Tribulation. "And he shall make fire come down from heaven in the sight of men."[23] Victorinus' reference to the satanic miracle of bringing fire down from heaven (Revelation 13:13–14) is virtually identical to the interpretation found in the writings of modern prophecy teachers.

The Revival of the Roman Empire—
A Ten-Nation Superstate

Irenaeus clearly identifies the kingdom of the future Antichrist with the final revival of the Roman Empire, symbolized by the fourth beast of Daniel 7. He taught that the Antichrist will violently overthrow three of the ten kingdoms that will form a ten-nation superstate in the territory of the original Roman Empire during the last days. "In a still clearer light has John, in the Apocalypse, indicated to the Lord's disciples what shall happen in the last times, and concerning the ten kings who shall then arise, among whom the empire [Rome] which now rules (the earth) shall be partitioned. . . . It is manifest, therefore that of these (potentates), he who is to come shall slay three, and subject the remainder to his power, and that he shall be himself the eighth among them."[24]

Lactantius also confirmed that the prophets foretold that ten nations would join a superstate confederacy in the last days. "Then civil discords will perpetually be sown; nor will there be any rest from deadly wars, until ten kings arise at the same time, who will divide the world, not to govern, but to consume it."[25]

In his commentary on Revelation, Victorinus also wrote about the seven kings of the revived Roman Empire who survive after the first three of the original ten kings are destroyed by the Antichrist. "His seven heads were the seven kings of the Romans, of whom also is Antichrist, as we have said above. 'And ten horns.' He says that the ten kings in the latest times are the same as these, as we shall more fully set forth there."[26]

Daniel's Seventieth Week—
The Seven Years of Tribulation and the Gap of Years

Some critical writers have stated that the teaching about a gap, or "parenthesis," of many years occurring between the end of Daniel's sixty-ninth week (at the time of Israel's rejection of the Messiah) and the commencement of the final seventieth week, the last seven years of this age (the beginning of the seven-year Tribulation), is a new theory that was unknown before modern times. However, a careful examination of the prophetic writings during the first few centuries of the Church era reveals that a number of writers also understood that the critical events of the last days will be fulfilled during Daniel's seventieth week of seven years.

In his commentary on Daniel 9:24–27, Irenaeus refers to the prophesied seventieth "week" of seven years as the duration of the future Antichrist's tyranny: "And in the midst of the week, he says, the sacrifice and the libation shall be taken away, and the abomination of desolation (shall be brought) into the temple: even unto the consummation of the time shall the desolation be complete. Now three years and six months constitute the half-week."[27]

In another early Church commentary, Lactantius confirmed that Satan would supernaturally empower the Antichrist with evil power during the last half (three and one-half years) of Daniel's seventieth week: "Power will be given him to desolate the whole earth for forty-two months."[28]

The writer Hippolytus wrote a detailed commentary about the prophecies and noted the clear prophecy of Daniel about the final seven-year Tribulation:

He intimated also of old in this Daniel. For he says, "I shall make a covenant of one week, and in the midst of the week my sacrifice and libation will be removed." For by one week he indicates the showing forth of the seven years which shall be in the last times. And the half of the week the two prophets, along with John, will take for the purpose of proclaiming to all the world the advent of Antichrist, that is to say, for a "thousand two hundred and sixty days clothed in sackcloth;" and they will work signs and wonders.[29]

In another manuscript, Hippolytus wrote about Daniel's vision of the seventy weeks and clearly revealed his understanding that the final "week" of seven years (the Tribulation) will occur after a long gap of time from the ending of the sixty-ninth week, when Christ had first come. Hippolytus commented on Daniel's prophecy that the time between "the commandment to restore and build Jerusalem unto the Messiah the Prince shall be seven weeks" (Daniel 9:25). Hippolytus wrote, "For when the threescore and two weeks are fulfilled, and Christ is come, and the Gospel is preached in every place, the times being then accomplished, there will remain only one week, the last, in which Elias will appear, and Enoch, and in the midst of it the abomination of desolation will be manifested, viz., Antichrist, announcing desolation to the world. And when he comes, the sacrifice and oblation will be removed, which now are offered to God in every place by the nations."[30]

In this same manuscript, Hippolytus identified the last half of Daniel's seventieth week (Daniel 9:27) with the Antichrist's persecution of the saints after the ministry of the two witnesses. "As also it was announced to Daniel: 'And one week shall confirm a covenant with many; and in the midst of the week it shall be that the sacrifice and oblation shall be removed'—that the one week might be shown to be divided into two. The two witnesses, then, shall preach three years and a half; and Antichrist shall make war upon the saints during the rest of the week, and desolate the world, that what is written may be fulfilled."[31]

It is intriguing to note that the ancient Jewish sages also interpreted the prophecy of Daniel 9:24–27 to teach that the Messiah, "the son of David," will literally appear at the end of a seven-year period of great troubles, suffering, and distress. For example, the Babylonian Talmud contains the following statement regarding the return of the Messiah: "Our rabbis taught: In the seven-year cycle at the end of which the son of David will come . . . at the conclusion of the septennate [7 year period] the son of David will come."[32] In another passage, the *Babylonian Talmud* reported, "The advent of the Messiah was pictured as being preceded by years of great distress."[33]

The Mark of the Beast

Irenaeus also commented on the mark of the Beast and 666: "The number is 666, that is, six times a hundred, six times ten, and six units. (He gives this) as a summing up of the whole of that apostasy which has taken place during six thousand years. For in as many days as this world was made, in so many thousand years shall it be concluded. And for this reason the Scripture says: Thus the heaven and the earth were finished, and all their adornment. And God brought to a conclusion upon the sixth day the works that He had made; and God rested upon the seventh day from all His works. This is an account of the things formerly created; as it is a prophecy of what is to come. For the day of the Lord is as a thousand years; and in six days created things were completed: it is evident, therefore, that they will come to an end at the year sixth thousand."[34] Irenaeus indicates in this passage his belief that Christ would establish His rule approximately two thousand years after His first coming.

Irenaeus wrote that some writers had speculated that the number 666 (Revelation 13:18) may refer to the name *Lateinos* (the Latin) or *Teitan* (Titan) but he wisely refused to speculate about the name of the Antichrist. "We will not, however, incur the risk of pronouncing positively as to the name of Antichrist: for if it were necessary that his name should be distinctly revealed in this present time, it would have been announced by him who beheld the apocalyptic vision. For that was seen no very long time since, but almost in our day, towards the end of Domitian's reign."[35]

Victorinus wrote in his commentary that both John and Daniel prophesied about the satanic system of population control that the Antichrist will employ involving the mark. "Moreover, he himself shall contrive that his servants and children should receive as a mark on their foreheads, or on their right hands, the number of his name, lest any one should buy or sell them. Daniel had previously predicted his [the Antichrist's] contempt and provocation of God."[36]

Lactantius wrote in his *Divine Institutes* about the last three and a half years of terror during the Great Tribulation under the Antichrist's mark of the Beast system: "As many as shall believe him and unite themselves to him, shall be marked by him as sheep; but they who shall refuse his mark will either flee to the mountains, or, being seized, will be slain with studied tortures. He will also enwrap righteous men with the books of the prophets, and thus burn them; and power will be given him to desolate the whole earth for forty-two months."[37]

The Temple will be Rebuilt in Jerusalem

Lactantius wrote in *Divine Institutes* that there will be a rebuilt Temple in the last days that will be defiled by the Antichrist during the Tribulation when he will persecute the Jewish people. "Then he will attempt to destroy the temple of God, and persecute the righteous people; and there will be distress and tribulation such as there never has been from the beginning of the world."[38]

Irenaeus also refers to the Antichrist sitting in a rebuilt Temple in Jerusalem: "In which (Temple) the enemy shall sit, endeavoring to show himself as Christ, as the Lord." He quotes Jesus' words in Matthew 24 that refer to Daniel 9:24–27: "When ye therefore shall see the abomination of desolation, spoken of by Daniel the prophet, stand in the holy place, (whoso readeth, let him understand)."[39]

The Rebirth of Israel

It is interesting to note that several of the early Christian writers correctly interpreted the ancient prophecies that Israel would once again become a nation when the Jewish exiles returned to the Promised Land. Irenaeus acknowledged that Israel would become a nation again in his book *Against Heresies*: "And again the same speaks thus: 'These things saith the Lord, I will gather Israel from all nations whither they have been driven . . . and they shall dwell in their own land, which I gave to my servant Jacob."[40] Hippolytus wrote the following statement in his book *Treatise on Christ and Antichrist*: "For he will call together all the people to himself out of every country of the dispersion, making them his own, as though they were his own children, and promising to restore their country and establish again their kingdom and nation in order that he may be worshipped by them as God."[41]

The Fig Tree Represents Israel

For many years the critics of modern prophecy teachers have denied that the prophetic passage of Christ's message in Matthew 24 regarding the "fig tree" actually referred to the rebirth of the nation Israel. Many critics suggest that there was no persuasive evidence that the "fig tree" actually refers to Israel and its restoration to the Promised Land in the last days. The Bible used the "fig tree," "fig," and "figs" numerous times as an obvious symbol of the nation Israel. For example, the book of Jeremiah used the "fig tree" as a symbol of the Jewish people. "Thus saith the Lord, the God of Israel; Like these good figs, so will I acknowledge them that are carried away captive of Judah, whom I have sent out of this place into the land of the Chaldeans for their good" (Jeremiah 24:5). Another significant use of the fig symbolically occurs in the repeated prophetic image of the Messianic dominion through the phrase, "But they shall sit every man under his vine and under his fig tree" (Micah 4:4). Jesus alluded to the same well-known messianic image of Israel at peace when He chose Nathanael to be His disciple, "When thou wast under the fig tree, I saw thee" (John 1:48).

However, a careful examination reveals there is clear and unequivocal evidence from the teachings of the primitive Church that they understood Christ's prophecy to definitely refer to Israel as the "fig tree." One of the Church writings that appeared in the first century following Jesus Christ clearly identifies the fig tree as a prophetic symbol of Israel. The ancient book known as the *Apocalypse of Peter*, which is an early second century (A.D. 110–140) commentary on the Gospel of Matthew, was discovered for the first time in 1887 in a Greek text, and an Ethiopian version was found in 1910. The *Apocalypse of Peter* comments on Christ's specific words used in the Matthew 24 Mount of Olives passage, when Jesus gave one of His most detailed messages regarding the Second Coming. Of particular note are the prophetic symbols used by Christ in this passage, especially His use of the "fig tree" symbol. This early Christian document states the following:

> And ye, receive ye the Parable of the fig-tree thereon: as soon as its shoots have gone forth and its boughs have sprouted, the end of the world will come. And I, Peter, answered and said unto him, "Explain to me concerning the fig-tree, [and] how we shall perceive it, for throughout all its days does the fig-tree sprout and every year it brings forth its fruit [and] for its master. What (then) meaneth the parable of the fig-tree? We know it not. And the Master answered and said unto me, "Dost thou not understand that the fig-tree is the house of Israel?"[42]

> Hast thou not grasped that the fig-tree is the house of Israel? Verily, I say to you that when its boughs have sprouted at the end, then shall deceiving Christs come, and awaken hope (with the words): "I am the Christ, who am (now) come into the world."[43]

A later comment in the *Apocalypse of Peter* on Christ's vital prophecy reveals that early Christian commentators understood that Jesus' plan was to restore the nation of Israel before the final "last days" crisis when the Antichrist will appear. Another interesting comment is found in the statement in *The Apocalypse of Peter* that the two witnesses, "Enoch and Elias [Elijah]," will play key roles in the last days: "Then shall the boughs of the fig-tree, i.e. the house of Israel, sprout, and there shall be many martyrs by His hand: they shall be killed and become martyrs. Enoch and Elias will be sent to instruct them that this is the deceiver who must come into the world and do signs and wonders in order to deceive."[44] *A small note of correction:* Despite the statement, the evidence is compelling that Enoch will *not* be one of the two witnesses because he was not a Jew and his rapture to heaven did not uniquely qualify him for the role as one of the two witnesses. Elijah and Moses appeared together with Jesus Christ revealing the glory of His coming kingdom on the Mount of Transfiguration. This fact strongly suggests that Elijah and Moses, who previously caused drought and plagues, will be the Two Witnesses of the last days described in Revelation 11:3–13. Malachi's prophecy about Elijah also mentions the role of Moses (Malachi 4:4–5).

This statement of Christ about the parable of the figs from the earliest days of the apostolic Church provides compelling evidence that believers who lived closest to the apostles understood the words of Christ in Matthew 24:30 to prophetically foretell the rebirth of Israel in the last days.

The prophetic teachings of the great theologians of the primitive Church provide compelling evidence that they understood the prophecies about the return of Christ and the future millennial dominion as we do today. Therefore, we can have confidence that our own prophetic interpretation about the coming Antichrist, the seven-year Tribulation, the mark of the Beast, and Christ's triumphant victory over Satan to establish His millennial kingdom are biblically valid and consistent with the Word of God as understood and taught by the first Christians.

Notes

1. Irenaeus, "Against Heresies,"*Ante-Nicene Library*, 10 vols. (Grand Rapids: Wm. B. Eerdmans Publishing Co., 1987).
2. Justin Martyr, "First Apology," *Ante-Nicene Library*, 10 vols. (Grand Rapids: Wm. B. Eerdmans Publishing Co., 1987).
3. Richard Rothe, *Dogmatic* (1863) 58.
4. James Donaldson, *History of Catholic Doctrine and Literature*, 2:261.
5. Philip Schaff, *History of the Apostolic Church*, 275.
6. Joseph Ernst Renan, *Life of Paul*, 250.
7. Karl A. Auberlen, *Prophecies of Daniel* (1854) 372.
8. Johann A. W. Neander, *Addendum to History of the Planting of Christian Churches*, ed. Bolin, 2:65.
9. Irenaeus, "Against Heresies,"*Ante-Nicene Library*, 10 vols. (Grand Rapids: Wm. B. Eerdmans Publishing Co., 1987) 554–555.
10. Hippolytus, "Treatise on Christ and Antichrist," *Ante-Nicene Library* 10 vols. (Grand Rapids: Wm. B. Eerdmans Publishing Co., 1987) 5:208.
11. John Mosheim, *Institutes of Ecclesiastical History* (1844) 1:89.
12. "Didache" *Ante-Nicene Library*, 10 vols. (Grand Rapids: Wm. B. Eerdmans Publishing Co., 1987) vol. 5.
13. "The Reliques of the Elders," *Ante-Nicene Library*, 10 vols. (Grand Rapids: Wm. B. Eerdmans Publishing Co., 1987) 1:1, 5.
14. "The Epistle of St. Clement to the Corinthians," *Ante-Nicene Library*, 10 vols. (Grand Rapids: Wm. B. Eerdmans Publishing Co., 1987).
15. Hippolytus, "Appendix," *Ante-Nicene Library*, 10 vols. (Grand Rapids: Wm. B. Eerdmans Publishing Co., 1987).
16. Edward Gibbon, "The Decline and Fall of the Roman Empire," *Great Books of the Western World* (Chicago: Encyclopedia Britannica, 1980) 187.
17. William B. Riley, *The Evolution of the Kingdom* (New York: Chas. C. Cook, 1913).
18. Hippolytus, "Appendix to the Works of Hippolytus," *Ante-Nicene Library*, 10 vols. (Grand Rapids: Wm. B. Eerdmans Publishing Co., 1987) vol. 5.

19. Lactantius, "Divine Institutes," *Ante-Nicene Library*, 10 vols. (Grand Rapids: Wm. B. Eerdmans Publishing Co., 1987) vol. 7.

20. Lactantius, "Divine Institutes," *Ante-Nicene Library*, 10 vols. (Grand Rapids: Wm. B. Eerdmans Publishing Co., 1987) vol. 7.

21. Irenaeus, "Against Heresies," *Ante-Nicene Library*, 10 vols. (Grand Rapids: Wm. B. Eerdmans Publishing Co., 1987) vol. 1.

22. Lactantius, "Divine Institutes," *Ante-Nicene Library*, 10 vols. (Grand Rapids: Wm. B. Eerdmans Publishing Co., 1987) vol. 7.

23. Victorinus, "Commentary on Apocalypse," *Ante-Nicene Library*, 10 vols. (Grand Rapids: Wm. B. Eerdmans Publishing Co., 1987).

24. Irenaeus, "Against Heresies," *Ante-Nicene Library*, 10 vols. (Grand Rapids: Wm. B. Eerdmans Publishing Co., 1987) vol. 1.

25. Lactantius, "Divine Institutes," *Ante-Nicene Library*, 10 vols. (Grand Rapids: Wm. B. Eerdmans Publishing Co., 1987) vol. 7.

26. Victorinus, "Commentary on Apocalypse," *Ante-Nicene Library*, 10 vols. (Grand Rapids: Wm. B. Eerdmans Publishing Co., 1987).

27. Irenaeus, "Against Heresies," *Ante-Nicene Library*, 10 vols. (Grand Rapids: Wm. B. Eerdmans Publishing Co., 1987) vol. 1.

28. Lactantius, "Divine Institutes," *Ante-Nicene Library*, 10 vols. (Grand Rapids: Wm. B. Eerdmans Publishing Co., 1987) vol. 7.

29. Hippolytus, "Appendix to the Works of Hippolytus," *Ante-Nicene Library*, 10 vols. (Grand Rapids: Wm. B. Eerdmans Publishing Co., 1987) vol. 5.

30. Hippolytus, "Commentary on Daniel, Fragments," *Ante-Nicene Library*, 10 vols. (Grand Rapids: Wm. B. Eerdmans Publishing Co., 1987).

31. Hippolytus, "Commentary on Daniel, Fragments," *Ante-Nicene Library*, 10 vols. (Grand Rapids: Wm. B. Eerdmans Publishing Co., 1987).

32. Sanhedrin, 97a, *The Babylonian Talmud* (London: Soncino Press, 1935) 654.

33. Shabbath, 118a, *The Babylonian Talmud* (London: Soncino Press, 1938).

34. Irenaeus, "Against Heresies," *Ante-Nicene Library*, 10 vols. (Grand Rapids: Wm. B. Eerdmans Publishing Co., 1987) vol. 1.

35. Irenaeus, "Against Heresies," *Ante-Nicene Library*, 10 vols. (Grand Rapids: Wm. B. Eerdmans Publishing Co., 1987) vol. 1.

36. Victorinus, "Commentary on Apocalypse," *Ante-Nicene Library*, 10 vols. (Grand Rapids: Wm. B. Eerdmans Publishing Co., 1987).

37. Lactantius, "Divine Institutes," *Ante-Nicene Library*, 10 vols. (Grand Rapids: Wm. B. Eerdmans Publishing Co., 1987) vol. 7.

38. Lactantius, "Divine Institutes," *Ante-Nicene Library*, 10 vols. (Grand Rapids: Wm. B. Eerdmans Publishing Co., 1987) vol. 7.

39. Irenaeus, "Against Heresies," *Ante-Nicene Library*, 10 vols. (Grand Rapids: Wm. B. Eerdmans Publishing Co., 1987) vol. 1.

40. Irenaeus, "Against Heresies," *Ante-Nicene Library*, 10 vols. (Grand Rapids: Wm. B. Eerdmans Publishing Co., 1987) vol. 1.

41. Hippolytus, "Treatise on Christ and Antichrist," *Ante-Nicene Library* (Grand Rapids: Wm. B. Eerdmans Publishing Co., 1987).

42. Wilhelm Schneemelcher, ed., *The New Testament Apocrypha* (Philadelphia: The Westminster Press, 1964) 668–669.

43. Wilhelm Schneemelcher, ed., *The New Testament Apocrypha* (Philadelphia: The Westminster Press, 1964) 669.

44. Wilhelm Schneemelcher, ed., *The New Testament Apocrypha* (Philadelphia: The Westminster Press, 1964) 669.

4

The Time of Christ's Return

> This same Jesus, which is taken up from you into heaven,
> shall so come in like manner as ye have seen him go
> into heaven. (Acts 1:11)

Careful study of the Scriptures and Church history confirms
that the Bible teaches and the faithful teaching of the orthodox
Church in all generations has affirmed the hope of the return of
Christ. The churches in all major Christian traditions—Catholic,
Protestant, Orthodox, and Coptic—acknowledge the scriptural
teaching of the Second Advent. Consequently, virtually all
Christians acknowledge the Second Coming of Christ. However,
the controversy involves the question as to the timing and
the literal details surrounding this critically important event,
which is prophesied in numerous passages throughout the
Old and New Testament.

One of the most intriguing prophecies concerning the
promise of His coming is that the final generation that
experiences the fulfillment of the events of the "last days"
will also witness an astonishing denial of the literal truth of
the return of our Lord by scoffers who will openly deny the

Bible's prophecies about the return of Christ. Specifically, the apostle Peter warned, "There shall come in the last days scoffers, walking after their own lusts, And saying, Where is the promise of his coming? for since the fathers fell asleep, all things continue as they were from the beginning of the creation" (2 Peter 3:3–4). In other words, in the last days, "scoffers" would appear in the Church who will deny the scriptural truth of a literal, future coming of Christ on the basis that a long period of time had passed since the original prophecies were given and the prediction remains unfulfilled.

As mentioned in the first few chapters, we are now witnessing an amazing proclamation by a group of scholars calling themselves preterists. Extreme or full preterists strongly deny the truth of the literal and future Second Coming. However, partial preterists believe that the prophecies of Matthew 24 and the book of Revelation were almost completely fulfilled when Jerusalem was destroyed in A.D. 70, but they suggest some kind of a Second Coming will occur in the far distant future. Rather than deny the truth of the hundreds of prophecies about the Second Advent, preterists claim these specific predictions were actually fulfilled almost two thousand years ago when the Roman legions burned Jerusalem. For example, a major full preterist writer, David Chilton, wrote, "The Olivet Discourse is not about the Second Coming of Christ. It is a prophecy of the destruction of Jerusalem in A.D. 70."[1] He also declared, "The Book of Revelation is not about the Second Coming of Christ. It is about the destruction of Israel and Christ's victory over His enemies in the establishment of the New Covenant Temple."[2]

However, it is obvious that the detailed prophecies in Matthew 24, 2 Thessalonians and the book of Revelation about Christ's return were not literally fulfilled by the limited historical events that transpired during the destruction of Jerusalem. Over 1,250,000 Jewish citizens of Jerusalem were starved, burned, and slaughtered by the brutal legions of Rome following the Jews' ill-considered revolt against the overwhelming military power of imperial Rome. The only way that the preterists can claim that the numerous prophecies about Christ's Second Coming were fulfilled during the burning of Jerusalem is to interpret the words contained in these numerous predictions in a totally allegorical, metaphorical, and symbolic manner.

This method of allegorical interpretation of the prophecies is totally contradicted by the normal principles of scriptural interpretation that are used by all orthodox Christian scholars, including preterists, to interpret all other non-prophetic scriptural passages. Curiously, the preterists interpret the language of the Scriptures about the death and resurrection of Christ in a totally literal and natural manner, but they abandon this fundamental principle of biblical interpretation when they interpret the prophecies about the Second Coming. This inconsistency of interpretation is logically indefensible and biased by their desire to escape the clear teaching of the prophecies regarding the literal and future Second Coming to set up Christ's millennial rule. (See Chapter 2 for a complete discussion of why the literal method of interpretation is the most accurate.)

The Scriptures declare that there will be a growing "spirit of Antichrist" in the last days (1 John 4:3). The Bible reveals that one of the characteristics of the spirit of Antichrist is that it denies that Jesus Christ comes in the flesh. Obviously, anyone who denies that Jesus Christ was incarnated into human flesh by being supernaturally born to His mother Mary is denying Christ's fundamental claim that He is both the Son of Man and the Son of God. That is "the spirit of Antichrist." In answer to this, John wrote:

> Beloved, believe not every spirit, but try the spirits whether they are of God: because many false prophets are gone out into the world. Hereby know ye the Spirit of God: Every spirit that confesseth that Jesus Christ is come in the flesh is of God: And every spirit that confesseth not that Jesus Christ is come in the flesh is not of God: and this is that spirit of antichrist, whereof ye have heard that it should come; and even now already is it in the world. Ye are of God, little children, and have overcome them: because greater is he that is in you, than

he that is in the world. They are of the world: therefore speak they of the world, and the world heareth them. We are of God: he that knoweth God heareth us; he that is not of God heareth not us. Hereby know we the spirit of truth, and the spirit of error. (1 John 4:1–6)

This passage, 1 John 4:2–3, which declares, "Every spirit that confesseth that Jesus Christ is come in the flesh is of God" also refers to His prophesied return in the last days. The New Testament confirms that just as Jesus truly came into this world as a physical human being, lived His life as a human, died, and rose from the dead, He will also return to the earth physically at the conclusion of the Battle of Armageddon. Therefore, the denial of the literal reality of the return of Christ is a fundamental characteristic of the spiritual opposition to God that will manifest during the last days leading up to His return from heaven.

It is surely significant that the New Testament contains repeated warnings about the danger of spiritual deception in the final days. The apostle John specifically warned about deception in the last days regarding the nature of Jesus Christ's Second Coming (2 John 7–8). It should not, then, be surprising that in our generation we are witnessing an astonishing claim that denies the literal reality of the hundreds of prophecies that affirm that Jesus Christ will return in the flesh from heaven to defeat the Antichrist and establish His rule on earth.

The Dating of Revelation

In Chapter 2, we briefly touched on the basic weakness of preterism, that is, its complete dependence upon Revelation being written before the A.D. 70 destruction of Jerusalem. Naturally, if John wrote his prophecy after the fall of the Holy City, then their argument falls apart. Thomas Ice summed up the preterist problem in the book *Dominion Theology: Blessing or Curse*:

It must be pointed out that if Revelation was written before A.D. 70, then Chilton's view may be correct. But if the Apocalypse was penned before A.D. 70, it would not by itself rule out the futurist and premillennial view (i.e., Revelation is still prophetic of the future). The futurist view could still be correct if it was written when Chilton says it was, since the date is not determinant to the validity of its view. However, if Revelation was written even one day after the fall of Jerusalem, then it ceases to be a prophecy concerning the destruction of Jerusalem.[3]

The preterists themselves understand that their theory cannot be true if John wrote his prophecies in the book of Revelation at any point in time after the Romans destroyed Jerusalem, as the well-known preterist Ken Gentry admitted. "If it could be demonstrated that Revelation was written twenty-five years after the fall of Jerusalem, Chilton's entire labor would go up in smoke."[4]

To get past the fundamental weakness in their position, the preterists have come up with several arguments to place John's writing of Revelation before A.D. 70 when both Jerusalem and the Temple were destroyed by Rome. Their main points are as follows.

The Preterist's Claim that the Temple was still Standing

The preterists argue that the apostle John's accurate description of the Temple in the book of Revelation can only be explained on the basis that the Temple was still standing when he wrote his book. In David Chilton's *Days of Vengeance*, he writes, "St. John's intimate acquaintance with the minute details of Temple worship suggests that 'the book of Revelation and the Fourth Gospel must have been written before the Temple services had actually ceased.'"[5]

A careful examination of the text of Revelation reveals only two verses that directly refer to the actual Temple in Jerusalem. Both of these references are found in Revelation 11, which clearly describes John's prophetic vision of a future Temple that will exist in the years just prior to Christ's return at the Battle of Armageddon. These genuine references to the Temple in Jerusalem are as follows: "And there was given me a reed like unto a rod: and the angel stood, saying, Rise, and measure the temple of God, and the altar, and them that worship therein. But the court which is without the temple leave out, and measure it not; for it is given unto the Gentiles: and the holy city shall they tread under foot forty and two months" (Revelation 11:1–2). All other specific references in Revelation to the Temple are either symbols or they clearly refer to the Temple in heaven. Those who wish to examine the evidence will find a number of verses that refer to the Temple in heaven including: Revelation 3:12; 7:15; 11:19; 14:15, 17; 15:5–6, 8; 16:1; 16:17; 21:22.

Could John have accurately described the Temple in A.D. 96 if it was destroyed approximately twenty-six years earlier? I believe so, for the following reasons.

As a righteous Jew, John would have attended the major Temple feasts (Passover, Pentecost, and Tabernacles) for a significant portion of his life, roughly fifty years from his being an adult until the Temple was destroyed. This means that John would have attended Temple services about 150 times, providing more than enough visits for him to accurately remember and describe the Temple service.

The gospel of John declares that John was a friend of the high priest, which would have afforded him additional opportunities to visit the Temple. This again would provide ample reason for his accurate description. In addition, as a disciple and important Christian teacher, John taught often in the Temple for many years following the ascension of Christ. Acts 3 through 6 show several instances of John's presence at the Temple. Unless the preterists argue that John suffered from Alzheimer's or some other specific memory problem, there is no reason to believe that John could not remember the few details regarding the Jewish Temple that are recorded in Revelation, regardless of whether the Temple was still standing at the time of his writing the book of Revelation.

A careful evaluation of the Temple imagery found in the Apocalypse finds that virtually every single detail is also found in the extensive Temple imagery found in the books of Chronicles, Kings, Daniel, Ezekiel, Joel, and Zechariah. If the preterists used the same argument they use to attack John to attack the prophetic vision of Ezekiel, they would be forced to argue that the enormous Temple of Ezekiel's vision (Ezekiel 40–46) must have been standing in Israel (and must have been visited by Ezekiel) during the prophet's exile during the Babylonian Captivity, to account for Ezekiel's highly detailed description and exact measurements of the future messianic Temple. However, all serious biblical scholars acknowledge that Ezekiel described in astonishing precision an inspired prophecy about a future Temple that will only come into existence at some point in the future when the Messiah returns. John would naturally have known the details of the Old Testament prophets' visions about the Temple. This scriptural knowledge can easily account for the few details regarding the Temple that are found in the book of Revelation, if his personal memories were not sufficient.

Finally, since those who support preterism accept that the Scriptures, including Revelation, are divinely inspired by the Holy Spirit, there is no reason to believe that God would have allowed John to inaccurately record details about the Temple service, regardless of the state of the prophet's memory or whether the Temple was still standing when John penned his inspired book. In John's Gospel, the Lord promised that He will inspire and "guide you into all truth." He said, "Howbeit when he, the Spirit of truth, is come, he will guide you into all truth: for he shall not speak of himself; but whatsoever he shall hear, that shall he speak: and he will show you things to come" (John 16:13). Furthermore, John specifically affirms in his Revelation that he "heard and saw these things" and then recorded in his inspired writing what the angel had shown him in divine vision. Therefore, the inspiration of the Holy Spirit is sufficient to account for John's accurate description of the Temple and his use of Temple imagery without any need for John to visit the Temple and see it with his own eyes before recording his divinely inspired visions. Logically, therefore, there is no basis for denying that John could accurately record the divine visions he received from the Holy Spirit.

Critics Claim Irenaeus' Testimony is Ambiguous

Despite the clear testimony of Irenaeus, that Revelation was written by John "toward the end of Domitian's reign," which was accepted universally by the early Church, David Chilton wrote: "Although some scholars have uncritically accepted the statement of St. Irenaeus (120–202) that the prophecy appeared 'toward the end of Domitian's reign' (i.e., around 96), there is considerable room for doubt about his precise meaning (he may have meant that the Apostle John himself 'was seen' by others). The language of St. Irenaeus is somewhat ambiguous; and, regardless of what he was talking about, he could have been mistaken."[6] However, no one ever suggested that Irenaeus was "ambiguous" or "mistaken" until the recent appearance of preterism and its need to deny his compelling testimony that John wrote his prophecy during the tyranny of Emperor Domitian.

While Irenaeus is the earliest historical source for the 96 date, there are numerous other historical sources from reliable early Church fathers that provide powerful evidence regarding the late date (as we will discuss in the next section). Indeed, no church historians disputed Irenaeus' statement about the Apocalypse for many centuries. In comparison, there are no historical sources from the second or third century that claim that John wrote the Apocalypse during the reign of Nero.

To try to make their point, the preterists quibble over semantics. David Chilton and other preterists reject the normal interpretation that Irenaeus' statement refers to John's prophetic vision as recorded in the book of Revelation. Rather, they suggest that the word *that*, which is part of Irenaeus' phrase "For *that* was seen no very long time since, but almost in our day, towards the end of Domitian's reign," actually refers to the apostle John himself, not his vision or his book. The Greek word translated "that" is an impersonal pronoun in the neuter gender, which is consistent with the interpretation of "that" referring to the book of Revelation. When we consider the nature of the Greek word "him," which is part of the phrase "it would have been announced by *him* who beheld the apocalyptic vision," we see that it is in the masculine gender. Therefore, the neuter gender of the original Greek word translated "that" cannot logically refer to the apostle John. In Greek grammar a word such as "that" will almost always refer to the nearest antecedent unless there is a clear reason not to do so based on the context. Irenaeus' statement must therefore refer to the Apocalypse itself, which again is consistent with a late date of 96.

Preterists' Claim Others Depend Solely upon Irenaeus

Since they have already impugned Irenaeus' credibility, the preterists dismiss other Church fathers' testimonies as relying solely upon Irenaeus for their facts. David Chilton wrote:

> St. Irenaeus, incidentally, is the only source for this late dating Revelation; all other "sources" are simply quoting from him. It is thus rather disingenuous for commentators to claim, as Swete does, that "Early Christian tradition is almost unanimous in assigning the Apocalypse to the last years of Domitian." Certainly, there are other early writers whose statements indicate that St. John wrote the Revelation much earlier, under Nero's persecution.[7]

Refuting the A.D. 68 Date of Revelation

Despite Chilton's hopes, there is ample historical evidence from numerous independent sources that supports the 96 date. In addition, the historical evidence demonstrates that Irenaeus is not the sole source. Most of the other witnesses regarding the date of the Apocalypse do not even mention Irenaeus, let alone quote him. The record of the early Church fathers and historians who supported the 96 date for the writing of Revelation is unanimous until approximately 367. There is also evidence from the Scriptures that support the 96 dating of Revelation. Furthermore, the following material will demonstrate that the first clear statement, and only non-contradictory source, that supports the date of Nero appeared in approximately A.D. 550, almost 450 years after the Apocalypse was written.

Irenaeus (160)

Irenaeus stated that John wrote the Revelation during the final years of Emperor Domitian's tyranny. In approximately 160, Irenaeus wrote about John's prophecies in Revelation concerning the name and number of the Antichrist. After warning against trying to identify the name of the Antichrist, he clearly identified "the apocalyptic vision," Revelation, as a book that appeared not long ago "almost in our day, towards the end of Domitian's reign."

> We will not, however, incur the risk of pronouncing positively as to the name of Antichrist; for if it were necessary that his name should be distinctly revealed in this present time, it would have been announced by him who beheld the apocalyptic vision. For that was seen no very long time since, but almost in our day, towards the end of Domitian's reign.[8]

Irenaeus' declaration is consistent with the traditional 96 date for Revelation (the date of Domitian's death). However, his evidence definitely contradicts the preterists' suggested date of 66–68. As an educated scholar in the Roman Empire, Irenaeus described the appearance of the book of Revelation at the end of the reign of Domitian. Because he was born only thirty-five years after Domitian's death, the well-respected Irenaeus is an extremely reliable historical source.

We also view Irenaeus as a very credible source because he was a student of Polycarp, who had been personally   tutored by the apostle John. There was a direct link of transmitted knowledge from the apostle John, to his disciple Polycarp, and ultimately to Irenaeus. Therefore Irenaeus' declaration regarding the authorship of the Apocalypse and the 96 date is of tremendous historical value. An article on Revelation in *The Interpreter's Dictionary of the Bible* states: "The earlier church writers converged on a date in the reign of Domitian (81–96); such appears to be the united testimony of Melito of Sardis, Irenaeus, Clement of Alexandria, Origen, Victorinus, and

Eusebius—church fathers ranging from the second to the fourth century. Jerome too knows of this tradition."[9]

Clement of Alexandria (190)

In approximately 190, Clement of Alexandria also confirmed that John wrote the Apocalypse in 96. He referred to an encounter between John and a backslidden robber, which occurred when the apostle returned from exile on Patmos "after the death of the tyrant."[10] Since two Roman emperors were tyrants during the first century of the Christian era, the word tyrant could logically refer to either Nero or Domitian. However, in the same writing Clement repeatedly referred to John as being a very old and infirm man.[11] John was less than sixty years old during the reign of Nero. Sixty would hardly be considered old and infirm. Thus, it is clear from Eusebius' *Ecclesiastical History* that Eusebius understood that Clement of Alexandria taught in his *Quis Dives Salvetur* that John was imprisoned on Patmos during the reign of Domitian.

Hippolytus (200)

Hippolytus, the bishop of Portus (170–236), was a Greek but is associated with the Latin Church. He was a disciple of Irenaeus and wrote extensively about the prophecies. A remarkable marble statue of Hippolytus sitting on a chair was discovered near the Tiburtine Road outside Rome in 1551. On the back of the marble chair, archeologists discovered a list of Hippolytus's books, demonstrating the breadth of his scholarship. Unfortunately, many of his works have not survived. Hippolytus was an important Christian leader, and as he lived so close to the time of the apostle John, his testimony (given in approximately 200) supporting the Domitian date for the Apocalypse is significant.

In 1888 Professor John Gwynn from Dublin, Ireland, discovered five fragments of an ancient Syriac manuscript belonging to Hippolytus. It is entitled *Capita Adversus Caium* and rests now in the British Museum (section Cod. Mus. Brit. Orient. 560). Later that year, Professor Gwynn wrote an article in the *Trinity College Dublin Review*, entitled *Hermathena*, referring to the writings of Dionysius Barsalibi, the Bishop of Amid. Dionysius' manuscript states that Hippolytus and Irenaeus believed that John wrote the Apocalypse during his banishment under Emperor Domitian in 96.[12] Professor John B. Lightfoot (1602–1675), vice-chancellor of Cambridge University, also refers to this manuscript in his authoritative series on ancient Christian writings entitled *Apostolic Fathers*. Professor Lightfoot wrote: "Dionysius Barsalibi states that Hippolytus, like Irenaeus, holds the Apocalypse to have been written by John the Evangelist under Domitian (Gwynn; *Hermathena* vii. p. 137)."[13] This previously unknown confirmation from Hippolytus provides additional and compelling evidence in support of the A.D. 96 date for the Apocalypse.

Tertullian (200)

Tertullian (160–240) was an important Christian theologian in the city of Carthage in North Africa. Tertullian's writings clearly support a 96 date for the Apocalypse in his references to the persecutions of the apostles.

> But if thou art near to Italy, thou hast Rome, where we also have an authority close at hand. What an happy Church is that! on which the Apostles poured out all their doctrine, with their blood: where Peter had a like Passion with the Lord; where Paul hath for his crown the same death with John; where the Apostle John was plunged into boiling oil, and suffered nothing, and was afterwards banished to an island.[14]

Tertullian declared that Emperor Nero martyred Paul and Peter, yet he does not mention John's banishment to Patmos during this first imperial persecution of the sword by Nero. However, Tertullian specifically described the later banishment of Christians, which was the punishment meted out to the apostle John "afterwards," when he described the persecution that occurred during the last two years of Emperor Domitian's reign (95–96). Tertullian described John's miraculous survival from boiling oil during the persecution of Nero in A.D. 66 when Peter and Paul were killed. Hovever, Tertullian then mentioned

John's banishment "to an island," which occurred "afterwards." Numerous sources confirm this banishment occurred during the tyranny of Domitian in A.D. 96. Possibly confusion developed centuries later regarding these two separate persecutions under Nero and Domitian, both of which were experienced by the apostle John.

Origen (225)

Origen was one of the greatest scholars of the early Church. He produced an incredible number of books during his long career as a teacher, theologian, and writer in Alexandria, Egypt. Writing in about 225, Origen confirmed the fact that John was banished during the reign of the brutal Domitian. In writing his commentary on the book of Matthew, Origen made the following statement about John's banishment:

> The King of the Romans, as tradition teaches, condemned John, who bore testimony, on account of the word of truth, to the isle of Patmos. John, moreover, teaches us things respecting his testimony, without saying who condemned him when he utters these things in the Apocalypse. He seems also to have seen the Apocalypse . . . in the island.[15]

While one might wish that Origen had been more specific regarding his identification of the "King of the Romans," it is most probable that he referred to Emperor Domitian. Knowing that Irenaeus had clearly identified Domitian as the one who banished John to Patmos, and that this conclusion was widely taught in the early Church (see Clement of Alexandria, Hippolytus, et cetera), it is logical that Origen would have specifically named another emperor if it were so. Origen's comment therefore tends to confirm that Domitian is "the King of the Romans" who "condemned John." R. H. Charles, in his commentary on the Apocalypse, discussed the preponderance of evidence that leads to this conclusion. "Neither in Clement nor Origen is Domitian's name given, but it may be presumed that it was in the mind of the writers."[16]

Victorinus (280)

Another Christian writer, Victorinus (240–303), bishop of Petau, wrote an extensive *Commentary on the Apocalypse*. In this book, Victorinus, who lived during the persecution under Emperor Diocletian, confirmed that John wrote his prophecy during the reign of Domitian. Victorinus' ministry overlapped that of early Church authorities such as Irenaeus, who personally knew those who were taught by the apostle John. Victorinus commented:

> When John said these things he was in the island of Patmos, condemned to the labour of the mines by Caesar Domitian. There, therefore, he saw the Apocalypse; and when grown old, he thought that he should at length receive his quittance by suffering, Domitian being killed, all his judgments were discharged. And John being dismissed from the mines, thus subsequently delivered the same Apocalypse which he had received from God.[17]

Bishop Victorinus commented on his interpretation of the seven kings described in Revelation 17. In Victorinus' commentary he wrote about the time of their appearance in history: "The time must be understood in which the written Apocalypse was published, since then reigned Caesar Domitian; but before him had been Titus his brother, and Vespasian, Otho, Vitellius, and Galba. These are the five who have fallen. One remains, under whom the Apocalypse was written—Domitian, to wit."[18]

Eusebius (325)

The early Church historian Eusebius (265–339) quoted the passage from Irenaeus that was referred to earlier in this chapter. Once again, it confirms Revelation as being written "towards the end of Domitian's reign." It is worthwhile to note that Eusebius, who had available to him all of the records of the early Christian Church, personally and directly testified that John wrote his Apocalypse under the reign of Emperor Domitian. In his historical chapter that details the cruelty of Domitian toward Christians, Eusebius wrote:

> It is said that in this [Domitian's] persecution the apostle and evangelist John, who was still alive, was condemned to dwell on the island of Patmos in consequence of his testimony to the divine word. ... To such a degree, indeed, did the teaching of our faith flourish at that time that even those writers who were far from our religion did not hesitate to mention in their histories the persecution and the martyrdom which took place during it. And they, indeed, accurately indicated the time. For they recorded that in the fifteenth year of Domitian Flavia Domitilla, daughter of a sister of Flavius Clement, who at that time was one of the consuls of Rome, was exiled with many others to the island of Pontia in consequence of testimony borne to Christ.[19]

While he questioned John's authorship at an earlier point in his life, Eusebius later concluded that the apostle John was the true author of the Apocalypse. He wrote about John's book of Revelation as follows:

> But after Domitian had reigned fifteen years and Nerva succeeded to the empire, the Roman Senate, according to the writers that record the history of those days, voted that Domitian's honors [decrees] should be cancelled, and that those who had been unjustly banished should return to their homes and have their property restored to them. It was at this time that the apostle John returned from his banishment in the island and took up his abode in Ephesus, according to an ancient Christian tradition.[20]

> After Emperor Nerva had reigned a little more than a year, he was succeeded by Emperor Trajan.[21]

> At that time the apostle and evangelist John, the one whom Jesus loved, was still living in Asia and governing

the churches of that region, having returned after the death of Domitian from his exile on the island. And that he was still alive at that time may be established by the testimony of two witnesses. They should be trustworthy who have maintained the orthodoxy of the Church; and such indeed were Irenaeus and Clement of Alexandria.[22]

It is noteworthy that Eusebius is the only early Christian historical source who directly referred to the evidence provided by Irenaeus in his own statement.

Jerome (385)

The uniform tradition of the early Church is that the apostle John was born near the time of Christ's birth, possibly later, which would be consistent with him being in his sixties during Nero's reign. For example, the writer Jerome (c. 345–c. 419), one of the greatest writers in the early Church, refers to this apostle as follows: "Yet John, one of the disciples, who is related to have been the youngest of the Apostles, and who was a virgin when he embraced Christianity, remained a virgin."[23] In the same passage in Book I, Jerome refers to John as "a youth, I may say almost a boy" at the time of the formation of the Church following Christ's resurrection. In this passage Jerome refers to John as "a prophet, for he saw in the island of Patmos, to which he had been banished by the Emperor Domitian as a martyr for the Lord an Apocalypse containing the boundless mysteries of the future."[24]

The clearest historical statement is Jerome's declaration: "We may be sure that John was then a boy because ecclesiastical history most clearly proves that he lived to the reign of Trajan, that is, fell asleep in the sixty-eighth year [A.D. 100] after our Lord's passion."[25]

In his book *Lives of Illustrious Men*, Jerome wrote about John's banishment.

In the fourteenth year then after Nero, Domitian having raised a second persecution, he was banished to the island of Patmos, and wrote the Apocalypse, on which Justin Martyr and Irenaeus afterwards wrote commentaries. But Domitian having been put to death and his acts, on account of his excessive cruelty, having been annulled by the Senate, he [John] returned to Ephesus under Pertinax and continuing there until the time of the emperor Trajan, founded and built churches throughout all Asia, and, worn out by old age, died in the sixty-eighth year after our Lord's passion and was buried near the same city. [26]

Another very important reference to the date of John's writing of the Apocalypse is found in *Jerome's Works*, Vol. iv. ii. p. 549 (Bened. Ed.), as recorded in *Epistle 44 Paulœ et Eustochii ad Marcellam*, where Jerome specifically describes the Apocalypse as being written *"after the destruction of Jerusalem."*

Sulpicius Severus (401)

Another interesting report by the Christian scholar Sulpicius Severus, in approximately 401, declares: "John, the Apostle and Evangelist, was banished by Domitian into the isle of Patmos; where he had visions, and where he wrote the book of the Revelation, which is either foolishly or wickedly rejected by many."[27]

Primasius (540)

During the sixth century, Primasius was the bishop of Hadrumentum in north Africa until his death in approximately 560. He wrote a major commentary on the Apocalypse (around 540), which was partly based on the earlier commentary of Bishop Victorinus. In the preface to his commentary, Primasius wrote that John received his apocalyptic visions while he was banished and imprisoned in the mines on the island of Patmos under Caesar Domitian (96). Primasius wrote: "Moreover, he was unfortunately seen to be deserving, [having been] sent on account of Christ to the island of Patmos under Caesar Domitian, to be condemned to the mine and incarcerated there until the end [of his sentence]."[28]

Isodore of Seville (596)

Isodore of Seville became the archbishop of the Spanish city Seville in approximately 600. As a prolific author, Isodore wrote numerous theological works including an important manual of Church doctrine as well as a twenty-volume encyclopedia. In his *Chronicle* in 596, Isodore wrote a history about a number of the apostles during the first century. He wrote about the martyrdom of Peter under Emperor Nero and the banishment of the apostle John under Emperor Domitian.

> Peter, as before said, went to Rome in the reign of Claudius, to oppose Simon Magus. Here the dispute with Simon Magus, and his death, are placed in the reign of Nero, and near the end of it; for about that time the martyrdom of the two forementioned apostles are supposed to have happened. Of Domitian, whose reign is computed to have from 81 to 96, he says, "He raised a persecution against the Christians. In his time the apostle John, having been banished into the island Patmos, wrote the Revelation."[29]

Venerable Bede (700)

The Venerable Bede (Baeda Bede, 673–735) was a famous Church leader and considered the "father of English history." Despite living in the neighborhood of Northumbria (northern England) throughout his life, Bede became known as the most learned man in Europe. He wrote a comprehensive Church history of the English people. After completing his famous translation of John's Gospel, he died. His fame continued to spread after his death and he was finally called "Venerable Bede" in recognition of his special spiritual qualities. Writing about John's Apocalypse, Bede stated the following: "John wrote his epistles, and his gospel, all about the same time; for after the death of Domitian, being returned from his exile, he found the Church disturbed by heretics, which had arisen in his absence, whom, in his epistles, he often calls antichrists."[30]

Other Historical Testimony

Another fascinating comment on the date of the Apocalypse is found in a curious historical source. An Anglican scholar, Daniel Whitby (1638–1726), who wrote *Paraphrase and Commentary on the New Testament,* commented on the fact that the old *Roman Martyrology* records that the Christian known as "Antipas" in John's Apocalypse (2:13) suffered martyrdom under the reign of Domitian. Obviously, if the Apocalypse of John included information about the death of Antipas during the persecution of Emperor Domitian (A.D. 95–96), then John must have published the book of Revelation at some point after his release from the island of Patmos.[31]

Contradiction With the Spiritual State of the Seven Churches

Another contradiction with the preterist theory is revealed in the spiritual state and history of the seven churches in Asia that John writes to in the first three chapters of Revelation. In 66, the apostle Paul was writing his second letter to Timothy at a time prior to John's involvement with these churches. Consider John's first letter to the church at Ephesus (Revelation 2:1–7); John declares that Ephesus has "left [their] first love," that they have "fallen," and that they must return to "the first works" and "repent." This spiritual condition could only occur after the passing of a number of years following the initial establishment of the church during Paul's missionary trips. The description of the church's spiritual challenges is consistent with a church that has existed for decades.

When Paul wrote to the Ephesians in the late 60s, the spiritual life of this church bore no resemblance to the spiritual backsliding described by John in Revelation. For example, in John's letter he warns of the Nicolaitans, while Paul makes no mention of them. The obvious conclusion is that John wrote Revelation much later, as an encouragement to the Church to stand against the terrible persecution of Domitian and the trials that would follow and to confront the teachings destroying their faith.

Preterist Claims in Support of A.D. 68 Date

A careful examination of the historical records of the early Church during the first few centuries following the resurrection of Christ fails to reveal any reliable and undisputed Christian authority that supports the preterists' view. Surely if John, the well-known disciple and bishop of seven churches, had truly written his Apocalypse before the destruction of Jerusalem, there would be ample surviving testimony to this fact. In addition, one would expect to discover several commentaries on Revelation that would have adopted the interpretation whereby John's predictions applied to the events concerning the destruction of Jerusalem and the Temple. The total absence of historical references to Jerusalem's destruction in any early Church commentaries on the book of Revelation provides compelling evidence that this theory was unknown to the Christians who lived closest to the life, ministry, and death of the apostle John.

While they have failed to find historical references in the first few centuries of the Christian era, preterists do suggest several later historical sources they claim support their position.

Epiphanius (367)

The first suggestion that the apostle John wrote the Apocalypse prior to the destruction of Jerusalem in A.D. 70 appears in the writings of Epiphanius (315–403), the bishop of Salamis (Cyprus) in A.D. 367. Epiphanius wrote that "John prophesied, or had the Revelation, in the Isle of Patmos, in the reign of Claudius" [who ruled Rome from 41–54].[32] Since there is no historical evidence about the persecution of Christians during the reign of Emperor Claudius, Epiphanius' statement is an obvious mistake with no historical credibility. In my research on this subject, I have not found any scholars who accept that Epiphanius was correct in assigning John's banishment to Patmos during the reign of Emperor Claudius; there is not the slightest evidence that any significant persecution of Christians occurred during the reign of this Roman emperor. In light of the fact that Epiphanius does not refer to Emperor Nero at all, nor to the period just before the destruction of Jerusalem, his evidence provides no credible support for the preterist position of the 68 date.

Another significant problem of inconsistency regarding Epiphanius' writing is the fact that he referred to John returning from the isle of Patmos "after ninety years of age." This statement reveals an internal contradiction—John's old age of ninety supports the 96 date. Since John was among the youngest of Christ's disciples he could not have been ninety years old in A.D. 68. Rather than dismiss Epiphanius' obvious error and ignoring his false statement, preterists have illogically argued that his incorrect testimony about Emperor Claudius should still be used to support an early A.D. 68 date for the Apocalypse.

Significantly, John Lawrence von Mosheim, one of the greatest Christian historians and evaluators of early Christian writings, wrote that Epiphanius' manuscripts were "full of blots and errors, through the levity and ignorance of the author."[33]

A Sixth-Century Syriac Version of the Apocalypse (550)

Preterists also point to the Syriac version of the Apocalypse, translated about the sixth century. It contains a subscription or title that refers to Emperor Nero. The subscription to the translation states: "The Revelation which was made by God to John the Evangelist in the island of Patmos, whither he was banished by the Emperor Nero." This is the first and, in fact, the only clear and non-contradictory historical evidence that supports the preterist argument. However, the weakness of this evidence is that the Syriac version of the Apocalypse was actually translated for the first time about the sixth century, more than four hundred years after the banishment of the apostle John to Patmos. The Church historian Johann David Michaelis notes, "The Syriac version of the Apocalypse is now known to be a part of the Philoxenian version, which was made by Polycarp at the beginning of the sixth century."[34] Therefore, while this is interesting, preterists still fail to provide any reliable evidence from the first few centuries of the Christian Church in support of their A.D. 68 date.

As noted earlier, Tertullian described the Apostle John's participation and supernatural survival from boiling oil during the persecution of Nero in A.D. 66 when Peter and Paul were killed. He then mentioned his banishment "to an island," which occurred "afterwards," that numerous other historical sources confirm occurred during the tyranny of Domitian in A.D. 96. It is possible that there was some confusion four centuries after the life of John regarding the two different persecutions experienced by the Apostle which may have resulted in the writer of the Syrian translation of the Apocalypse in the sixth century mistakenly believing that John composed the Apocalypse during the first persecution under Nero when he survived rather than the correct date of A.D. 96 during the second wave of persecution when he was banished by Domitian.

Arethas (762 or possibly later)

One of the important sources cited by the preterists is the Christian writer Arethas, who they claim wrote his *Commentary about the Apocalypse* around 540. While some scholars, such as Moses Stuart and Andrew Robert Fausset, agree with the 540 date, others such as Henry Barclay Swete suggest that Arethas lived up to three centuries later (approximately 914).

There is some evidence that Arethas was the archbishop of Caesarea and wrote a commentary on the Apocalypse in approximately 800. However, Arethas wrote his commentary on the beast of Revelation (13:2), and mentioned the Saracen capital city of Baghdad near ancient Babylon.[35] In light of the historical fact that Baghdad was only built by the Saracen dynasty in 762, it appears that Arethas must have composed his commentary on the Apocalypse at some point in time after this late date.

Arethas claimed that the Revelation was written "before the destruction of Jerusalem."[36] However, Arethas contradicts this statement in his earlier comment on Revelation 1:9. There Arethas approvingly quotes Eusebius, referring to the Apocalypse as being written by the apostle John at the island of Patmos under the tyranny of Emperor Domitian, "sub Domitiano."[37] Unfortunately for the preterists, the evidence of Arethas is hopelessly contradictory, and was written over seven centuries after the Apocalypse. It does not support their argument.

Therefore, the sole non-contradictory evidence in favor of Nero's banishment of John remains the sixth-century translation of the Apocalypse. However clear it may be, it was written over four centuries after John wrote his book.

Preterists Claim Domitian's Persecution of Christians Was Not Sustained

David Chilton wrote the following in his book *Days of Vengeance*: "A good deal of the modern presumption in favor of a Domitianic date is based on the belief that a great, sustained period of persecution and slaughter of Christians was carried on under his rule. This belief, cherished as it is, does not seem to be based on any hard evidence at all."[38]

However, this argument is quite irrelevant to the issue in question. The issue of the 96 date for the Apocalypse does not depend at all on a "great, sustained period of persecution and slaughter of Christians." Chilton's argument is weak and somewhat bizarre in that the Bible does not describe the details about this persecution other than to refer to the fact that John was banished to Patmos. Therefore, the ample historical evidence about Domitian's banishment of Christians is sufficient to support the conclusion that the apostle John was indeed imprisoned by Domitian. The historical records reveal that Nero killed Christians near Rome in relatively large numbers. However, there are no early historical sources that support the preterist assumption that widespread banishment of Christians occurred during the limited persecution during the short reign of Nero.

Preterists Claim John Referred to Nero in Revelation 17:9–10

According to David Chilton in his book *Days of Vengeance*:

> Our safest course, therefore, must be to study the Revelation itself to see what internal evidence it presents

regarding its date. As we will see throughout the commentary, the Book of Revelation is primarily a prophecy of the destruction of Jerusalem by the Romans. This fact alone places St. John's authorship somewhere before September of A.D. 70. Further, as we shall see, St. John speaks of Nero Caesar as still on the throne—and Nero died in June 68.[39]

This argument is circular and without serious merit. Chilton first concludes, without compelling evidence, that Nero is clearly mentioned in John's prophecy (because he accepts the 68 date) and *then* he uses his own assumption as evidence for his premise that John must therefore have written his prophecies in the Apocalypse during the reign of Nero.

Critics Claim God's Revelation was "sealed up" (Daniel 9:24)

To again quote from the preterist David Chilton:

> More important than any of this, however, we have a priori teaching from Scripture itself that all special revelation ended by A.D. 70. The angel Gabriel told Daniel that the "seventy weeks" were to end with the destruction of Jerusalem (Daniel 9:24-27); and that period would also serve to "seal up the vision and prophecy" (Daniel 9:24). In other words, special revelation would stop—be "sealed up"—by the time Jerusalem was destroyed. The Canon of Holy Scripture was entirely completed before Jerusalem fell.[40]

However, the Word of God does not teach that "inspired revelation was sealed" in A.D. 70. The evidence of the Scriptures reveals that the prophecies extend to the final events at the end of this age, which will culminate in the return of Jesus Christ at the Battle of Armageddon. The prophet Daniel wrote: "Seventy weeks are determined upon thy people and upon thy holy city, to finish the transgression, and to make an end of sins, and to make reconciliation for iniquity, and to bring in everlasting righteousness, and to seal up the vision and prophecy, and to anoint the most Holy" (Daniel 9:24).

We need to analyze this important prophecy to determine when these vital messianic predictions will finally be fulfilled. The six prophecies are: (1) to finish the transgression; (2) to make an end of sins; (3) to make reconciliation for iniquity; (4) to bring in everlasting righteousness; (5) to seal up the vision and prophecy; and (6) to anoint the most Holy. If you were to ask any person unfamiliar with the controversy if these six conditions were fulfilled at any previous point in history, it is highly unlikely that they would choose the Roman army's destruction of Jerusalem in A.D. 70 as the event that fulfilled these six important predictions. Most people will acknowledge that sins are still being committed and that "everlasting righteousness" would not precisely describe the times we live in that are reported daily in our newspapers, the Internet, and the television news.

An Evaluation of the Preterist Position

These main arguments of the preterists are actually astonishingly weak when we consider the absence of strong historical or scriptural evidence for their position. Despite their lack of conclusive evidence, the preterists assert in the strongest terms that their position for a 68 date for the Apocalypse is absolutely proven. However, even some of the top preterists admit that David Chilton's arguments in favor of an A.D. 68 date for the Apocalypse are quite weak.

One of the most interesting books in defense of the doctrine of preterism is *The Parousia* by J. Stuart Russell, first published anonymously in 1878.[41] This book has been republished from 1983 through 1999. Russell's book strongly supports the full preterist theory that all prophecy was fulfilled by A.D. 70. He suggests that the Second Coming and the rest of Revelation's prophecies were either fulfilled in the destruction of Jerusalem or they were fulfilled "spiritually." Russell honestly admitted that his "explanation of the predictions of the New Testament, instead of relieving the difficulty, embarrasses and perplexes us more than ever." Russell even acknowledged the objections of many orthodox Christians when they consider the preterist view that all of these powerful prophecies were fulfilled spiritually, without any observed historical events: "But how can we be expected to believe in fulfillments which are said to have taken place in the region of the spiritual and invisible when we have no witnesses to depose the facts?" There is not one example in the Bible of a prophecy that was fulfilled in an allegorical, non-historical manner.

Answering Objections to the Literal Kingdom

Critics who reject the Millennial Kingdom often raise objections to its literal nature because they claim several scriptural passages support their view that the kingdom of God is purely spiritual.

Jesus stated: "My kingdom is not of this world."

In John 18:36 Jesus declared, "My kingdom is not of this world." Some suggest that Jesus affirmed in this passage the non-material and purely spiritual nature of His kingdom. However, Christ revealed that His coming kingdom is not part of this present, sinful, spiritual "world" system. His kingdom will be announced on earth at His glorious and triumphant return with His saints. "For all that is in the world, the lust of the flesh, and the lust of the eyes, and the pride of life, is not of the Father, but is of the world" (1 John 2:16). The Lord sharply defined the difference between His future kingdom and the present world of sinful rebellion. The gospel of John revealed Christ's separate view of this present sinful world in contrast to the glorious sinless kingdom of God which will be revealed at His Second Coming. "And he said unto them, Ye are from beneath; I am from above: ye are of this world; I am not of this world" (John 8:23).

"Behold, the kingdom of God is within you."

Some claim that Christ's words "Behold, the kingdom of God is within you" (Luke 17:21) support their view that the kingdom of God exists only in the souls of believers. However, this is incorrect. Jesus was not stating that the holy kingdom of God existed in the hearts or spirits of the wicked Pharisees who rejected His Messianic claims. The Amplified Bible renders this verse as, "the kingdom of God is within you and among you." Jesus was referring to the promise of the kingdom of God as existing in the midst of the Jewish nation at that very time because Christ as the Messianic King represented that coming kingdom.

"The Kingdom of God is not meat and drink."

Others point to Paul's words, "For the kingdom of God is not meat and drink; but righteousness, and peace, and joy in the Holy Ghost"(Romans 14:17). In other words, Paul was saying that the Kingdom of God is not simply public observances. These inspired words of the apostle cannot mean what the critics suggest-that the future kingdom will not involve physical reality such as eating and drinking. For example, Jesus declared, "Blessed is he that shall eat bread in the kingdom of God" (Luke 14:15). In another passage, the Lord stated, "And I appoint unto you a kingdom, as my Father hath appointed unto me; That ye may eat and drink at my table in my kingdom, and sit on thrones judging the twelve tribes of Israel" (Luke 22:29–30).

"Flesh and blood cannot inherit the kingdom of God."

Those who believe in a purely spiritual kingdom claim support from the passage where Paul warns that "Flesh and blood cannot inherit the kingdom of God" (1 Corinthians 15:50). They suggest this passage teaches that Christ's kingdom is not a real one. However, the Scriptures repeatedly declare that the coming kingdom will exist on earth under the direct rule of Jesus Christ as "King of Kings." Paul revealed that our present mortal and corruptible bodies are not designed for the holy and eternal kingdom of God. Jesus will supernaturally resurrect the bodies of all believers to enable us to rule and reign with Christ forever in His eternal kingdom. "Behold, I show you a mystery; We shall not all sleep, but we shall all be changed, In a moment, in the twinkling of an eye, at the last trump: for the trumpet shall sound, and the dead shall be raised incorruptible, and we shall be changed. For this corruptible must put on incorruption, and this mortal must put on immortality" (1 Corinthians 15:51–53).

The kingdom of God will be ushered in at the return of the Messiah, the Lord Jesus Christ. "Then shall the King say unto them on his right hand, Come, ye blessed of my Father, inherit the kingdom prepared for you from the foundation of the world" (Matthew 25:34).

The Preterist Denial of the Imminent Second Coming of Christ

Though we have discussed in depth the issue of the date when Revelation was written, the implication of the preterist's teaching must not be lost. The point of the preterist's claim that the writing of Revelation occurred in the year 68 is to show that Revelation was fulfilled in 70, when Rome destroyed Jerusalem and the Temple. They argue that Revelation holds no promise of the imminent return of Christ. Their additional points are as follows.

The Preterist Argument—The Time Texts

Preterist scholars reject the teaching of a future premillennial return of Christ and specifically point to New Testament phrases such as "the Lord is at hand," "the coming of the Lord draweth nigh," et cetera. They argue that such phrases demand that the Lord must have returned within a very short time of the original utterance of these prophecies or the prophecies would be false.

The problem of the proper interpretation of these time passages has led to several unfortunate responses: (1) Some have chosen to ignore the prophecies of the Second Advent on the grounds that they are vague and not literal. (2) Others have rejected these prophecies as false because Christ did not return in the generation when these specific predictions were given. (3) Finally, some have chosen to interpret these "time prophecy" passages as being fulfilled in the Roman destruction of Israel and Jerusalem. The preterists argue that these predictions specifically demand that the prophesied events must be fulfilled within a few years of the original prophecy.

Preterists often refer to three specific texts that they claim show that the Second Coming of Christ must have occurred in the first century (i.e., 70).

First Time Text—Matthew 10:23

"But when they persecute you in this city, flee ye into another: for verily I say unto you, Ye shall not have gone over the cities of Israel, till the Son of man be come" (Matthew 10:23).

They claim this passage clearly points to the coming of "the Son of Man" in the lifetime of the disciples. However, many scholars admit that Matthew arranged his Gospel according to subject rather than a strict chronological sequence. The prophecy of Matthew 10 relates to the prophecy given by Christ on the Mount of Olives, recorded in Matthew 24. The prophecy of Matthew 10:21–23 will be fulfilled when the Jews preach the "gospel of the Kingdom" during the tribulation, ending with the Second Coming. The prophecy's use of the title the "Son of Man" always appears as a reference to the Second Coming of Christ. This prophetic phrase, expressing Jesus' humanity, points to His visible, personal coming. Nothing corresponding to Christ's visible and personal coming as described in numerous prophecies including Matthew 24 and Revelation 19 ever occurred at the destruction of Jerusalem, according to the historical records of Flavius Josephus, who lived at the time and wrote *The Jewish War*. For example, Jesus prophesied that, "For then shall be great tribulation, such as was not since the beginning of the world to this time, no, nor ever shall be. And except those days should be shortened, there should no flesh be saved: but for the elect's sake those days shall be shortened" (Matthew 24:21–22).

The destruction of Jerusalem in A.D. 70 was indeed horrific with the death of an estimated 1,250,000 Jewish citizens. However, Jesus prophesied an unprecedented global "great tribulation" so devastating that if He delayed His return "no flesh [would] be saved." Revelation's prophecies declare, "behold a pale horse: and his name that sat on him was Death, and Hell followed with him. And power was given unto them over the fourth part of the earth, to kill with sword, and with hunger, and with death, and with the beasts of the earth" (Revelation 6:8). If words have any meaning whatsoever, then we must reject the claim of the preterists and amillennialists who declare that these scriptural predictions and numerous others about the coming Tribultion were fulfilled in A.D. 70. Obviously, these prophecies must be fulfilled at some point in the future.

Second Time Text—Matthew 16:27–28

For the Son of man shall come in the glory of his Father with his angels; and then he shall reward every man according to his works. Verily I say unto you, There be some standing here, which shall not taste of death, till they see the Son of man coming in his kingdom. (Matthew 16:27–28)

Many amillennialists and postmillennial preterists who state that the kingdom of God appeared spiritually (including the Second Coming) at the destruction of Jerusalem point to Christ's words in both the Gospels of Matthew and Mark. These critics of the millennial kingdom suggest that Christ's statement demands that the Second Coming must occur during the lifetime of those disciples who heard His prophecy and wrongly conclude that Jerusalem's destruction is the correct fulfillment. However, the very next verse in the passage provides the correct answer to the question. "And after six days Jesus taketh Peter, James, and John his brother, and bringeth them up into an high mountain apart, And was transfigured before them: and his face did shine as the sun, and his raiment was white as the light. And, behold, there appeared unto them Moses and Elias [Elijah] talking with him" (Matthew 17:1–3). Only six days after His prophecy, the same disciples, Peter, James, and John accompanied Jesus up into a mountain and they personally saw the glory of the Lord revealed as they witnessed, "the Son of man coming in his kingdom."

To emphasize the glory of His appearing to the disciples, God the Father announced in "a voice out of the cloud, which said, This is my beloved Son, in whom I am well pleased; hear ye him" (Matthew 17:5). The Scriptures repeatedly refer to the glorification of the resurrected saints at Christ's appearing. The apostle Paul taught of the glorification of the resurrected saints as follows: "If so be that we suffer with him, that we may be also glorified together. For I reckon that the sufferings of this present time are not worthy to be compared with the glory which shall be revealed in us. For the earnest expectation of the creature waiteth for the manifestation of the sons of God" (Romans 8:17–19). The transfiguration of Christ together with the appearance of the resurrected saints, Elijah and Moses, provided powerful confirmation to His disciples that God will resurrect and glorify all of those who place their faith and trust in Christ when He ushers in the kingdom of God

Third Time Text—Matthew 24:34

"Verily I say unto you, This generation shall not pass, till all these things be fulfilled" (Matthew 24:34)

Preterists such as Ken Gentry wrote about Matthew 24:34: "This statement of Christ is indisputably clear and absolutely demanding of a first-century fulfillment of the events in the preceding verses, including the Great Tribulation."[45] However, the question of the correct time indicated by Christ when He refers to "this generation" in Matthew 24:34 is clarified when we consider the related phrase "all these things," which appears in this verse as well as the preceding verse, "So likewise ye, when ye shall see all these things, know that it is near, even at the doors." In other words, Jesus Christ prophesied that the "last days" generation that sees "all these things" occur will not cease to exist as a generation until every one of the events of the future tribulation period are literally fulfilled. Jesus is ultimately speaking to those who will be living in the generation that will personally witness the fulfillment of the prophetic signs of Matthew 24.

Understanding The Time Texts

The correct solution to the problem of these "time texts" is found in the understanding that these prophets were writing with the specific style used in the Old Testament Jewish prophetic form.

Israel's ancient prophets, such as Isaiah, Joel, and Zechariah, prophesied about God's promise of ultimate national salvation, the coming day of the Lord, and the coming of the Messiah in prophetic language that pointed to its being close at hand. However, both history and the New Testament reveal that a number of these specific prophecies were fulfilled centuries after the prediction was given. It is significant that no scholar has ever objected to the language of these Old Testament prophets on the basis that these predictions referred to events far in the future, despite the fact that the prophecy used language that described events as though they were about to be fulfilled.

Obviously God, who is eternal, views time quite differently than we do. The Word of God specifically refers to this phenomenon in the following passages: "For a thousand years in thy sight are but as yesterday when it is past, and as a watch in the night" (Psalms 90:4). "But, beloved, be not ignorant of this one thing, that one day is with the Lord as a thousand years, and a thousand years as one day" (2 Peter 3:8).

For example, consider the "time text" references found in the language of several Old Testament prophecies:

"Howl ye; for the day of the Lord is at hand; it shall come as a destruction from the Almighty" (Isaiah 13:6).

"For the day is near, even the day of the Lord is near, a cloudy day; it shall be the time of the heathen" (Ezekiel 30:3).

"Alas for the day! for the day of the Lord is at hand, and as a destruction from the Almighty shall it come"(Joel 1:15).

"Blow ye the trumpet in Zion, and sound an alarm in my holy mountain: let all the inhabitants of the land tremble: for the day of the Lord cometh, for it is nigh at hand" (Joel 2:1).

"Multitudes, multitudes in the valley of decision: for the day of the Lord is near in the valley of decision" (Joel 3:14).

"For the day of the Lord is near upon all the heathen: as thou hast done, it shall be done unto thee: thy reward shall return upon thine own head" (Obadiah 15).

"Hold thy peace at the presence of the Lord God: for the day of the Lord is at hand: for the Lord hath prepared a sacrifice, he hath bid his guests. . . . The great day of the Lord is near, it is near, and hasteth greatly, even the voice of the day of the Lord: the mighty man shall cry there bitterly" (Zephaniah 1:7, 14).

"Behold, the day of the Lord cometh, and thy spoil shall be divided in the midst of thee" (Zechariah 14:1).

It is obvious that each of these Old Testament prophecies contains prophetic language dealing with time ("the day of the Lord is at hand") that is very similar to the language used by the New Testament prophecies in reference to the nearness of Christ's Second Coming. The language of these inspired prophets contain phrases such as "near," and "at hand," yet these inspired prophecies were given by God twenty-five centuries ago. The language confirms that the prophesied event is as certain in its future fulfillment as if it had already happened.

Implications of the Preterists' Beliefs

In David Chilton's book *Paradise Restored*, he revealed the implications of his rejection of this historic hope of the Church. Speaking about God's promise of the coming Messiah, he said:

> The God of the covenant told His people that He would bless them to the thousandth generation of their descendants (Deuteronomy 7:9). That promise [the Second Coming] was made (in round figures) about 3,400 years ago. If we figure the biblical generation at about 40 years, a thousand generations is forty thousand years. We've got 36,600 years to go before this promise is fulfilled.[46]

Incredibly, some preterists such as David Chilton actually claim that Jesus Christ will not return for over 36,000 years! Tragically, the rejection of the truth of the premillennial and imminent return of Christ leaves those who embrace this teaching to face a future that offers little hope of a dramatic spiritual victory over the forces of Satan. While all Christians rejoice at the wonderful growth of the Church in the Third World in these last days, we also observe the tragic growth of unrestrained evil. The world is filled with historically unprecedented evil developments including devastating chemical, biological, and nuclear weapons of mass destruction,[47] the genocide of millions in Africa, concentration camps holding millions (including many innocent Christians) in China for "re-education,"[48] the harvesting of organs from Chinese prisoners,[49] partial birth and forced tri-semester abortions,[50] the slavery of millions in Africa and other nations,[51] and the sexual abuse of millions of young children.[52]

The preterists who reject the literal teaching of the scriptural prophecies that Christ's Second Coming is imminent and future are left with a viewpoint that teaches that Satan will continue his powerful and evil opposition to Christ for many thousands of years. They claim that their view is optimistic in that they believe that the Church will eventually, after thousands of years, Christianize the world and then deliver the kingdom to Christ. However, I believe this view is, in reality, pessimistic because it inevitably accepts the continued growth of evil in this world for thousands of years while the majority of humans will continue to be lost to an eternity in hell. If someone believes that Christ will not return until a thousand years after the world is converted to Christianity, it is difficult to see how the doctrine of the Second Coming can seriously motivate their witnessing, their daily walk in holiness, or their hope for His return.

Yet Jesus Christ taught His followers to watch constantly for His return because, although He might tarry, He will definitely return for us. Jesus warned:

> For the Son of man is as a man taking a far journey, who left his house, and gave authority to his servants, and to every man his work, and commanded the porter to watch. Watch ye therefore: for ye know not when the master of the house cometh, at even, or at midnight, or at the cock crowing, or in the morning: And what I say unto you I say unto all, Watch. (Mark 13:34–35, 37).

Pessimism or Optimism?

Postmillennial and amillennial critics of the premillennial return of Christ often complain that our view is somehow pessimistic.

For example, the preterist, post-millennial writer David Chilton claimed that those who believe in the premillennial Second Coming (such as this author and most prophecy teachers) are supporters of "pessimillennialism." Chilton declared that the "pessimillennialists" are "content to remain historical (pre-second coming) losers." The truth is that both postmillennialism and amillennialism represent a real surrender to theological "pessimism" because they reject the hope of Christ's imminent return in favor of their spiritually pessimistic view that the world shall continue in sinful rebellion for many thousands of years while they gradually Christianize the world. These critics deny the hope of the prophesied triumphant return of Christ to usher in the glorious kingdom of God.

Those who long for Christ's imminent premillennial return totally reject this false characterization that we are pessimistic. Our optimism is based on our confidence in the inspired Word of God and its glorious promises that Jesus will triumph over evil when He returns as King of Kings. Premillennialists *are* pessimistic about the likelihood of this present evil world becoming truly Christian before Christ's return because the Scriptures deny this. However, we are totally optimistic about the Bible's prophecies that Christ will triumphantly return suddenly in an evil generation such as ours. Then Christ will defeat Satan and usher in the kingdom of God with righteousness and justice forever. The message of prophecy is not a pessimistic view of "doom and gloom" but rather a glorious announcement that the Church's time of waiting is almost over. The King is coming to victoriously set up His long awaited kingdom.

As we contemplate the prophetic events that are being fulfilled in our generation we are reminded that Jesus Christ commanded His followers: "And when these things begin to come to pass, then look up, and lift up your heads; for your redemption draweth nigh" (Luke 21:28). Someday soon the angels will proclaim the glorious truth: "The kingdoms of this world are become the kingdoms of our Lord, and of his Christ; and he shall reign for ever and ever" (Revelation

11:15). This is truly the greatest and most optimistic message ever proclaimed.

Notes

1. David Chilton, *Days of Vengeance: An Exposition of the Book of Revelation* (Fort Worth: Dominion Press, 1987).

2. David Chilton, *Days of Vengeance: An Exposition of the Book of Revelation* (Fort Worth: Dominion Press, 1987).

3. Tommy D. Ice, *Dominion Theology: Blessing or Curse?* (Portland: Multnomah Press, 1988).

4. Kenneth L. Gentry, *The Council Chalcedon* 11:11.

5. David Chilton, *Days of Vengeance: An Exposition of the Book of Revelation* (Fort Worth: Dominion Press, 1987) 3.

6. David Chilton, *Days of Vengeance: An Exposition of the Book of Revelation* (Fort Worth: Dominion Press, 1987) 3.

7. David Chilton, *Days of Vengeance: An Exposition of the Book of Revelation* (Fort Worth: Dominion Press, 1987) 4.

8. Irenaeus, "Against Heresies," *Ante-Nicene Library*, 10 vols. (Grand Rapids: Wm. B. Eerdmans Publishing Co., 1987) vol. 5.

9. Editors of *The Interpreters Dictionary of the Bible* (New York: Abingdon Press, 1962) 60.

10. Clement of Alexandria, "Quis Dives Salvetur," rpt. by Eusebius, "Ecclesiastical History," *Ante-Nicene Library*, 10 vols. (Grand Rapids: Wm. B. Eerdmans Publishing Co., 1987) vol. 3.

11. Clement of Alexandria, "Quis Dives Salvetur," rpt. by Eusebius, "Ecclesiastical History," *Ante-Nicene Library*, 10 vols. (Grand Rapids: Wm. B. Eerdmans Publishing Co., 1987) vol. 3.

12. John Gwynn, *Hermathena* (Dublin, 1888) 137.

13. J. B. Lightfoot, ed., *Apostolic Fathers*, 5 vols. (Peabody: Hendrickson, 1989) 1:394.

14. Tertullian, "Exclusion of Heretics," *Ante-Nicene Library*, 10 vols. (Grand Rapids: Wm. B. Eerdmans Publishing Co., 1987) vol. 3.

15. Origen, "Comment on Matthew," *Ante-Nicene Library*, 10 vols. (Grand Rapids: Wm. B. Eerdmans Publishing Co., 1987) vol. 4.

16. R. H. Charles, "The Revelation of St. John," *The International Critical Commentary* (Edinburgh: T. & T. Clark, 1920) 1: xciii.

17. Victorinus, "Commentary on the Apocalypse," *Ante-Nicene Library*, 10 vols. (Grand Rapids: Wm. B. Eerdmans Publishing Co., 1987).

18. Victorinus, "Commentary on the Apocalypse," *Ante-Nicene Library*, 10 vols. (Grand Rapids: Wm. B. Eerdmans Publishing Co., 1987).

19. Eusebius, "Ecclesiastical History," *Ante-Nicene Library*, 10 vols. (Grand Rapids: Wm. B. Eerdmans Publishing Co., 1987) vol. 3.

20. Eusebius, "Ecclesiastical History," *Ante-Nicene Library*, 10 vols. (Grand Rapids: Wm. B. Eerdmans Publishing Co., 1987) vol. 3.

21. Eusebius, "Ecclesiastical History," *Ante-Nicene Library*, 10 vols. (Grand Rapids: Wm. B. Eerdmans Publishing Co., 1987) vol. 3.

22. Eusebius, "Ecclesiastical History," *Ante-Nicene Library*, 10 vols. (Grand Rapids: Wm. B. Eerdmans Publishing Co., 1987) vol. 3.

23. Jerome, "Against Jovinianus," *Ante-Nicene Library*, 10 vols. (Grand Rapids: Wm. B. Eerdmans Publishing Co., 1987) 1:365.

24. Jerome, "Against Jovinianus," *Ante-Nicene Library*, 10 vols. (Grand Rapids: Wm. B. Eerdmans Publishing Co., 1987) 1:366.

25. Jerome, "Against Jovinianus," *Ante-Nicene Library*, 10 vols. (Grand Rapids: Wm. B. Eerdmans Publishing Co., 1987) 1:366.

26. Jerome, "Lives of Illustrious Men," *Ante-Nicene Library*, 10 vols. (Grand Rapids: Wm. B. Eerdmans Publishing Co., 1987) vol. 1.

27. Sulpicius Severus, *Works of N. Lardner*, 11 vols. (London: 1788).

28. *Bibliotheca Maxima Patrum*, 9 vols. (Lyons, 1677) 288

29. Isodore of Seville, *Works of N. Lardner*, 11 vols. (London: 1753) 5:309.

30. Bede, "Homily on St. John the Evangelist," *Works of N. Lardner*, 11 vols. (London) 5:314.

31. E. B. Elliott, *Horæ Apocalyptic* (London: Seeley, Burnside, and Seeley, 1846).

32. Epiphanius, "Heresies," *Works of N. Lardner*, 11 vols. (London: 1788) 9: 316.

33. John Lawrence von Mosheim, *Institutes of Ecclesiastical History* (New York: Harper & Brothers, 1845) 4: 2.2.9.

34. Johann David Michaelis, *Introduction to the New Testament* (1750) 521.

35. *Bibliotheca Maxima Patrum*, 9 vols. (Lyons, 1677) 771.

36. Arethas, "Commentary about the Apocalypse," *Bibliotheca Patrum Maxima*, 9 vols. (Lyons, 1677) 7: 759.

37. *Bibliotheca Maxima Patrum*, 9 vols. (Lyons, 1677) 743.

38. David Chilton, *Days of Vengeance: An Exposition of the Book of Revelation* (Fort Worth: Dominion Press, 1987) 4.

39. David Chilton, *Days of Vengeance: An Exposition of the Book of Revelation* (Fort Worth: Dominion Press, 1987) 4.

40. David Chilton, *Days of Vengeance: An Exposition of the Book of Revelation* (Fort Worth: Dominion Press, 1987) 5.

41. J. Stuart Russell, *The Parousia* (Grand Rapids: Baker House, 1983).

42. Charles H. Spurgeon, *The Sword and the Trowel* Oct. 1879: 553.

43. Charles H. Spurgeon, *The Restoration & Conversion of the Jews* MTP, 10:429.

44. Charles H. Spurgeon, *Justification & Glory* MTP (1865) 11: 249.

45. Tommy Ice and Ken Gentry, *The Great Tribulation Past or Future?* (Grand Rapids: Kregel Publications, 1999).

46. David Chilton, *Paradise Restored* (Ft. Worth, TX: Dominion Press, 1985).

47. "Biological Weapons, Chemical weapons, nuclear wars, robot wars," http://www.futurestuff.net/ccwars/

48. "Democide in Communist China, 38 million people killed," http://www.freedomsnest.com/rummel_prc.html

49. "Organ Harvesting," http://www.laogai.org/news/organs/

50. http://www2.cwrl.utexas.edu/~bill/306/pennington/abort.html

51. "Global Slavery Resource Centre," http://www.anti-slavery.org/global/index.html

52. "Child Sexual Exploitation,"http://www.casa-alianza.org/EN/human-rights/sexual-exploit/press/index.html/

5

The Second Coming of Christ Will Be Premillennial

The Millennial kingdom of the coming Messiah is perhaps the most misunderstood subject in the whole field of prophecy. The nature of the Millennium is the issue that has divided Christian scholars and prophecy writers into three great positions: amillennial, postmillennial, and premillennial. The premillennial position teaches that Christ will actually return to establish his millennial kingdom. It is the oldest of the three views and was taught consistantly by the leaders of the early Church. The premillennial return of Christ is the only view consistent with the literal interpretation of the prophecies of the Old and New Testament. The amillennial position suggests that the Millennium is only symbolic and that it refers to Christ spiritually ruling the kingdom of God from heaven. This amillennial view was popularized by Augustine (A.D. 354–430) and gradually replaced the teaching of the premillennial return of Christ throughout the medieval Church for over a thousand years. Amillennialists teach that Christ will only return after the Church has Christianized the population of earth. The third view, the postmillennial position, is somewhat similar to amillenialism in that it teaches that the Millennial Kingdom will occur as a result of the conquest of the Church over the secular world. The postmillennial view was first introduced only two centuries ago by Daniel Whitby in 1800 and teaches that Christ will not return until *after* the Church establishes the Millennial Kingdom on earth for a thousand years. These two theories are contradicted by numerous prophecies throughout the Scriptures. An excellent comprehensive presentation of the three millennial views and a very persuasive case for premillennialism is given by Dwight Pentecost in his book *Things to Come*.[1]

The Scriptures teach that Jesus Christ, who suffered crucifixion at His first advent, "shall come in his glory, and all his angels with him, then shall he sit upon the throne of his glory" (Matthew 25:31). The New Testament contains a great number of specific predictions about the future kingdom of God that have not yet been fulfilled. For example, the prophecies declare that the Second Coming of Christ will usher in an unprecedented time of universal righteousness and true peace on earth. After this, the prophecy of the book of Revelation will finally be fulfilled, "And the seventh angel sounded; and there were great voices in heaven, saying, The kingdoms of this world are become the kingdoms of our Lord, and of his Christ; and he shall reign for ever and ever" (Revelation 11:15).

If we are to understand the hundreds of specific prophecies about the divine plan of God to establish His kingdom on earth, we must first attempt to understand the fundamental biblical truth regarding the Second Coming and its relation to the time of the coming Millennium. For example, King David wrote about the future global rule of the coming Messiah over all nations using the words "all nations shall serve him." David declared:

He shall have dominion also from sea to sea, and from

the river unto the ends of the earth. They that dwell in the wilderness shall bow before him; and his enemies shall lick the dust. The kings of Tarshish and of the isles shall bring presents: the kings of Sheba and Seba shall offer gifts. Yea, all kings shall fall down before him: all nations shall serve him. (Psalms 72:8–11)

If we carefully examine God's plan for the redemption of the earth and a lost humanity, we will see that the prophecies of the Scriptures encompass the vast panorama from paradise lost in the Garden of Eden to paradise restored in Revelation's astonishing visions of the future triumph of Christ.

The word "millennium" is derived from the Latin word *mille* for "one thousand" and the word *annum* for "year." The Greeks used the word *chiliast*, meaning "one thousand" to describe the period of one thousand years that John described in Revelation 20. Ultimately, the word millennium became the common term used to describe the period of one thousand years during which Jesus Christ would rule the earth from His throne in Jerusalem. Charles Ryrie described the basic principles of premillennialism: "Its duration will be 1,000 years; its location will be on this earth; its government will be theocratic with the personal presence of Christ reigning as King; and it will fulfill all the yet-unfulfilled promises about the earthly kingdom."[2]

While virtually all Christians in the early Church, as well as in later centuries, acknowledge that the apostle John taught about a period of one thousand years under the rule of Christ, there is a great deal of controversy regarding the meaning, duration, and the point in time when this prophesied Millennium will occur. It is interesting to note that the very popular medieval hymn "Te Deum" included these words, acknowledging that Jesus Christ will come to the earth in the future to establish His rule over the nations: "We believe that Thou shalt come to be our Judge."

The ancient prophets of Israel taught that the Messiah would come to establish His kingdom on earth forever. The prophet Isaiah declared:

For unto us a Child is born, Unto us a Son is given;

and the government shall be upon his shoulder: and his name shall be called Wonderful, Counsellor, The mighty God, The everlasting Father, The Prince of Peace. Of the increase of his government and peace there shall be no end, upon the throne of David, and upon his kingdom, to order it, and to establish it with judgment and with justice from henceforth even for ever. The zeal of the Lord of hosts will perform this. (Isaiah 9:6–7)

The Scripture's promise has ultimately focused on the prophecy about the kingdom of God on earth under the rule of the Messiah. From the moment the Lord made His first covenant with Abraham, He confirmed His covenant with humanity to establish a theocratic kingdom on earth where man would ultimately enjoy the restoration of the state of paradise, which was lost after the rebellious sin of our first parents, Adam and Eve. Through all of the generations from the patriarch Abraham to the time of Jesus of Nazareth, Israel longed for the coming of their Messiah and the establishment of His glorious rule from the throne of David in Jerusalem.

According to the Word of God, an evil world empire will be established under the satanic rule of Antichrist in the last days. Then Jesus Christ will return to earth as the conquering Messiah. He will descend from heaven with a powerful army of resurrect saints and angels and will destroy the Antichrist and His enemies forever (Revelation 19:11–21). The Church will not defeat this evil world system. The role of the Church is to preach the Gospel to everyone so that the Holy Spirit will call out a remnant of souls who will repent and find salvation through the forgiveness of Christ.

The prophet Daniel was given a divine interpretation of the dream of Nebuchadnezzar, the King of Babylon, regarding the future of gentile world political rule. The Lord provided Daniel with a detailed prophetic outline that predicted the history of the last twenty-five hundred years of gentile world empires. Daniel recorded that four Gentile world empires would succeed each other in the course of human history until a final crisis when

Jesus Christ would return to defeat the final revived Roman Empire under the tyrannical rule of the Antichrist.

According to the prophecy, the fourth world empire, Rome, will be revived in a unique political form of a ten-nation superstate in the last days and will be led by the world dictator, the Antichrist. Daniel declared that Christ will appear from heaven and will suddenly destroy this empire. The stone in Daniel's vision (Daniel 2:40–45) represents the Second Coming and the millennial "kingdom of God" under Christ's rule. Jesus will suddenly destroy the world empire of the Antichrist when He returns to the earth to save Israel from the armies of the Antichrist during the Battle of Armageddon. "The Lord will then judge the nations in the Valley of Jehoshaphat [the valley where Jehovah judges]" (Joel 3:2, 12). This judgment by Christ of the Gentiles will follow the Battle of Armageddon and the Gentile survivors will be judged on the basis of their treatment of His chosen people, Israel and the tribulation saints.

Premillennial Tradition in Jewish Teaching

Interestingly, the beliefs about the literal Millennium were held by orthodox Jewish believers centuries before and after the life of Christ. Hundreds of years before John wrote the Apocalypse, the Jewish sages taught that the Scriptures revealed God's plan to set up a messianic kingdom under the rule of the Son of David that would endure for one thousand years. This Jewish doctrine of a future Millennium rest, under the rule of the Messiah king, was obviously related to their acceptance of the tradition of the "Great Week of Human History" in which the Messiah would rule during the last Sabbath day—lasting "one thousand years," before the end of this age. Anyone who examines the Scriptures will be impressed with the fact that there are many divisions of time into sevens and into "weeks" of years in the Word of God, beginning with the week of Creation in Genesis and concluding with the various sevenfold divisions in the Apocalypse. God's command to Israel to honor the weekly Sabbath day of rest is derived from the original week of Creation and God's rest on the seventh day. Even the Feast of Pentecost is based on a week of weeks (forty-nine days) interval between the Feast of Firstfruits and the day of Pentecost. The Year of Jubilee was based on a cycle of forty-nine years (seven sevens) and the fiftieth year of rest and restitution that followed.

It is important to note that this widely held view of the Great Week of History that was taught by some Jewish and Christian writers does not provide any basis for any "date-setting" regarding the time of the return of the Messiah. Numerous calendar changes make this impossible. This view simply points generally to our time as the generation when we should see prophetic signs pointing toward the Second Coming and the approaching Millennial Kingdom.

It is obvious that a sacred cycle of sevens governs the laws and religious life of ancient Israel. That is why the inspired writer of the book of Hebrews referred to the coming Millennium using the term *Sabbath*, or *rest*. Speaking of the prophesied Sabbath, the book of Hebrews declared, "There remaineth therefore a rest to the people of God. For he that is entered into his rest, he also hath ceased from his own works, as God did from his. Let us labour therefore to enter into that rest, lest any man fall after the same example of unbelief" (Hebrew 4:9–11). The context makes it clear that this biblical reference in Hebrews is related to the Jewish anticipation of the coming one-thousand-year Sabbath "rest to the people of God."

In the book of Psalms, King David prophesied, "For a day in thy courts is better than a thousand. I had rather be a doorkeeper in the house of my God, than to dwell in the tents of wickedness" (84:10). In another passage the Psalmist refers to this important principle that God views time differently than we do. "For a thousand years in thy sight are but as yesterday when it is past, and as a watch in the night" (90:4). This widely held ancient Jewish belief in a Great Week of God's dealing with humanity that would conclude with a Sabbath rest of one thousand years was reinforced in the New Testament in the prophecy of the apostle Peter. "But, beloved, be not ignorant of this one thing, that one day is with the Lord as a thousand years, and a thousand years as one day" (2 Peter 3:8). Peter's prophecy is given in the context of our anticipation of Christ's return.

The Jewish belief in the coming millennial reign of the

Messiah was espoused by many of the greatest orthodox Jewish rabbis. These rabbis recorded their work in the Oral Law—the Talmud, composed over a period of five hundred years (from 100 B.C. to A.D. 400). The Talmud confirms that these religious Jews looked expectantly for the Messiah to establish a period of righteousness on earth that would last one thousand years. The German scholar H. Graetz notes in his book *Geschichte der Juden* that during medieval debates with Christians, the Jewish scholars of Spain argued that Jesus could not have been the promised Messiah because according to their traditional Jewish interpretation of the Messianic passages in the Bible the Messiah would not appear until the seventh millennium. In his book *Contra Judaeos*, the Christian writer Julian of Toledo, described the rabbis' interpretation at great length. This evidence suggests that the Jewish concept of the Messiah's appearance in the seventh millennium must have been fairly widely held.[3]

There is an ancient Jewish millennial tradition attributed to a famous rabbi named Elias, who lived two centuries before the birth of Jesus of Nazareth. The Talmud records that Rabbi Elias declared that God's great plan for man involved a great Sabbath Week concluding with a thousand years of peace. "The world endures six thousand years: two thousand years before the Law; two thousand years under the Law and two thousand under the Messiah. This period is called Yemoth ha-Mashiah."[4]

Another ancient rabbi, Rabbi Ketina, is referred to in a commentary upon the Talmud: "The world endures six thousand years, and one thousand it shall be laid waste, [that is the enemies of God shall be destroyed,] whereof it is said, (Isaiah 2:11) 'The Lord alone shall be exalted in that day.'" The Jewish tradition about Rabbi Ketina declares that he taught that "as out of seven years every seventh is the year of remission, so out of the seven thousand years of the world the seventh millennary shall be the millennary of remission, that God alone may be exalted in that day."[5]

The Early Church and the Premillennial
Return of Christ

It was to Jews who shared this widely held belief that Jesus brought His unique message about His coming kingdom. It is inconceivable that Jesus would have departed from the orthodox Jewish biblical teaching. He supported the Old Testament's scriptural law as it related to the Jews on many occasions. Jesus only broke with the religious leaders when their teachings had strayed from God's intentions. As Matthew recorded, Jesus plainly stated, "Think not that I am come to destroy the law, or the prophets: I am not come to destroy, but to fulfill. For verily I say unto you, Till heaven and earth pass, one jot or one tittle shall in no wise pass from the law, till all be fulfilled" (Matthew 5:17–18). Likewise, it is inconceivable that all of the teachers of the early Church would have taught the premillennial return of Christ if Jesus and the apostles had not clearly taught this doctrine.

We have testimony from many writers in the early Church that support the premillennial Second Coming of Christ to set up the Kingdom of God.

Papias

Papias (60–130) was a disciple of the apostle John. He often sat at the foot of the beloved disciple and other saints who had personally met Jesus. Papias recorded their statements from memory. Tragically, his five known books have been lost to history, so we are limited to those few portions of his writings recorded by the Church historian Eusebius. Eusebius reported in his *Ecclesiastical History* that Papias wrote, "There will be a millennium after the resurrection of the dead, when the personal reign of Christ will be established on earth."[6] Papias' statement provides clear evidence of the very early teaching of the premillennial doctrine in the apostolic Church within a few years of John writing his Apocalypse in A.D. 96.

Barnabas

An early Christian writer, Barnabas (not the Barnabas of the New Testament) wrote a fascinating epistle in the early second century (100–120) that clearly taught the premillennial return of the Lord. The *Epistle of Barnabas*, though it was never part of the canonical New Testament, is historically valuable as extrabiblical evidence concerning the early Christian teachings. Many important early Church leaders, including Origen and Jerome, believed this document was authoritative and quoted from it.

In his epistle, Barnabas wrote about the creation account recorded in Genesis:

> And God made in six days the works of His hands; and He finished them on the seventh day, and He rested on the seventh day and sanctified it. Consider, my children, what that signifies, He finished them in six days. The meaning of it is this: that in six thousand years the Lord God will bring all things to an end. For with Him, one day is a thousand years; as Himself testifieth, saying, behold this day shall be as a thousand years. Therefore children, in six days, that is, in six thousand years, shall all things be accomplished. And what is it that He saith, and He rested the seventh day; He meaneth this; that when His Son shall come, and abolish the season of the wicked one [the Antichrist], and judge the ungodly; and shall change the sun and the moon, and the stars, then He shall gloriously rest in that seventh day.[7]

This statement provides compelling proof of the widespread acceptance of this premillennial doctrine regarding Christ's return as taught in the early decades of the second century.

Irenaeus

The respected early Church scholar, Irenaeus (A.D. 120–202), who supported the late authorship of Revelation, also taught about the Second Coming and a literal Millennium. In his *Against Heresies*, he declared the truth of the one thousand years known as the Millennium in his reference to the great week of God's plan of redemption for humanity. "This is an account of the things formerly created, as also it is a prophecy of what is to come. For the day of the Lord is as a thousand years; and in six days created things were completed; it is evident, therefore, that they will come to an end at the sixth thousand years."

In another passage about the future Tribulation period, Irenaeus wrote:

> When Antichrist shall have devastated all things in this world, he will reign for three years and six months, and sit in the temple at Jerusalem, and then the Lord will come from heaven in the clouds, in the glory of the Father, sending this man to the lake of fire, but bringing in for the righteous the times of the kingdom, the rest, the hallowed seventh-day, and restoring to Abraham the promised inheritance in which kingdom the Lord declared, that 'many coming from the east and from the west should sit down with "Abraham, Isaac, and Jacob."'[8]

This passage confirms both the doctrine of the Millennial Kingdom and belief in the Antichrist's evil tyranny will endure in the last three and a half years of the Great Tribulation.

Justin Martyr

Justin Martyr (A.D. 110–165) was an important Church leader during the second century. Justin wrote *Dialogue with Trypho*, which recorded his extensive debate about Christian beliefs with the pagan philosopher Trypho in Ephesus. In addition to his statement confirming that the apostle John wrote the Apocalypse, Justin also taught the premillennial return of Christ and the resurrection of the righteous before the beginning of the thousand-year kingdom that will conclude with the resurrection of the wicked dead for final judgment at the Great White Throne.

> Now we have understood that the expression used among these words, "According to the days of the tree

[of life] shall be the days of my people; the works of their toil shall abound" obscurely predicts a thousand years. For as Adam was told that in the day he ate of the tree he would die, we know that he did not complete a thousand years. We have perceived, moreover, that the expression, "The day of the Lord is as a thousand years," is connected with this subject. There was a certain man with us, whose name was John, one of the apostles of Christ, who prophesied by a revelation that was made to him, that those who believed in our Christ would dwell a thousand years in Jerusalem and that thereafter the general, and, in short, the eternal resurrection, and judgment of all men would likewise take place.[9]

In this debate, Justin also confirmed that he and other "right-minded Christians" believed in the literal doctrine of the thousand-year reign of Christ in the Millennium. "But I and others, who are right-minded Christians on all points, are assured that there will be a resurrection of the dead, and a thousand years in Jerusalem, which will then be built, adorned, and enlarged, [as] the prophets Ezekiel and Isaiah and others declare."

Tertullian

Tertullian (145–220) was a prominent Church theologian in North Africa at the beginning of the third century. In his book *Against Marcion*, Tertullian wrote about the Millennium and the New Earth that will follow the renewal of the earth by fire:

But we do confess that a kingdom is promised to us upon the earth, although before heaven, only in another state of existence; inasmuch as it will be after the resurrection for a thousand years in the divinely-built city of Jerusalem, 'Let down from heaven,' which the apostle also calls 'our mother from above;' and while declaring that our citizenship, is in heaven, he predicates of it that it is really a city in heaven. This both Ezekiel had knowledge of and the Apostle John beheld.[10]

This extraordinary statement from the early Church affirms the literal reality of both the thousand-year kingdom of Christ on earth as well as the reality of the New Jerusalem as "really a city in heaven."

Commodianus

Commodianus was a bishop in North Africa (240) who taught about the Millennium in his book entitled *Instructions of Commodianus*. He wrote about God's final judgment on His enemies at the end of this age: "Flames on the nations, and the Medes and Parthians burn for a thousand years, as the hidden words of John declare. For then after a thousand years they are delivered over to Gehenna; and he [Satan] whose work they were, with them burnt up."[11]

Lactantius

Lactantius (A.D. 260–330) was a great Christian scholar who lived just prior to the Council of Nicea (325). He personally tutored the son of the Roman emperor Constantine after the remarkable conversion of the emperor. Lactantius wrote about the future Millennium in his seventh *Book of Divine Institutions:*

> Therefore, since all the works of God were completed in six days, the world must continue in its present state through six ages, that is, six thousand years. For the great day of God is limited by a circle of a thousand years, as the prophet shows, who says, 'In Thy sight, O Lord, a thousand years are as one day.'. . . And again, since God, having finished His works, rested the seventh day and blessed it, at the end of the six thousandth year all wickedness must be abolished from the earth, and righteousness reign for a thousand years. . . . [12]

The Council of Nicea (325)

After three centuries of savage pagan imperial persecution, the Church was finally relieved of torment by the unusual conversion of the Roman emperor Constantine, who became a Christian in 312. He called all of the bishops of the Christian

Church throughout the Roman Empire to participate in an ecumenical Church council in the city of Nicea in 325. His goal at this meeting was to refute the heresies that had gradually arisen and to confirm the true apostolic Christian faith as it had been handed down through three centuries since Christ's death and resurrection. Those who wish to understand what the whole Church believed and taught at that critical moment when Christianity was transformed from being a persecuted faith in hiding to becoming the publicly supported state religion throughout the Roman empire should find the following statement of tremendous interest.

> Gelasius Cyzicus, a Greek historian in the fifth century (A.D. 476), was fortunately able to gather together the historical records of the teachings endorsed by the Council of Nicea. Cyzicus published a history of the council that demonstrated the Church's adherence to the doctrine of the resurrection and the premillennial return of Christ. Despite years of attacks on the doctrine of the Millennium and the authority of John's Apocalypse by the new teachers of the allegorical interpretation (supported by the Gnostics and Origen's school at Alexandria), the orthodox bishops of the Council of Nicea (representing the churches of the Western and Eastern Roman Empire) strongly endorsed the book of Revelation as canonical, including its teaching on the coming Millennium. Cyzicus demonstrated that the pastors and bishops throughout the Roman Empire prepared the following Ecclesiastical Form known as the *Diatyposis*. It would be read in every church.[13]

This statement of the genuine faith of the early church, the *Diatyposis*, was confessed by the orthodox believers as well as ministers. It was widely taught throughout the Church, confirming belief in the coming literal Kingdom of God in "the land of the living." It reads as follows:

> We expect a New Heaven and Earth, according to the Scriptures, when the Appearing and Kingdom of the

great God and our Saviour, Jesus Christ, shall have shone forth. Then, as Daniel says, the saints of the Most High shall receive the Kingdom. And the earth shall be pure and holy, a land of the living and not of the dead, which David, foreseeing, exclaimed: 'I believe I shall see the goodness of the Lord in the land of the living, land of the meek and humble.' For, 'Blessed,' says Christ, 'are the meek, because they shall inherit the earth.' And the prophet says: 'The feet of the meek and humble shall tread it.'[14]

Abandonment of Premillennialism After Origen and Augustine

It is very difficult to imagine how all of the early Church teachers, many of whom were personally taught by the apostles or by those who had sat at the feet of apostles, could be totally mistaken about the correct interpretation of the prophecies. Surely, if these first-, second-, and third-century teachers had misunderstood the correct prophetic doctrine of the apostles, there would be ample evidence in the writings of the Church regarding a strong debate between those who espoused premillennialism and those who opposed it (such as we find written against false teachings such as Gnosticism, Docetism, and Donatism). However, even those who deny the premillennial return of Christ have been unable to find *any* historical evidence that *anyone* denied this premillennial doctrine during the early centuries of the Church Age.

The first major Christian teacher who rejected the premillennial doctrine was the theologian Origen, as discussed in earlier chapters. Despite the respect Church leaders had for Origen's scholarship, the major councils of the Church—the Council of Nicea (325) and the Council of Constantinople (381)—rejected his allegorical interpretation of Revelation 20.

However, during the centuries following Origen, there was a gradual and widespread institutionalization of his allegorical method of biblical interpretation. The teaching of St. Augustine and his important book *The City of God*[15] (greatly influenced by

Origen and Ambrose) dominated the doctrine of the Church for the next thousand years. The medieval Church often ignored the literal promises of Christ's coming kingdom on earth. Consequently, as the Church formed powerful alliances with the kings of Europe, it lost interest in the literal prophecies about Christ's coming Kingdom. The Church began to focus primarily on the role of Christ as the head of the Church, and leaders of the medieval Church set out to change humanity and to rule the world themselves and in alliance with Christian rulers. Because most Christians, both laymen as well as clergy, could not read the Scriptures in their own language (for they were written in Latin) and because the Bible was unavailable to the vast majority of believers, it was very difficult to counteract the unscriptural teaching that rejected the truth of the Second Coming and the Millennium.

Significantly, the Protestant Reformation, which reached a boiling point when Martin Luther posted his Ninety-five Theses in 1520, produced a powerful "back to the Bible" movement within Christendom. The invention of the Gutenberg Press greatly facilitated the distribution of printed Bibles, liberating the Christians of Europe to discover God's Word and read His prophecies for themselves. It produced a spiritual revolution that is still having profound consequences throughout the world as billions now read the Word of God. This spiritual reformation movement was characterized by the widespread printing and distribution of the Scriptures in the common language of the people of Europe. For the first time in a thousand years, most of the Christians of Europe could read the Scriptures in their own language and determine what the Bible actually taught. It is no coincidence that as people read the prophecies for themselves, the doctrine of premillennialism re-emerged. Where would the idea have come from if not from the Word of God itself? In the centuries that followed the Reformation, millions of Christians in many denominations throughout the nations rediscovered the ancient prophetic teaching as it had been taught by the early Church; Christ clearly promised that He would return to establish His kingdom on earth for a thousand years.

The New Testament Teaches
the Premillennial Return

If the Scriptures truly taught the postmillennial view that the Millennium was to occur during the age of Grace, before the return of Jesus Christ from heaven, one would expect to find numerous biblical references to such an important doctrine. The lack of scriptural texts about a Millennium appearing prior to the Second Advent indicates that this postmillennial view was not the teaching of the New Testament. In addition, no one ever taught this theory until Daniel Whitby first proposed his "New Hypothesis" in 1800.

In a similar manner, the amillennial view that rejects the literal millennial kingdom is directly contradicted by numerous scriptural prophecies regarding a literal Kingdom of God on earth. Despite the attempts of many amillennialists to find biblical support for their position, they have failed. Surely, if Christ and His apostles believed that the Church would succeed in converting the world's population to Christianity before His return in glory, we would find ample evidence for this doctrine prominently displayed in the writings of the New Testament. However, we find nothing of the kind. There is not one passage that clearly teaches that the world will be converted to the Kingdom of God before the return of our Lord to this earth.

Growing Opposition to Christians Before His Return

Jesus warned His disciples about the growing religious opposition to their proclamation of the Gospel message. Rather than prophesy that the Church would triumphantly usher in the coming Kingdom of God on earth, Jesus foretold the final apostasy and growing iniquity within the Church and the waning love for God and others that would characterize the saints. He prophesied that "the love of many shall wax cold" and that "iniquity shall abound" in the last days. In fact, the state of apostasy will become so prevalent in the last days that Christ warned the saints that they would "be hated of all men for my name's sake: but he that shall endure unto the end, the same shall be saved" (Mark 13:13). Christ's message indicates that the Church will be involved in a profound spiritual crisis at the end of this age when He will return in glory. In Christ's prophecy to His disciples regarding the events to transpire in the final crisis of the last days, Jesus declared, "And this gospel of the kingdom shall be preached in all the world for a witness unto all nations; and then shall the end come" (Matthew 24:14). These passages and their proper interpretation will be dealt with later.

The Bible does not state that there will be an extended period of global triumph of spiritual righteousness led by the Church before Christ's return in glory. In fact, the New Testament repeatedly and positively affirms that Christ's return from heaven is imminent. Furthermore, His imminent return is held forth as an ever-present hope and earnest expectation of the saints. It is significant that the return of Christ in glory is constantly connected with the Scripture's affirmation of the introduction of His kingdom on earth. The critics of the premillennial return of Christ teach that a thousand years of Christian domination and spiritual victory by the Church over evil throughout the earth will precede His return. However, this concept is clearly contradicted by Christ's own proclamation:

> For yourselves know perfectly that the day of the Lord so cometh as a thief in the night. For when they shall say, Peace and safety; then sudden destruction cometh upon them, as travail upon a woman with child; and they shall not escape. But ye, brethren, are not in darkness, that that day should overtake you as a thief. Ye are all the children of light, and the children of the day: we are not of the night, nor of darkness. Therefore let us not sleep, as do others; but let us watch and be sober. (1 Thessalonians 5:2–6)

Canon Ryle, one of the evangelical leaders of the Church of England, considered the implications of the promises of the Scriptures concerning the coming Millennium. He suggested, "I believe, finally, that it is for the safety, happiness, and comfort, of all true Christians to expect as little as possible from churches, or governments, under the present dispensation, to hold themselves ready for tremendous conversions and changes of all things established, and to expect their good things only from Christ's Second Advent."[16]

Jesus Christ will Defeat Antichrist Before the Millennium

The Scriptures clearly teach that Christ will return from heaven to defeat Satan's Antichrist. John taught in the Apocalypse that Jesus will descend with His heavenly army of resurrected saints to destroy the armies of the Antichrist, casting him and the False Prophet into the Lake of Fire.

> And the armies which were in heaven followed him upon white horses, clothed in fine linen, white and clean. . . . And I saw the beast, and the kings of the earth, and their armies, gathered together to make war against him that sat on the horse, and against his army. And the beast was taken, and with him the false prophet that wrought miracles before him, with which he deceived them that had received the mark of the beast, and them that worshipped his image. These both were cast alive into a lake of fire burning with brimstone. (Revelation 19:14, 19–20)

Only two verses later, John continues his prophecy by telling us about the commencement and nature of the coming Millennium. Therefore, it is clear that Christ premillennially comes to earth first and then establishes His millennial kingdom.

This sequence of events is so definite that those who deny the doctrine of the premillennial return of Christ are forced to allegorize or spiritualize the language of this prophecy to evade its clear statement. The disciple Matthew recorded Jesus' prophecy of His Second Coming, stipulating the sequence of prophetic events including the premillennial return of Christ to establish His kingdom. Here Jesus declares that His coming will occur immediately after the Tribulation:

> Immediately after the tribulation of those days shall the sun be darkened, and the moon shall not give her light,

and the stars shall fall from heaven, and the powers of the heavens shall be shaken: And then shall appear the sign of the Son of man in heaven: and then shall all the tribes of the earth mourn, and they shall see the Son of man coming in the clouds of heaven with power and great glory. (Matthew 24:29–30)

Christ's Prophecy of the Wheat and the Tares

Jesus taught about this kingdom of God in a number of parables. In His famous parable of the wheat and the tares, Christ spoke of a farmer whose enemy secretly planted "tares" (weeds, representing evil) within his fields of wheat.

He said unto them, An enemy hath done this. The servants said unto him, Wilt thou then that we go and gather them up? But he said, Nay; lest while ye gather up the tares, ye root up also the wheat with them. Let both grow together until the harvest: and in the time of harvest I will say to the reapers, Gather ye together first the tares, and bind them in bundles to burn them: but gather the wheat into my barn. (Matthew 13:28–30)

In this prophecy Jesus directly affirmed that the "tares," representing evil, will continue growing side by side with the "wheat," representing the saints, "until the harvest," God's final judgment of humanity. Therefore, since Christ taught that evil will continue to flourish until the end, it is impossible that the Millennium of one thousand years of peace, holiness, and justice could occur before the final harvest judgment of God. Logically, Christ's teaching of the "wheat and the tares" indicates that His return must be premillennial. It is significant that while we are never told to look expectantly for the coming Millennium, the Scriptures continually command believers to wait with anticipation for the imminent return of Christ.

The Bible's Teaching about the Resurrection

A careful analysis of the Scripture's teaching about the first resurrection of the saints and the second resurrection of those who have rejected God's offer of salvation provides overwhelming evidence that the Millennium will occur after the first resurrection of believers, which will occur before Christ's Second Coming with the saints at Armageddon. The apostle Paul taught that God's plan involves a distinct order of several resurrections that began with the rise of Christ from the tomb two thousand years ago.

> For as in Adam all die, even so in Christ shall all be made alive. But every man in his own order: Christ the firstfruits; afterward they that are Christ's at his coming. Then cometh the end, when he shall have delivered up the kingdom to God, even the Father; when he shall have put down all rule and all authority and power. For he must reign, till he hath put all enemies under his feet. The last enemy that shall be destroyed is death. (1 Corinthians 15:22–26)

After describing the resurrection of the saints ("they that are Christ's at his coming"), Paul revealed that "then [afterwards] cometh the end" referring to the last resurrection (of the wicked; Revelation 20:11–15) "when he shall have delivered up the kingdom to God."

In Paul's first epistle to the church at Thessalonica, he taught that the resurrection of the saints would be separate from and prior to the resurrection of the unrepentant sinners. The apostle confirmed that "the dead in Christ shall rise first" and immediately be followed by the resurrection of all living believers (I Thessalonians 4:16). Finally, in the Apocalypse, John clearly taught that the Millennium will take place in the interval between the first resurrection of the living and departed saints (Rapture) and the final resurrection of the wicked dead (the Great White Throne judgement).

> And I saw thrones, and they sat upon them, and judgment was given unto them: and I saw the souls of them that were beheaded for the witness of Jesus, and for the word of God, and which had not worshipped the beast, neither his image, neither had received his mark upon their foreheads, or in their hands; and they lived

and reigned with Christ a thousand years. But the rest of the dead lived not again until the thousand years were finished. This is the first resurrection. Blessed and holy is he that hath part in the first resurrection: on such the second death hath no power, but they shall be priests of God and of Christ, and shall reign with him a thousand years. And when the thousand years are expired, Satan shall be loosed out of his prison. . . . And I saw a great white throne, and him that sat on it, from whose face the earth and the heaven fled away; and there was found no place for them. And I saw the dead, small and great, stand before God; and the books were opened: and another book was opened, which is the book of life: and the dead were judged out of those things which were written in the books, according to their works. And the sea gave up the dead which were in it; and death and hell delivered up the dead which were in them: and they were judged every man according to their works. And death and hell were cast into the lake of fire. This is the second death. (Revelation 20:4–7, 11–14)

This passage clearly describes the fact that the thousand years of Christ's millennial kingdom will occur between the first and the second resurrection.

It is interesting to note that the phrase "the second death" appears in four passages in the Apocalypse (Revelation 2:11, 20:6, 20:14, 21:8). This phrase also appears in the *Targum of Jonathan Ben Uzziel*, an ancient Jewish paraphrase or Aramaic commentary of Deuteronomy 33:6: "Let Reuben live, and not die." It reads, "Let him not die the second death by which the wicked die in the world to come." This ancient Jewish acknowledgment of the fact that the "second death" resurrection is different than the resurrection of the righteous saints supports Revelation's teaching that the two resurrections, that of the saints and that of the wicked, occur at different times (separated by the Millennium).

Christ's Command to Watch for
His Second Coming

The New Testament is filled with commands to obediently watch for the imminent return of the Lord. This command to watch encourages us to study the prophecies about His return and to be motivated by His Second Coming, to walk in holiness as well as to witness with urgency in light of the nearness of His advent. In His great Mount of Olives prophecy about the events that will transpire in the last days, Jesus declared, "Watch therefore: for ye know not what hour your Lord doth come" (Matthew 24:42). Then He announced, "Watch therefore, for ye know neither the day nor the hour wherein the Son of man cometh" (Matthew 25:13). Finally, Jesus concluded the New Testament with the book of Revelation that foretold the millennial kingdom that would follow His triumphant return in glory to defeat Satan's Antichrist. Christ promises a blessing on all those Christians who obediently watch for His imminent return. "Behold, I come as a thief. Blessed is he that watcheth, and keepeth his garments, lest he walk naked, and they see his shame" (Revelation 16:15). This statement regarding the need for constant vigilance regarding His return appears to be an allusion to the punishment that was given to a night guard in the Temple who fell asleep at his post. Rabbi Elieser ben Jacob declared that his uncle was punished for falling asleep by having the captain of the Temple guards actually set his clothes on fire.[17]

Christ's command to constantly "watch" for His return from heaven contradicts the position of those who suggest that a thousand years or more of millennial peace will intervene before His return. The only logical and consistent interpretation of Christ's repeated commands to watch for His return is to believe that He will return to earth and establish His millennial kingdom as the early Church taught during the early centuries.

Answering the Critics' Objections
to Premillennialism

Many critics of the Millennium deny that the apostolic Church believed in and looked expectantly for the imminent premillennial return of Christ. For example, the preterist and postmillennialist theologian David Chilton wrote in his book *Days of Vengeance* the following astonishing and incorrect statement:

> In this objective sense, therefore, orthodox Christianity has always been postmillennialist. That is to say, regardless of how 'the Millennium' has been conceived (whether in a heavenly or an earthly sense)—i.e., regardless of the technical exegesis of certain points in Revelation 20—orthodox Christians have always confessed that Jesus Christ will return after ('post') the period designated as 'the thousand years' has ended.[18]

David Chilton then falsely stated that the orthodox Church never taught the premillennial return of Christ. Chilton wrote:

> The historic Church has always rejected the heresy of Millenarianism (in past centuries, this was called *chiliasm*, meaning *thousand-year-ism*). The notion that the reign of Christ is something wholly future, to be brought in by some great social cataclysm, is not a Christian doctrine. It is an unorthodox teaching, generally espoused by heretical sects on the fringes of the Christian Church.[19]

However, the unanimous evidence of the New Testament and of the extensive writings of the Early Church is that the Scriptures and the apostolic Church repeatedly taught that the premillennial Second Coming (although it could be delayed) was always imminent. The apostle Paul encouraged the Christians in the church at Corinth to wait expectantly for Christ's return: "So that ye come behind in no gift; waiting for the coming of our Lord Jesus Christ" (1 Corinthians 1:7). In another passage Paul taught that we should "wait for his Son from heaven, whom he raised from the dead, even Jesus, which delivered us from the wrath to come" (1 Thessalonians 1:10). This prophecy reveals that the return of Christ at the Rapture will deliver the living Christians in the last generation from "the wrath to come" (a reference to the wrath of God upon unrepentant sinners during the seven-year Tribulation that will follow the Rapture of the Church).

The critics suggest the Millennium is only a symbolic picture of the triumphant and spiritually victorious Church that will precede the Second Advent. However, this is directly contradicted by the Bible's prophecies that the establishment of the Millennial Kingdom will occur at the Second Coming of Christ when He destroys the Antichrist. The New Testament contains many prophecies by Jesus and the apostles that declare that the cataclysmic events of the Great Tribulation will precede His return to set up His kingdom. For example, the Gospel of Luke records:

> And there shall be signs in the sun, and in the moon, and in the stars; and upon the earth distress of nations, with perplexity; the sea and the waves roaring; men's hearts failing them for fear, and for looking after those things which are coming on the earth: for the powers of heaven shall be shaken. And then shall they see the Son of man coming in a cloud with power and great glory. And when these things begin to come to pass, then look up, and lift up your heads; for your redemption draweth nigh. (Luke 21:25–28)

Jesus' words describe His Second Coming as occurring at a time of massive global crisis in which there will be chaos on earth and sea with "distress of nations" and even the heavens being "shaken." None of these detailed prophecies were fulfilled at the destruction of Jerusalem in A.D. 70 as preterists claim. This prophecy also totally contradicts both the amillennial and postmillennial positions. His prophecy is, however, completely consistent with the premillennial return of Christ.

One of the most powerful prophetic passages in the Word of God is quite specific about Christ's return.

> But those things, which God before had shewed by the mouth of all his prophets, that Christ should suffer, he hath so fulfilled. Repent ye therefore, and be converted,

that your sins may be blotted out, when the times of refreshing shall come from the presence of the Lord; and he shall send Jesus Christ, which before was preached unto you: Whom the heaven must receive until the times of restitution of all things, which God hath spoken by the mouth of all his holy prophets since the world began. (Acts 3:18–21)

Luke began by pointing out that the prophecies of Christ's first coming were genuine, literally fulfilled, and accurate. Then he encourages his readers to accept salvation while there is still time before "the times of refreshing shall come from the presence of the Lord." In addition to this definite statement describing the sequence of events, the passage concludes with the absolutely clear statement, "he shall send Jesus Christ . . . whom the heaven must receive until the times of restitution of all things." One could hardly ask for a more definite statement that Jesus' second advent will usher in the long-awaited millennial kingdom, "the times of restitution of all things" that has been the goal of God's plan of redemption for humanity "since the world began."

It is important to note that our Lord commanded Christians to pray the Lord's Prayer, composed of these words, "Thy kingdom come. Thy will be done in earth, as it is in heaven" (Matthew 6:10). The truth about the Second Coming is so fundamental to the Church that Jesus Christ commanded His followers to acknowledge His coming millennial kingdom every time they celebrated the Lord's Supper at Communion. The Lord declared during the Last Supper, "For as often as ye eat this bread, and drink this cup, ye do shew the Lord's death till he come" (1 Corinthians 11:26).

The apostle John's Apocalypse begins with the promise of the imminent Second Coming: "Behold, he cometh with clouds; and every eye shall see him, and they also which pierced him: and all kindreds of the earth shall wail because of him. Even so, Amen" (Revelation 1:7). Significantly, Christ's final prophetic message to His Church concludes with this message:

"Surely I come quickly. Amen. Even so, come, Lord Jesus" (Revelation 22:20).

The critics suggest the Millennium will take place on earth during the Church Age before the Second Coming. This is clearly contradicted by the New Testament. The Scriptures contain numerous passages in which Jesus Christ confirmed that He will finally return to earth at His return to defeat Satan's Antichrist and establish His millennial kingdom on earth. Jesus Himself repeatedly prophesied to His disciples and followers that He would return at some future time that was imminent but unknowable to us.

Jesus declared, "Watch therefore: for ye know not what hour your Lord doth come" (Matthew 24:42). The writer Luke recorded another prophecy of Christ, "And then shall they see the Son of man coming in a cloud with power and great glory" (Luke 21:27). Why would Christ prophetically announce, "Watch therefore, for ye know neither the day nor the hour wherein the Son of man cometh" (Matthew 25:13) if His plan were to gradually introduce the kingdom of God on earth over the centuries?

Obviously, there are numerous biblical prophecies that describe a very literal return of Christ to defeat the Antichrist and to establish His kingdom on earth. These predictions totally contradict the amillennialist and postmillennial doctrines that suggest the Millennium is to be interpreted allegorically as an indefinite period when the Church has finally prospered over the forces of evil and established a Christian dominated world government.

One of the critics' main objections to the biblical doctrine of the Millennial Kingdom is their claim that the Millennium was only taught in one short passage in Revelation, Chapter 20. Furthermore, the critics argue that the symbolic nature of many of the prophecies in the Apocalypse should dissuade us from taking the prophecy about the Millennium literally. But the apostle John was given a very detailed vision about the future Millennium recorded in Revelation, and he was inspired to describe the kingdom of God as lasting precisely "one thousand years" six times in this passage. This strongly suggests that the number of years is an accurate measurement.

> And I saw an angel come down from heaven, having the key of the bottomless pit and a great chain in his hand. And he laid hold on the dragon, that old serpent, which is the Devil, and Satan, and bound him a thousand years, And cast him into the bottomless pit, and shut him up, and set a seal upon him, that he should deceive the nations no more, till the thousand years should be fulfilled: and after that he must be loosed a little season. And I saw thrones, and they sat upon them, and judgment was given unto them: and I saw the souls of them that were beheaded for the witness of Jesus, and for the word of God, and which had not worshipped the beast, neither his image, neither had received his mark upon their foreheads, or in their hands; and they lived and reigned with Christ a thousand years. But the rest of the dead lived not again until the thousand years were finished. This is the first resurrection. Blessed and holy is he that hath part in the first resurrection: on such the second death hath no power, but they shall be priests of God and of Christ, and shall reign with him a thousand years. And when the thousand years are expired, Satan shall be loosed out of his prison. (Revelation 20:1–7)

One of the clearest prophetic teachings about the Second Coming and the setting up of His kingdom is found in the book of Acts. Luke wrote,

> Repent ye therefore, and be converted, that your sins may be blotted out, when the times of refreshing shall come from the presence of the Lord; and he shall send Jesus Christ, which before was preached unto you: Whom the heaven must receive until the times of restitution of all things, which God hath spoken by the mouth of all his holy prophets since the world began. (Acts 3:19–21)

This prophecy clearly connects the Second Coming with "the times of restitution" (the promised millennial kingdom of God). The immediate connection between Christ's return and His establishment of His Kingdom is revealed in Paul's epistle to Timothy: "I charge thee therefore before God, and the Lord Jesus Christ, who shall judge the quick and the dead at his appearing and his kingdom" (2 Timothy 4:1).

Notes

1. Dwight Pentecost, *Things To Come* (Grand Rapids: Zondervan Publishing House, 1958).

2. Charles C. Ryrie, *Basic Theology: A Popular Systematic Guide To Understanding Biblical Truth* (Wheaton: Victor Books, 1986) 450.

3. H. Graetz, *Geschichte der Juden* (Leipsig: 1897) 15.

4. *Talmud, Sanhedrin* 97a.

5. *Talmud,* Gemara commentary, *Sanhedrin.*

6. Eusebius, "Ecclesiastical History," *Ante-Nicene Library,* 10 vols. (Grand Rapids: Wm. B. Eerdmans Publishing Co., 1987) 3:39.

7. "The Epistle of Barnabas," *Ante-Nicene Fathers,* 10 vols. (Grand Rapids: Wm. B. Eerdmans Publishing Co., 1987) 146.

8. Irenaeus, "Against Heresies," *Ante-Nicene Fathers,* 10 vols. (Grand Rapids: Wm. B. Eerdmans Publishing Co., 1987) 1: 560.

9. Justin Martyr, "Dialogue With Trypho," *Ante-Nicene Fathers,* 10 vols. (Grand Rapids: Wm. B. Eerdmans Publishing Co., 1987) 1: 239.

10. Tertullian, "Against Marcion," *Ante-Nicene Fathers,* 10 vols. (Grand Rapids: Wm. B. Eerdmans Publishing Co., 1987) 4: 342.

11. Commodianus, "Instructions of Commodianus," *Ante-Nicene Fathers,* 10 vols. (Grand Rapids: Wm. B. Eerdmans Publishing Co., 1987) 4: 211.

12. Lactantius, "Book of Divine Institutions," *Ante-Nicene Fathers,* 10 vols. (Grand Rapids: Wm. B. Eerdmans Publishing Co., 1987) 7:211.

13. Nathanial West, *Premillennial Essays* (Chicago: F. H. Revell, 1879) 347.

14. Gelasius Cyzicus, *Commentarius Actorum Concilii, Nicae,* vol. 2.

15. Augustine, "The City of God," *Nicene and Post-Nicene Fathers,* 3 vols. (Grand Rapids: Wm. B. Eerdmans Publishing Co., 1987) vol. 2.

16. Canon Ryle, *Coming Events and Present Duties,* preface.

17. Rabbi Elieser ben Jacob, *Middoth,* i.2.

18. David Chilton, *Days of Vengeance: An Exposition of the Book of Revelation* (Fort Worth: Dominion Press, 1987) 494.
19. David Chilton, *Days of Vengeance: An Exposition of the Book of Revelation* (Fort Worth: Dominion Press, 1987) 494.

6
The Millennial Kingdom of God

The purpose of the coming kingdom of God, which encompasses the Millennium and the eternal New Earth to follow forever after, is another essential yet misunderstood subject. The history of humanity is, in fact, the history of God's plan to redeem a willing remnant of a rebellious humanity from the consequences of their sinful rebellion through the sacrificial atonement of Jesus Christ on the Cross. The Scriptures record the history of humanity's first and continued rebellion against God, its tragic consequences in sin, violence, and death. Finally the Scriptures reveal the prophecies of God regarding the final conflict and its resolution when Jesus Christ will appear and gloriously triumph over the armies of Antichrist at the Battle of Armageddon. All of the prophetic revelations of the Bible regarding the progressive unfolding of God's truth and His plan of redemption will culminate in the return of the Messiah to defeat Satan and his allies. Then, following the Messiah's destruction of the Antichrist's armies, Jesus Christ will establish His glorious millennial kingdom. Christ's Second Coming will usher in the long-awaited kingdom of God that will endure throughout eternity.

The kingdom of God on earth provides the spiritual key to explaining human history, from the fall of Adam and Eve, to Jesus' First Coming, and until the final appearance of Christ at the end of this age. The prophecies about the coming kingdom provide the key to the true understanding of the Scriptures and God's plan for redeeming humanity from the curse of sin.

Throughout the Scriptures, God repeatedly promises His followers that the goal is the coming millennial kingdom and the New Earth to follow forever. The prophecies in both the Old and New Testament teach that this promised Kingdom will be a real global kingdom on the earth. The kingdom is not simply an allegorical picture of a spiritual state of mind. Tragically, beginning with Origin and St. Augustine during the third and fourth centuries after Christ, the allegorical method of scriptural interpretation gradually became the general teaching of the western Church. Following St. Augustine's book, *The City of God*, which rejected the future premillennial return of Christ to defeat Antichrist and establish His kingdom, the medieval Church generally abandoned a literal interpretation of the Bible's prophecies.

Jude, the brother of Jesus, knowing that the Church would someday abandon these biblical principles, wrote the following message to believers two thousand years ago: "It was needful for me to write unto you, and exhort you that ye should earnestly contend for the faith which was once for all delivered unto the saints" (Jude 3). How should we evaluate all teachings that are presented to us regarding the doctrines of the Word of God? The best and most certain answer is found in the words of the Bible itself. We should evaluate all teachings according to this principle: "To the law and to the testimony: if they speak not according to this word, it is because there is no light in them" (Isaiah 8:20).

It is very significant that every single Old Testament messianic prophecy that came to fruition during the life of Jesus of Nazareth was fulfilled in a literal, common-sense way. Not one of the Old Testament prophecies about Jesus' birth, life, death, and resurrection was fulfilled in a purely allegorical manner. The apostolic Church clearly taught that a personal Antichrist will literally arise in the last days to rule for seven years leading to the final Battle of Armageddon. This battle will end in the triumphant victory of the heavenly army of Christ. Then, He will establish His Kingdom ruling from the throne of David in the city of Jerusalem. The Millennial Kingdom of Christ will ultimately produce the greatest blessings the world has ever known. All of humanity's longings for peace, prosperity, health, justice, and righteous government will finally be realized when Jesus Christ returns to establish His Kingdom.

The Kingdom of God Is Literal

The promise of our Lord's return and His establishment of the kingdom of God is so fundamental to the revealed plan of God that the failure to understand this foundational doctrine will prevent a proper appreciation of Christ's plan to redeem the earth from the curse of sin. The promise of the coming kingdom is a golden thread that runs through the Scriptures from Genesis to the last chapter of the book of Revelation. Beginning in Genesis, God announces His unbreakable covenants with Abraham and his descendants that will ultimately be realized in the future kingdom that will be ruled by the promised seed, the Messiah. King David and Solomon constantly affirm the reality of the future kingdom when Christ will finally rule this earth. Each of the Old Testament prophets added their inspired prophecies to reveal new details about the coming kingdom. Jesus Himself taught more about the Kingdom of God than any other topic. The Gospels and the epistles of Paul and Peter resound with assurances that Jesus will fulfill His covenants and promises in the last days. Finally, the prophet John was given the privilege of revealing the prophecies of Jesus Christ throughout the book of Revelation to enable us to see a clear vision of the coming Kingdom of God.

The New Testament revealed God's plan to use the Church to evangelize the world and call out a remnant of people to salvation in the name of Christ. The Church, by fulfilling Christ's command to go "into all the world, and preach the gospel" (Mark 16:15), has led hundreds of millions of souls to repentance and prepares the world for the coming kingdom of God. It would take another complete book to explore the events involving the Great Commission of His Church that have been fulfilled during the last two thousand years as the Gospel has been effectively "preached in all the world." However, the focus of this book is the prophetic truth concerning the Second Coming and the kingdom of God.

In a sense, the Church is designed for the present age of God's grace and Christ's offer of salvation to all those who will repent. However, the coming kingdom of God belongs to the future when Jesus Christ will return to earth to defeat the Gentile world empires and establish His righteous kingdom forever. When the kingdom of God arrives with the return of the Messiah, the Church of Christ will have completed its historical task of taking the gospel of salvation to the nations and calling out a remnant from all nations who will repent and be saved. Then the resurrected saints of the Church will take their promised exalted place as the "kings and priests" with Christ reigning over the billions of Jews and Gentiles that compose the worldwide kingdom of God ruled by His Messiah: "And hast made us unto our God kings and priests: and we shall reign on the earth" (Revelation 5:10).

The evidence is overwhelming that the Old Testament prophets understood that God intended to establish a literal kingdom on earth under the rule of the Messiah. The word *kingdom* is used 342 times throughout the entire Scriptures, appearing 127 times in the Gospels alone. The phrase "kingdom of God" appears 68 times, and "kingdom of heaven" is found 31 times. The angel Gabriel came to Mary and prophesied that Jesus will rule the kingdom from "the throne of his father David." The prophecy of Gabriel declares, "He shall be great, and shall be called the Son of the Highest: and the Lord God shall give unto him the throne of his father David: And he shall reign over the house of Jacob for ever; and of his kingdom there shall be no end" (Luke 1:32–33).

The Jews, both His followers and enemies, affirmed that Jesus came as their king. For example, when Jesus was born, the

Magi came to King Herod in Jerusalem and asked, "Where is he that is born King of the Jews?" (Matthew 2:2). Note that Herod's officials did not dispute their expectation that the Messiah, the "King of the Jews" should be born at that time. In fact, they immediately directed the Magi to Bethleham, the city of David where Micah had prophesied the Messiah would be born (Micah 5:2). During Jesus' trial, Matthew declares that Jesus accepted the title "king of the Jews." "And Jesus stood before the governor: and the governor asked him, saying, Art thou the King of the Jews? And Jesus said unto him, Thou sayest" (Matthew 27:11). Mark recorded that a sign reading "King of the Jews" was placed on the Cross above Christ's head (Mark 15:26).

Critics of the belief in a premillennial return of Christ have often argued that Jesus did not teach that this kingdom was literal but that He taught the kingdom was only spiritual. However, the evidence is overwhelming that the Old Testament prophets and the New Testament followers of Christ believed in a literal kingdom on earth. If, as the critics argue, all of these individuals were mistaken in their understanding of this kingdom, then it is inconceivable that Jesus and His inspired apostles would have failed to correct their mistake on such a fundamentally important topic.

A careful analysis of the Gospels reveals numerous occasions when Christ immediately corrected His disciples from their mistaken belief or misunderstanding of some other issue or doctrine. For example, when Lazarus died, Jesus' disciples misunderstood His words. Jesus "saith unto them, Our friend Lazarus sleepeth; but I go, that I may awake him out of sleep. Then said his disciples, Lord, if he sleep, he shall do well" (John 11:11–12). Immediately Jesus corrected their mistaken notion that Lazarus was only sleeping, "Then said Jesus unto them plainly, Lazarus is dead" (John 11:14). On another occasion Jesus warned them of the false doctrines of the Pharisees and Sadducees by saying, "Take heed and beware of the leaven of the Pharisees and of the Sadducees" (Matthew 16:6). When the disciples misunderstood His words as if He spoke about real leaven and bread, Jesus immediately corrected their mistake. "Then understood they how that he bade them not beware of the leaven of bread, but of the doctrine of the Pharisees and of the Sadducees" (Matthew 16:12).

Yet, Jesus never once challenged His disciples' repeated comments that revealed their belief in a literal coming kingdom. An example is found in the first chapter of Acts, which recorded Christ's teaching to His disciples following His resurrection. "They asked of him, saying, Lord, wilt thou at this time restore again the kingdom to Israel? And he said unto them, It is not for you to know the times or the seasons, which the Father hath put in his own power" (Acts 1:6–7). Jesus affirms that knowledge of the precise timing of the future establishment of His kingdom is retained solely by God. If the Kingdom was not literal, but only spiritual, this would have provided the perfect opportunity to clarify the issue. However, He did not tell His disciples that their expectation regarding the setting up of a literal kingdom of God on earth was incorrect.

Characteristics of the Kingdom of God

If the Lord wanted us to understand that the kingdom of God was purely spiritual and not a literal future kingdom, it is hard to explain why He repeatedly inspired His prophets and apostles to write about the kingdom in such literal and material language that was bound to convince readers of the real nature of the coming kingdom. If language is used meaningfully and purposefully in the Word of God, then the clear intent of the Lord is to teach us to expect a real kingdom of God. When you carefully examine the criticism of the preterists and amillennialists against the literal kingdom of God, you discover that many of them are emotionally uncomfortable with the concept of a real and earthly kingdom, as if this was too "material" or "carnal" for their liking. However, the real question for those who acknowledge that God alone is qualified to determine the proper nature of His future kingdom is this: Is the earthly kingdom of God taught clearly by Christ and the prophets in the Scriptures? If the answer is yes, then those who are faithful to His Word must acknowledge that the Lord intends to establish His real Kingdom of God on earth to complement His heaven above.

In considering the question as to whether the kingdom is material or spiritual in nature, let's look at the Scriptures that describe the characteristics of this kingdom:

- The kingdom will be ruled forever by Jesus Christ as king: "And he shall reign over the house of Jacob for ever; and of his kingdom there shall be no end" (Luke 1:33).
- The king will rule "upon the throne of David" (Isaiah 9:7).
- The kingdom will be ruled "with judgment and with justice" (Isaiah 9:7).
- It has a real government: "The government shall be upon his shoulder" (Isaiah 9:6).
- Jesus' disciples will administer the land of Israel: "Ye also shall sit upon twelve thrones, judging the twelve tribes of Israel" (Matthew 19:28).
- The faithful servants of Christ will administer cities of the kingdom: "Have thou authority over ten cities" (Luke 19:17).
- The saints will rule and reign with the Messiah during the Millennium and "shall reign with him a thousand years" (Revelation 20:6).
- The saints will continue to reign with Christ forever in the kingdom in the New Earth: "They shall reign for ever and ever" (Revelation 22:5).
- The kingdom will be ruled from the city of Jerusalem: "The Lord of hosts shall reign in mount Zion, and in Jerusalem" (Isaiah 24:23).
- The kingdom will govern territory: "He shall have dominion also from sea to sea, and from the river unto the ends of the earth" (Psalms 72:8).

The Kingdom of God will appear in the future at the dramatic and public Second Coming of Christ, which the whole world will observe as Jesus announced to His disciples during the Olivet discourse:

> For as the lightning cometh out of the east, and shineth even unto the west; so shall also the coming of the Son of man be. . . . Immediately after the tribulation of those days shall the sun be darkened, and the moon shall not

give her light, and the stars shall fall from heaven, and the powers of the heavens shall be shaken: And then shall appear the sign of the Son of man in heaven: and then shall all the tribes of the earth mourn, and they shall see the Son of man coming in the clouds of heaven with power and great glory. (Matthew 24:27, 29–30)

God's Eternal Covenant with Israel

All of the covenant prophecies and promises that God made with Abraham and His descendants—including the kingdom promises to David, Solomon, and all the prophets—will finally be realized during the millennial kingdom and the New Earth that will follow. These divine promises of peace, justice, prosperity, and eternal blessings for Israel and the Gentile nations will be fulfilled when Jesus Christ establishes His messianic throne in Jerusalem. In addition to these material promises, the Lord also promised a new spiritual covenant with Israel in which He would give them "a new heart," including the forgiveness of their sins and the divine empowering by the Holy Spirit of all the righteous inhabitants of the renewed nation. The prophet Ezekiel declared, "A new heart also will I give you, and a new spirit will I put within you: and I will take away the stony heart out of your flesh, and I will give you an heart of flesh" (Ezek. 36:26). This promised eternal kingdom of God will fulfill all of the hopes and dreams of the Chosen People forever. Zechariah and the other prophets affirm that all of the surviving Gentiles and their descendents will participate in these millennial kingdom promises as well.

The Millennium
The First 1000 Years of the Eternal Kingdom of God

Most Christians who accept the scriptural truth about the literal Millennium have unfortunately concluded that the Kingdom of Christ will only exist for a period of one thousand years. However, the Scriptures teach that Christ's Kingdom on earth and in heaven will be eternal. The Millennium will simply form the first chapter or portion in the eternal plan of God for humanity's future in the coming kingdom of Christ. Every one of the Old Testament prophecies concerning the coming kingdom of God are unlimited in duration. The apostle John was given a unique prophetic revelation of this initial period of Christ's rule that will last one thousand years. To emphasize its literal reality, the one-thousand-year duration of this initial period of Christ's kingdom is repeated six times in Revelation 20. John prophesied a number of specific events that would define this period of time. However, it is a fundamental error to believe that all of the Bible's many promises of the kingdom of God could ever be fulfilled in such a short period of time as one thousand years. The Old and New Testaments prophesy that the kingdom of God will truly commence with the Coming of the Messiah to usher in the millennial Kingdom and that it will continue forever.

> And I saw an angel come down from heaven, having the key of the bottomless pit and a great chain in his hand. And he laid hold on the dragon, that old serpent, which is the Devil, and Satan, and bound him a thousand years, and cast him into the bottomless pit, and shut him up, and set a seal upon him, that he should deceive the nations no more, till the thousand years should be fulfilled." (Revelation 20:1–3)

After Adam and Eve sinned against God, Satan received the dominion of this world from Adam and became "the god of this age" (2 Corinthians 4:4) and "the prince of the power of the air" (Ephesians 2:2). Christ will defeat Satan at His triumphant return at the Battle of Armageddon, and He will cast him into the bottomless pit for a thousand years. When the millennial kingdom begins, Jesus Christ will rule throughout this world in righteousness and justice. Humanity will still be tested as to obedience during this thousand-year period as they will live under the righteous government of Jesus Christ, but Satan cannot tempt them. Any sin will be dealt with judicially by Christ; John foretold that "she brought forth a man child, who was to rule all nations with a rod of iron" (Revelation 12:5). Even in this ideal spiritual condition, the Bible foretells that many of the people who survive Armageddon will fail this final test of obedience.

When the Millennium is almost concluded, Satan will be released from his imprisonment in the bottomless pit and set free for "a little season" (Revelation 20:3). During this time, Satan will gather a multitude of the sinful rebels of all nations throughout the earth to join in a last desperate attempt to defeat Christ in a great battle against "the beloved city" Jerusalem (Revelation 20:9). Satan will finally be defeated by Jesus Christ and will be sent to the "lake of fire" forever. John prophesies in the Apocalypse that God will renew the earth and the heavens with fire from heaven following His victory over Satan's final rebellion. In a similar manner, as God cleansed the earth from the pollution of sin with a great worldwide flood during the days of Noah, Christ will cleanse the earth and heaven from the pollution of sin with fire. Then the eternal kingdom of God, with Israel and the surviving Gentile nations, will continue throughout eternity to enjoy the blessings of God under the direct rule of Jesus the Messiah and the righteous saints of the resurrected Church acting as holy "priest-kings" of His divine kingdom.

Numerous passages throughout the Word of God confirm that God's plan is that the earth and His kingdom will endure forever. For example, the first book of the Bible, Genesis, reveals God's promise to Noah following the Flood that He would establish His unbreakable "everlasting covenant" with humanity and "every living creature of all flesh that is upon the earth" to never again "destroy all flesh" (Genesis 9:15–16). King Solomon wrote in Ecclesiastes the following statement: "One generation passeth away, and another generation cometh: but the earth abideth for ever" (Ecclesiastes 1:4). His father, King David, wrote the following statement affirming the eternal nature of God's creation: "They shall fear thee as long as the sun and moon endure, throughout all generations. . . . His name shall endure for ever: his name shall be continued as long as the sun: and men shall be blessed in him: all nations shall call him blessed. Blessed be the Lord God, the God of Israel, who only doeth wondrous things. And blessed be his glorious name for ever: and let the whole earth be filled with his glory; Amen, and Amen" (Psalms 72:5, 17–19). David also wrote: "And he built his sanctuary like high palaces, like the earth which he hath established for ever" (Psalms 78:69). In another passage David spoke of the Lord God as the Creator, "Who laid the foundations of the earth, that it should not be removed for ever" (Psalms 104:5).

These passages confirm that God will redeem the earth from the curse of evil after the Millennium. The renovated and sinless earth will continue forever as part of the eternal kingdom of God. Many Christians have misunderstood the scriptural references to the New Earth as if they taught that God would annihilate His original creation and replace it with a newly created New Earth. However, the numerous passages quoted above demonstrate that God created the original earth to exist forever as part of the eternal kingdom of God. When we examine the passages in the Bible that deal with the New Earth we find that the Lord plans to renovate the surface of the earth with fire similar to the renovation of the pre-Flood earth with water during the days of Noah. While the surface of the earth was transformed by the actions of the water, the original earth remained. Similarly, God will purge the earth with fire following Satan's final rebellion at the end of the thousand-year Millennium and present humanity with a New Earth cleansed of the pollution and remnants of humanity's sinful rebellion.

If this interpretation is correct, then the burning of the earth must be confined to the surface of the planet as occurred during the biblical Flood. The apostle John wrote: "And I saw a new heaven and a new earth, for the first heaven and the first earth had passed away" (Revelation 21:1). The Greek word used in this passage *Parerchomai* indicates something that is transformed from one condition into another, but the word does not suggest the annihilation and replacement by something completely new and different. The words of Revelation 21:1 do not prophesy the annihilation of the existing heaven and earth but rather declare that they "passed away." Just as "the world that then existed perished, being flooded with water" (2 Peter 3:6) in the days of Noah, the present earth will be burnt with fire after the

Millennium. While the ancient pre-Flood world "perished," the planet earth survived to be renovated following the Deluge. Similarly, God's plan for "the restitution of all things" will renovate His earthly creation into a holy and eternal kingdom of God on earth and in heaven. The inspired promise of God was recorded by Luke in the book of Acts: "And he shall send Jesus Christ, which before was preached unto you: Whom the heaven must receive until the times of restitution of all things, which God hath spoken by the mouth of all his holy prophets since the world began" (Acts 3:21).

Jesus Christ and His Kingdom

All of the Gentile nations, as well as Israel, will witness the coming glory of God when Jesus Christ returns from heaven at the Battle of Armageddon. Christ's glorious return will demonstrate both His humanity and His divinity. He will demonstrate His multiple roles as Judge, King, Teacher, Shepherd, and the promised Redeemer of humanity in the sight of all men. As the true "son of David," Jesus will finally take His rightful place as King of kings upon the throne of David. Jesus is truly both perfect man and perfect God. Christ will show His righteousness, holiness, mercy, and goodness as He rules the planet. He will then receive the full and worthy worship of all humanity and fulfill each of the remaining prophecies of the Old Testament. A perfect and just peace will issue forth from Jerusalem, "the City of Peace," because the Prince of Peace will rule humanity with holiness and justice forever.

The problem many scholars face when they consider the prophecies about this real millennial kingdom is similar to the problem faced by the Jews during the lifetime of Jesus. Many Jews truly believed that God would send His Messiah to the earth at that precise time in history based on the clear prophecies of Daniel. However, when Jesus actually stood before the Jewish religious leaders as the promised Messiah in the flesh, many of them had a very difficult time accepting His physical reality. The tremendous truth that God had revealed Himself to man in the form of "the Son of Man" with a "real" material body was very shocking to the Jews.

The same difficulty is paralleled in some measure by many scholars today as they contemplate the reality of both heaven and the millennial kingdom. The prophesied kingdom of Christ will be visible and concrete, yet it is at the same time spiritual in its context. The concept of a totally material and natural kingdom, divorced from the spiritual, is obviously unscriptural. However, the alternative suggested by some scholars of a purely spiritual kingdom, without any tangible, earthly, and material element, is contradicted by the plain declarations of many passages in the Word of God. Christ has promised in the clearest language possible that He will establish His kingdom of righteousness on this earth.

God's Holy Spirit will be poured out on Israel as well as the Gentile nations and will transform humanity forever: "And it shall come to pass afterward, that I will pour out my spirit upon all flesh; your sons and your daughters shall prophesy, your old men shall dream dreams, your young men shall see visions: And also upon the servants and upon the handmaids in those days I will pour out my spirit" (Joel 2:28–29). The Lord gave His Church the divine power of His Holy Spirit on the day of Pentecost, spiritually giving birth to and empowering the Church of Christ almost two thousand years ago. However, this supernatural empowerment of the Spirit was only the foretaste of the coming millennial kingdom, in which the spirits of all natural men and women who are believers will be eternally renewed by the Holy Spirit of God. The transforming power of the Holy Spirit will manifest Himself in the glorious praise, joy, and worship of the saints forever. The emotional, social, and religious barriers that separate believers today will be removed forever by the divine supernatural unity and fellowship of God's Holy Spirit. When the Lord pours out His Spirit upon the Chosen People of Israel, their hearts will overflow with the joy of a bride who finally sees her bridegroom. The Gentile nations will also bask in the great blessings granted to Israel. All of the redeemed will share in the glory of Christ's kingdom.

The Scriptures reveal that one of the greatest blessings that will flow from the millennial kingdom will be a true and lasting world peace. For the first time in human history, soldiers will truly lay down their weapons. They will be secure in the knowledge that their nations, homes, and families are safe at last. The prophet Micah prophesied that "he shall judge among many people, and rebuke strong nations afar off; and they shall beat their swords into plowshares, and their spears into pruninghooks: nation shall not lift up sword against nation, neither shall they learn war anymore" (Micah 4:3).

It appears that Micah may be referring to the enormous release of financial, scientific, material, and human resources from the task of war, which will then be utilized to meet the real needs of humanity. Almost one trillion dollars is spent annually on the military around the world. The allocation of such presently unimaginable sums of money for the use of all people will allow us to solve many of the greatest problems facing us today. Today, we cannot find the funds to provide for the homeless on the streets of our cities, or feed the starving millions throughout the Third World. It is a sad indictment on our national priorities that such enormous funds are available for weapons of war but not for the truly needy in our societies. After the global devastation during the Great Tribulation and the cataclysmic Battle of Armageddon, the cities and infastructure of our planet will need to be rebuilt. Then, finally, all of the energies of this incredibly productive world can be turned to achieve something positive: the rebuilding of the planet's environment and the feeding of its precious children.

Can you imagine what your life would be like if we were living today in the millennial Kingdom of God? There would be no need for locks on our doors and security systems in our homes to protect our innocent children and ourselves. When the Millennium is introduced by the dramatic return of Jesus Christ, the life of every single human will be transformed forever when the influence of Satan will be eliminated from our planet as the devil is confined to the bottomless pit for a thousand years. For the first time in the history of humanity, we will be able to live without the threat of violence, without fear of constant hunger and devastating plagues and disease, without the ever-present threat of death of our loved ones.

The Messiah, Jesus Christ, will create a just society for all of humanity. Some Christian writers have imagined that the verses that promise that the Church will "reign and rule" suggest that Christ will passively rule the earth from His throne. However, when you consider the practical nature of God's plan and the enormous number of resurrected saints who will be available, it is probable that resurrected Christians shall provide millennial leadership in a multitude of roles, including government. The greatest adventure we could ever imagine awaits us in the coming kingdom of Christ.

The curse of sin, and the resulting judgment that God placed upon the earth following the sin of Adam and Eve, will finally be lifted when the kingdom of God is established during the coming Millennium. The deserts will blossom and the earth will produce abundantly under the blessing of God. The prophet Isaiah foretold that all sickness would be eliminated (Isaiah 33:24). All of the deaf and the blind will be cured as Christ heals people in the future millennial kingdom. Even the devastated land of Lebanon shall become a fruitful and productive nation when the Messiah renews the earth from the curse of sin. "Is it not yet a very little while, and Lebanon shall be turned into a fruitful field, and the fruitful field shall be esteemed as a forest? And in that day shall the deaf hear the words of the book, and the eyes of the blind shall see out of obscurity, and out of darkness" (Isaiah 29:17–18).

7

The Rapture:
The Resurrection Prophecy

For the Lord himself shall descend from heaven with
a shout, with the voice of the archangel, and with the
trump of God: and the dead in Christ shall rise first:
Then we which are alive and remain shall be caught
up together with them in the clouds, to meet the Lord
in the air: and so shall we ever be with the Lord.
(1 Thessalonians 4:16–17)

During the last two thousand years, the vast majority of
Christians have believed in and longed for a future resurrection.
They have clung to the promise of the Scriptures that one day
they will be resurrected from death to join Jesus and all of the
saints in His heavenly home. Christians today call this future
resurrection the Rapture. When the Rapture occurs, the bodies
of all Christians living throughout the world will suddenly be
spiritually transformed and ascend from the earth to heaven to
join the other saints who were resurrected from their graves a
moment earlier. The Bible declares that all believers shall rise

to meet Jesus Christ when He descends to the air from heaven to meet the saints. There are a number of other prophecies that refer to this resurrection event; they include John 11:25–26; John 14:3; 1 Corinthians 15:51-52; Philippians 3:20-21; 2 Thessalonians 2:1; and 1 John 3:2.

The Rapture is the modern term used to describe the supernatural moment when Jesus Christ will transform the bodies of all living and departed believers into their new spiritual, immortal bodies that will "rise to meet him in the air." Naturally, the word "rapture" does not appear in the English translations of the Bible, yet the concept of the resurrection-rapture is taught in a number of passages. For the critics who deny the truth of the Rapture by claiming the term is not actually used in the Bible, it is important to note that the word "trinity" does not appear in the Bible either. However, most great theologians over the last two thousand years have declared that the concept of "a triune God" is revealed in numerous passages, from Genesis to Revelation. The word rapture is derived from the Latin word *rapere*, which means to "snatch away" suddenly or be "caught up." The Latin word *Rapere* was first used by the early Church writer Jerome (385) in his Latin translation of the phrase "caught up" as it appears in 1 Thessalonians 4:17: "Then we which are alive and remain shall be *caught up* together with them in the clouds."

The concept of the Rapture has been popularized in the past decade by many books and films. The most popular of these books has been the famous *Left Behind* series of prophetic novels written by my friend Tim LaHaye and Jerry Jenkins. Numerous recent books and films portray the supernatural resurrection of the saints. Millions of nonreligious people in North America have recently become aware of the fact that many evangelical Christians believe the Scripture's promise that Christ will return in the air to gather his people to heaven, whether they are living or dead. Although most non-Christians today reject the Bible's claims about Jesus Christ as well as its teaching about heaven and hell, they are intrigued by the Scripture's prophecies about end time events concerning the Second Coming of Christ.

The Reason Our Bodies Will Be Resurrected

When Jesus comes for His Bride, the Church will consist of two distinct groups—those who have previously died in the faith and those who are still alive. We cannot enter or live forever in an incorruptible heaven with a corruptible body, which is subject to sin, decay, and death. Paul said it best in 1 Corinthians: "For this corruptible [our natural body] must put on incorruption, and this mortal must put on immortality" (1 Corinthians 15:53).

We must receive a new spiritual body to experience all that Christ has prepared for us in heaven and the kingdom of God on earth where we shall rule with Him. Therefore, at the moment of His coming, He will transform the bodies of the living saints simultaneously as He transforms the bodies of those believers who have previously died. The spirits of those Christians who have died in the faith are now in heaven, the Paradise that Christ promised to the thief on the Cross when He said, "To day shalt thou be with me in paradise" (Luke 23:43). However, those saints living today in heaven do not yet have the resurrection body that they will receive on the day of the Rapture. "The dead in Christ will rise first" indicates that the spirits of the Christians in heaven will receive their newly resurrected bodies, which will rise to meet their descending spirits in the air. A moment after their spirits join their new resurrected spiritual bodies in the air, "we which are alive and remain shall be caught up together with them . . . in the air: and so shall we ever be with the Lord" (1 Thessalonians 4:17).

Our bodies will be transformed at the Rapture into a new supernatural resurrection body similar to the body of Jesus Christ after He rose from the empty tomb: "Beloved, now we are the sons of God, and it doth not yet appear what we shall be: but we know that, when he shall appear, we shall be like him; for we shall see him as he is" (1 John 3:2).

The Sequence of Prophetic Events

The precise chronology of the events of the Second Coming has always been a point of debate with biblical scholars. They have presented three different scenarios regarding the timing of the resurrection of the saints, popularly called the Rapture: pre-Tribulation, mid-Tribulation, or post-Tribulation. Will the Church be raptured to heaven before the Great Tribulation begins, or will Christians living in the last generation be subjected to God's wrath during the Tribulation together with nonbelievers? Many prophecy scholars, including this author, believe that the Bible teaches that the Rapture will precede the Great Tribulation. Some teachers suggest the resurrection will not occur until the midpoint of the seven years. Yet others believe that, while there will be a resurrection-rapture, it may not happen until the end of the seven-year Tribulation period at the final return of Christ at the Battle of Armageddon.

Some Christians have even suggested that the timing of the Rapture is unimportant, half-jokingly proclaiming their belief in a "pan-Tribulation" theory (that it will all somehow "pan out" in the end). However, that is an irresponsible attitude that dismisses the scriptural truth that the Tribulation will be a time of historically unparalleled persecution so terrible that Jesus Christ warned, "For then shall be great tribulation, such as was not since the beginning of the world to this time, no, nor ever shall be. And except those days should be shortened, there should no flesh be saved: but for the elect's sake those days shall be shortened" (Matthew 24:21–22).

I cannot agree that the timing of the Rapture is unimportant. The Tribulation will be a time of unparalleled horror for all those left behind to live through the final seven years of this age; everyone must either take the Antichrist's satanic "Mark of the Beast" or suffer terrible persecution including beheading. If the Rapture does not precede the Tribulation, then hundreds of millions of those Christians living in the last generation of the Church Age must experience mass martyrdom. Therefore, the timing of the rapture is a matter of great concern to determine the truth of God's revelation about this matter and this necessitates in-depth study of the relevant scriptural passages.

There are no biblical prophecies that reveal the precise date of the Rapture. The Lord has specifically hidden the time of the future resurrection of the saints. Jesus told us, "But of that day and hour knoweth no man, no, not the angels of heaven, but my Father only" (Matthew 24:36). By intentionally not revealing the time of the coming resurrection, the Lord has kept His Church waiting expectantly, in every generation for the last two thousand years, until the final day when we shall be called up in the air to join with all of the departed saints to return to heaven with Christ. We are simply instructed "to wait for his Son from heaven, whom he raised from the dead, even Jesus, which delivered us from the wrath to come" (1 Thessalonians 1:10).

The Rapture and the Revelation

The Rapture of the Church should not be confused with the Revelation of Christ's Second Coming. Although these two events are the two most significant occurrences connected with Christ's return in the last days, they are quite separate events involving separate participants, as well as different times, purposes, and locations.

The word *Rapture* known as *parousia* in Greek, denotes a personal presence or appearance of Jesus Christ. The use of this term is best exemplified in 1 Thessalonians 4:13–18. The *Parousia* provides a message of comfort to the righteous saints (1 Thessalonians 4:18). The Rapture will be announced with the voice of the archangel (1 Thessalonians 4:16) and will take place in the air as all living and departed saints rise to meet Christ and return to heaven (Matthew 25:10), while the Revelation of Christ at Armageddon will take place when He and His saints as part of His victorious army return to earth to defeat Antichrist at Armageddon (Revelation 19:7–9). The Rapture will precede the Tribulation. At the time of the Rapture, Christ will come to take His saints home. Only the saints will experience the Rapture; non-believers will not be aware of it until they witness the disappearance of the saints (1 Thessalonians 4:13–18). The Rapture will reveal the Lord's transformation of the mortal bodies of believers into new resurrection bodies for eternity (1 Thessalonians 4:16), while His Revelation at the Battle of Armageddon will reveal the glory of Jesus Christ as our returning Messiah.

The word *revelation*, known as the *apokalupsis* in Greek, denotes an unveiling and a time of "shining forth" of Christ's glorious return (2 Thessalonians 1:7). The apocalypse reveals a message of terror to the unrighteous (2 Thessalonians 1:7–8), as Jesus Christ and His mighty angels will come in judgment upon the wicked. Christ's Revelation will occur on the earth, at the Valley of Megiddo and, later, at the Mount of Olives opposite Jerusalem (Zechariah 14:4), and will victoriously end the Antichrist's seven-year Tribulation. At the time of His glorious Revelation, Christ will return from heaven with His enormous army of angels and resurrected saints (Revelation 19:11–16). Every person still surviving on earth at the end of the devastating Tribulation period will witness Christ's glorious Second Coming (Revelation 1–7). The Gospel of Matthew records Christ's prophecy: "For as the lightning cometh out of the east, and shineth even unto the west; so shall also the coming of the Son of man be. . . . Immediately after the tribulation of those days shall the sun be darkened, and the moon shall not give her light, and the stars shall fall from heaven, and the powers of the heavens shall be shaken. And then shall appear the sign of the Son of man in heaven: and then shall all the tribes of the earth mourn, and they shall see the Son of man coming in the clouds of heaven with power and great glory" (Matthew 24:27, 29–30). At His revelation, Jesus Christ will appear in glory, destroying the Antichrist and his wicked army before they can destory His Chosen People Israel (Matthew 13:41–43, 2 Thessalonians 2:8).

The Lord will save the believing remnant of the Jews in Israel who repent of their rejection of His messianic claims during the final devastating attack on the Jewish defenders of Jerusalem by the surviving forces of the Antichrist following the battle of Armageddon. When Jesus descends on the Mount of Olives, He will supernaturally destroy the remnants of the satanic forces who still desire to destroy the Chosen People. The prophet Zechariah declared: "And this shall be the plague wherewith the Lord will smite all the people that have fought against Jerusalem; Their flesh shall consume away while they stand upon their feet, and their eyes shall consume away in their holes, and their tongue shall consume away in their mouth. And it shall come to pass in that day, that a great tumult from the Lord shall be among them; and they shall lay hold every one on the hand of his neighbour, and his hand shall rise up against the hand of his neighbour. And Judah also shall fight at Jerusalem" (Zechariah 14:12–14).

Biblical Support for a Pre-Tribulation Rapture

The Scriptures clearly support a pre-Tribulation Rapture of believers. At the Second Coming at the Battle of Armageddon, Jesus Christ will return from heaven to earth in glory with His resurrected. In the book of Revelation John wrote, "And I saw heaven opened, and behold a white horse; and he that sat upon him was called Faithful and True, and in righteousness he doth judge and make war. . . . And the armies which were in heaven followed him upon white horses, clothed in fine linen, white and clean" (Revelation 19:11, 14).

Therefore, logically, if the Christian saints will join in Christ's heavenly army to participate in the Battle of Armageddon, then they must be translated to heaven and given their immortal resurrection body at some point in time prior to their leaving heaven with Christ to return to earth to defeat the armies of the Antichrist. The alternative theory developed by those who espouse the post-Tribulation Rapture suggests that the saints will be resurrected at the end of the Tribulation, rise in the air to meet Christ together with the souls of the departed saints, participate in the Bema Judgment seat and marriage supper of the Lamb in the air, and then instantaneously reverse direction to return to earth with Jesus Christ to participate in the Battle of Armageddon. A careful reading of Revelation 19 does not suggest the above post-tribulation scenario is at all credible or in agreement with the scriptural prophecy.

Significantly, John records that the angels will withhold their threatened judgment during the Tribulation until they first supernaturally seal the "servants of God" to protect them from the coming wrath of God (Revelation 7). This revelation is consistant with the complete biblical record that shows that God never pours His wrath upon the righteous. John reveals that those who are supernaturally sealed for protection against the wrath of God are 144,000 Jews (12,000 from each of the twelve tribes of Israel). However all Christians are also "the servants of God" as Peter affirmed, "For so is the will of God, that with well doing ye may put to silence the ignorance of foolish men: As free, and not using your liberty for a cloak of maliciousness, but as the servants of God" (I Peter 2:15–16). The question is this: Why would God supernaturally seal the 144,000 Jews to protect them only but leave hundreds of millions of Christians unprotected from His coming wrath? The only logical reason for not protecting the millions of Christians as "the servants of God" is that these Christians will no longer require supernatural protection. All Christians will already be raptured to heaven before the wrath of God is poured out upon unrepentant sinners during the Tribulation period.

The Church Age, the period of time from the birth of the Church at Pentecost in A.D. 32 until the future Rapture, is known as the Age of Grace. During this period, the Holy Spirit reveals there is "no difference between Jew and Greek" (Romans 10:12) because all genuine born-again Christians, regardless of race, are spiritually and truly one in Christ. Yet the prophecies in Daniel, Matthew, 2 Thessalonians, and Revelation that reveal the events that will occur during the final seven-year Tribulation focus repeatedly on Israel, Jerusalem, the Jews, and their separate identity from the surrounding Gentile nations. These prophetic passages discuss the Jews, Israel fleeing into the wilderness, the rebuilt Temple, the resumption of animal sacrifice, the purifying of the Levites, the Antichrist's claim to be Israel's Messiah, the False Prophet bringing fire down from heaven in imitation of the prophet Elijah, the Law, and the 144,000 Jewish witnesses. All of these issues concern Israel, not the Church.

From the day of Pentecost when the Church was first born, the Scriptures declared that the Holy Spirit, the Comforter of the Church, is restraining the mystery of iniquity, the appearance of Antichrist, the man of sin. Paul wrote, "And now ye know what withholdeth that he might be revealed in his time. For the mystery of iniquity doth already work: only he who now letteth will let, until he be taken out of the way. And then shall that Wicked be revealed, whom the Lord shall consume with the spirit of his mouth, and shall destroy with the brightness of his coming" (2 Thessalonians 2:6–8). The word "let" means hinder. Paul's use of the personal pronoun "he" in this verse proves that the restrainer of the Antichrist is a person, the Holy Spirit, not a political-military power such as the Roman Empire, as some scholars have suggested. Jesus Christ promised that He would give us the Holy Spirit as our Comforter and that the Holy Spirit will never leave the Church "comfortless." The apostle John recorded these words of Christ, "And I will pray the Father, and he shall give you another Comforter, that he may abide with you for ever. . . . I will not leave you comfortless: I will come to you" (John 14:16, 18). Since God affirms that the man of sin cannot appear until the Holy Spirit is removed from His role as restrainer of the Antichrist, and since Christ declares that the Holy Spirit will never leave His Church, the logical conclusion is that the Church must be taken to heaven at some point prior to the appearance of the Antichrist.

The Lord commands the Church to always be watchful for Christ's coming, which could happen at any moment. Jesus Christ commands us, "Therefore let us not sleep, as do others; but let us watch and be sober" (1 Thessalonians 5:6). This doctrine of watching expectantly for the imminent return of Christ to resurrect His saints is logically consistent with a pre-Tribulation Rapture. However, if the Lord intended that the Church should live through the terrible wrath of God as hundreds of detailed prophesied events unfold during the seven years of the Tribulation period, it would be misleading for the Scriptures to continually motivate Christian believers to "be ye therefore ready also: for the Son of man cometh at an hour when ye think not" (Luke 12:40).

If the Rapture will not occur until the future conclusion of the Battle of Armageddon (following the prophetic events of seven years involving global government, a world dictator, an ecumentical world religion, a rebuilt Temple in Jerusalem, resumption of animal sacrifice in the Temple, the Two Witnesses, and a final global war between the East and West, et cetera), as some critics suggest, there would have been no need for the Lord's command to believers to be ready and watchful for His imminent return. Even those sinners who reject Jesus Christ during the Tribulation will be fully aware of both the prophecies of the Second Coming and the obvious buildup for the cataclysmic and global Battle of Armageddon. If the Rapture will not happen until the end of the Tribulation period at the end of Armageddon, then there is a serious contradiction with the repeated scriptural warnings that the Rapture of the saints by Jesus Christ will come suddenly and without any warning.

When speaking to the Christians in the church at Thessalonica, the apostle Paul affirmed the fundamental importance of this imminent return of Christ as follows: "For what is our hope, or joy, or crown of rejoicing? Are not even ye in the presence of our Lord Jesus Christ at his coming?" (1 Thessalonians 2:19). It is significant that Paul described the resurrection of the saints in such positive terms. Paul certainly knew the truth concerning God's intention about the timing of the Rapture from the inspiration of the Holy Spirit. Paul encouraged all believers to look forward to the imminent resurrection of the saints through his use of words such as hope, joy, comfort, and rejoicing. Paul's words of hope and joy are consistant with his compelling teaching that the rapture of the Church will deliver the saints from this world into the presence of Christ in heaven. These terms "our hope, or joy, or crown of rejoicing" would have been totally inappropriate if the apostle Paul knew he needed to prepare the Christians living in the last days for the coming wrath of God which they would endure for the seven years of the Tribulation period. The only logical conclusion is that the apostle Paul knew and believed that the Lord would return imminently, without warning, to take His believers home to glory before the world will experience the Tribulation at the end of this age.

Jesus was the first to teach about the Rapture when He spoke to his friend Martha after the death of her brother Lazarus. Martha said, "Lord, if thou hadst been here, my brother had not died." Jesus responded by saying, "Thy brother shall rise again." Martha acknowledged her belief in the resurrection of the departed saints as taught by the Old Testament in her answer, "I know that he shall rise again in the resurrection at the last day." Jesus then declared, "I am the resurrection, and the life: he that believeth in me, though he were dead, yet shall he live." He closed this dialogue with this fascinating remark, "And whosoever liveth and believeth in me shall never die. Believest thou this?" (John 11:21–26).

For many years, when I read this well-known passage in the gospel of John, I thought that Christ was simply repeating Himself in His last sentence. However, upon closer examination and serious reflection, I believe that this remarkable passage contains the first teaching in the New Testament about the Rapture of the Church. Notice that Jesus is teaching about the destiny of two distinct groups of believers. The first group is made up of all of those believers who will have died during the period between the birth of the Church at Pentecost and the Second Coming of Christ: "He that believeth in me, though he were dead, yet shall he live." This statement of Jesus to Martha confirmed the doctrine of the Old Tesatment regarding the resurrection of the believers in the last days as taught by Job 19:25–26 and numerous other scriptural passages.

The second group of Christians as covered in Jesus' second statement includes all believers who will be living at the time of the return of Jesus Christ. This was an entirely new revelation: "And whoever liveth and believeth in me shall never die." Jesus revealed that there will be a generation of believers who will not have to pass through death to reach eternal life; the generation of Christians who are living at the resurrection will be "caught up together . . . to meet the Lord in the air" as Paul taught in 1 Thessalonians 4:15–18.

The apostle Paul reaffirms this great truth when he wrote to the Corinthian Christians during his third missionary journey, probably during the winter of 55.

> Behold, I shew you a mystery; We shall not all sleep, but we shall all be changed, in a moment, in the twinkling of an eye, at the last trump: for the trumpet shall sound, and the dead shall be raised incorruptible, and we shall be

changed. For this corruptible must put on incorruption, and this mortal must put on immortality. So when this corruptible shall have put on incorruption, and this mortal shall have put on immortality, then shall be brought to pass the saying that is written: Death is swallowed up in victory. (1 Corinthians 15:51–54)

In this passage, Paul taught about the Second Coming of the Lord and His promise of the Rapture of the saints. There are five new points that Paul revealed in his teaching. The first point is that not all Christians will die—many believers will be alive in the final generation at the moment when Christ returns to resurrect all of the saints. The second point is that Christ will first resurrect the bodies of those believers who have already died. The third point is that the resurrection will be instantaneous, in one-tenth of a second, in "the twinkling of an eye." Another is that this Rapture will be accompanied by the blowing of "the last trumpet." And the final point Paul makes is that all believers—both dead and alive—will be changed into their new supernatural, immortal, resurrection bodies. The Lord will transform our mortal, corruptible earthly bodies into incorruptible, immortal, heavenly bodies fit for heaven as well as the Kingdom of God on earth.

Early Church Teaching about the Rapture

The doctrine of the pre-Tribulation Rapture has produced conflict and debate during recent years as many Christians attempt to determine the truth about this vital doctrine about the resurrection of the saints in the last days. The Protestant Reformation was predominantly based on the rejection of centuries of accumulated man-made doctrines, church traditions, and a return to the authority of the Word of God as found in the Bible. The Latin phrase *Sola Scriptura*, meaning "Scripture Alone" became the rallying cry of the reformers who ignored centuries of medieval tradition and Church councils in their insistence that spiritual truth could only be discovered in the literal teaching of the Word of God. It is important to answer the arguments of those who disparage the blessed hope of the Rapture with misinformation claiming that no one ever taught or believed in the pre-tribulation rapture at any point prior to the 1800s.

During the last century, many post-Tribulation Rapture writers have attacked the pre-Tribulation Rapture doctrine by claiming that it cannot be valid because no Church writer or Reformer ever taught it until about 1830. The argument that no one ever taught the pre-Tribulation Rapture during the first eighteen hundred years of Church history has been very effective, and has caused many Christians to doubt or abandon their belief in this doctrine. However, this claim of the post-Tribulationists is false.

Many contemporary writers claim that the pre-Tribulation Rapture theory originated approximately 1812 to 1830. They ascribe the theory's initial creation to Emmanuel Lacunza (known as Ben Ezra, 1812), Edward Irving (1816), or Margaret Macdonald (1830), and finally to John Darby (1827). For example, Dave MacPherson stated in his 1975 book *The Incredible Cover-Up*: "Margaret Macdonald was the first person to teach a coming of Christ that would precede the days of Antichrist. . . . Before 1830 Christians had always believed in a single future coming, that the catching up of I Thessalonians 4 will take place after the Great Tribulation of Matthew 24 at the glorious coming of the Son of Man when He shall send His angels to gather together all of His Elect."[1] Another preterist, Rev. John Bray, in *The Origin of the Pre-Tribulation Rapture Teaching*, declared, "People who are teaching the pre-tribulation rapture teaching today are teaching something that never was taught until 1812 . . . Not one of those early church fathers taught a pre-tribulation rapture."[2]

Post-tribulation authors should correct their previous statements. A remarkable textual discovery conclusively proved that an important Christian teacher, living almost fourteen centuries before John Darby, clearly taught that the Rapture would occur before the Tribulation. During the summer of 1994, after more than a decade of diligent searching in libraries and rare bookstores throughout North America and Europe, I discovered an important manuscript that provides compelling evidence of the teaching of the pre-Tribulation Rapture more than a thousand years before the 1800s.

Ephraem the Syrian Taught the Pre-Tribulation Rapture in 373

Ephraem the Syrian (306–373) was a very important writer, poet, and theologian of the early Byzantine Church. He was born near Nisbis, in the Roman province of Syria, near present-day Edessa, Turkey. Ephraem displayed a profound love of the Scriptures in his writings as illustrated by several of his written comments quoted in the *Works of Nathaniel Lardner*, Vol. 4, 1788: "I esteem no man more happy than him, who diligently reads the Scriptures delivered to us by the Spirit of God, and thinks how he may order his conversation by the precepts of them."

After seventeen centuries, Ephraem's hymns and homilies are still used today in the liturgy of the Greek Orthodox and Middle Eastern Nestorian Church. The well-respected sixteen-volume *Post-Nicene Library* (which includes the most important Christian writings after the 325 Council of Nicea) contains a number of homilies and psalms by Ephraem. The editors noted that he also wrote a large number of biblical commentaries that have never before been translated into the English language

In Ephraem's *On the Last Times, the Antichrist, and the End of the World* (probably written A.D. 373 by Ephraem; but definitely written before 622), he reveals a literal method of scriptural interpretation regarding the prophecies about the Antichrist and the premillennial return of Christ to set up His kingdom of God on earth. Ephraem's text contains a very clear statement about the pre-tribulational return of Christ to take His elect saints home to heaven before the coming Tribulation and the horrors of the satanic persecution during the seven years leading to Armageddon: "For all the saints and Elect of God are gathered, prior to the tribulation that is to come, and are taken to the Lord lest they see the confusion that is to overwhelm the world because of our sins."

Ephraem also declared his belief in a Jewish Antichrist who will rule the Roman Empire during the last days, a rebuilt Temple, the Two Witnesses, and a literal Great Tribulation lasting 1,260 days. He also taught that the war of Gog and Magog (Ezekiel 38–39) would precede the Tribulation. In another text called *The Book of the Cave of Treasure*, Ephraem taught that Daniel's seventieth week would be fulfilled in the final seven years at the end of this age that will conclude with Christ's return at the Battle of Armageddon.

In 1995, after I discovered *On the Last Times, the Antichrist, and the End of the World,* I arranged for Dr. Cameron Rhoades of Tyndale Theological Seminary to translate it. This fascinating document states that the Lord will gather together the Elect of the Lord "before the tribulation" and that the saints will be "taken to the Lord" to escape "the confusion which overwhelms the world." Ephraem's text includes his understanding of the imminent return of Christ, the need to turn from worldly concerns.

> Most dearly beloved brothers, believe the Holy Spirit who speaks in us. Now we have spoken before, because the end of the world is very near, and the consummation remains. Has not the first faith withered away in men? . . .

> *We ought to understand thoroughly therefore, my brothers what is imminent or overhanging.* Already there have been hunger and plagues, violent movements of nations and signs, which have been predicted by the Lord, they have already been fulfilled, and there is not other which remains, except the advent of the wicked one in the completion of the Roman kingdom. Why therefore are we occupied with worldly business, and why is our mind held fixed on the lusts of the world or the anxieties of the ages? Why therefore do we not reject every care of earthly actions and prepare ourselves for the meeting of the Lord Christ, *so that He may draw us from the confusion, which overwhelms the world?* Believe you me, dearest brothers, because the coming of the Lord is nigh, believe you me, because the end of the world is at hand, believe me, because it is the very last time. . . . (Italics added)

Because all saints and the Elect of the Lord are gathered together before the tribulation which is to come and are taken to the Lord, in order that they may not see at any time the confusion which overwhelms the world because of our sins [italics added]. And so, brothers, most dear to me, it is the eleventh hour, and the end of this world comes to the harvest, and angels, armed and prepared, hold sickles in their hands, awaiting the empire of the Lord ... (Italics added)

When therefore the end of the world comes, there arise diverse wars, commotions on all sides, horrible earthquakes, perturbations of nations, tempests throughout the lands, plagues, famine, drought throughout the thoroughfares, great danger throughout the sea and dry land, constant persecutions, slaughters and massacres everywhere ...

When therefore the end of the world comes, that abominable, lying and murderous one is born from the tribe of Dan. He is conceived from the seed of a man and from a most vile virgin, mixed with an evil or worthless spirit.

But when the time of the abomination of his desolation begins to approach, having been made legal, he takes the empire. . . Therefore, when he receives the kingdom, he orders the temple of God to be rebuilt for himself, which is in Jerusalem; who, after coming into it, he shall sit as God and order that he be adored by all nations . . . then all people from everywhere shall flock together to him at the city of Jerusalem, and the holy city shall be trampled on by the nations for forty-two months just as the holy apostle says in the Apocalypse, which become three and a half years, 1260 days.

In these three years and a half the heaven shall suspend its dew; because there will be no rain upon the earth . . . and there will be a great tribulation, as there has not been, since people began to be upon the earth

... and no one is able to sell or to buy of the grain of the fall harvest, unless he is one who has the serpentine sign on the forehead or the hand. . .

And when the three and a half years have been completed, the time of the Antichrist, through which he will have seduced the world, after the resurrection of the two prophets, in the hour which the world does not know, and on the day which the enemy or son of perdition does not know, will come the sign of the Son of Man, and coming forward the Lord shall appear with great power and much majesty, with the sign of the word of salvation going before him, and also even with all the powers of the heavens with the whole chorus of the saints. . . . Then Christ shall come and the enemy shall be thrown into confusion, and the Lord shall destroy him by the Spirit of his mouth. And he shall be bound and shall be plunged into the abyss of everlasting fire alive with his father Satan; and all people, who do his wishes, shall perish with him forever; but the righteous ones shall inherit everlasting life with the Lord for ever and ever.

Ephraem's manuscript is unusual among ancient Church writings about prophecy in that it presents the events of the last days in a detailed chronological sequence. Significantly, Ephraem began his series of future events with the Rapture of the saints, saying it was "imminent or overhanging." He explained that God will rapture the Church before the tribulation in these words: "all saints and the Elect of the Lord are gathered together before the tribulation which is to come and are taken to the Lord, in order that they may not see at any time the confusion which overwhelms the world because of our sins." Ephraem used the word "confusion" as a synonym for the terrible persecution of the final seven-year tribulation period. Then he described the Great Tribulation, which will occur during the last three and a half years of the seven-year tribulation, under the Antichrist's tyranny, including the Mark of the Beast. He concluded his prophetic sequence of events with the Second

Coming of Christ from heaven to earth with His saints to defeat the Antichrist.

Dr. Paul Alexander, one of the most authoritative scholars studying the writings of the early Byzantine Church, concluded in his book, *The Byzantine Apocalyptic Tradition*, that Ephraem's text on the Antichrist taught that the Lord would supernaturally remove the saints of the Church from the earth "prior to the tribulation that is to come."[3] Dr. Alexander believed some unknown writer may have written this text in the sixth century and added the name Ephraem to it to honor the great teacher. Alexander concluded that it was derived from an original Ephraem manuscript from 373. However, one of the greatest scholars of eschatology, Wilhelm Bousett, accepted the 373 date and Ephraem's authorship as probably genuine.[4] In his book, *Alexander's Gate: Gog and Magog and the Enclosed Nations*, Professor Andrew R. Anderson also supports the early date of 373 for this important manuscript.[5]

Other scholars, including the German editor Professor C. P. Caspari, who wrote a German commentary on this ancient Latin manuscript in 1890, believed that the genuine Ephraem could have written this important manuscript in 373 but also suggested that some unknown writer might have written this manuscript based on Ephraem's original work at some point in the fifth or sixth century.[6] Regardless of whether this manuscript was written originally by Ephraem or by some unknown writer using his manuscripts as a source a few centuries later, most scholars agree that this was written at some point before the year 622 when Mohammed introduced the Islamic religion. This discovery also demonstrates that the pre-Tribulation Rapture was taught and attributed to Ephraem the Syrian, one of the greatest and most respected of the teachers of the ancient Greek Christian Church.

Why a Pre-Trib Rapture?

In the great purging of evil civilizations recorded throughout the Scriptures, God has never once poured out His wrath upon His faithful and righteous followers. The wrath of God has always fallen solely upon unrepentant sinners; it has never fallen upon the righteous. This is demonstrated clearly in the accounts of Noah's flood and the destruction of Sodom and Gomorrah. It would be a contradiction of God's holiness and just character if He exposed His saints to seven years of His wrath during the future Tribulation.

> And as it was in the days of Noe, so shall it be also in the days of the Son of man. They did eat, they drank, they married wives, they were given in marriage, until the day that Noe entered into the ark, and the flood came, and destroyed them all. Likewise also as it was in the days of Lot; they did eat, they drank, they bought, they sold, they planted, they builded; But the same day that Lot went out of Sodom it rained fire and brimstone from heaven, and destroyed them all. Even thus shall it be in the day when the Son of man is revealed. (Luke 17:26–30)

As recorded in the book of Genesis, God withheld His wrathful judgment upon the wicked and rebellious population of the world until the righteous Noah and his family entered the ark. Signifcantly, the wrath of God unleashed the Flood only after "the Lord shut him in" for protection. God supernaturally destroyed the wicked city of Sodom, but only after Lot and his family escaped from the city. The angel warned Lot, "Haste thee, escape thither; for I cannot do any thing till thou be come thither" (Genesis 19:22). This significant passage reminds us of a fundamental principle of God's dealing with mankind—despite the wickedness of Sodom, the angel declared that he could not destroy the evil city and its perverse population until the righteous Lot and his family escaped.

The wrath of God is reserved for those who reject the Lord's offer of salvation. When Abraham asked God for mercy for the other citizens of Sodom, he pled, "That be far from thee to do after this manner, to slay the righteous with the wicked: and that the righteous should be as the wicked, that be far from thee: Shall not the Judge of all the earth do right?" (Genesis 18:25). In Paul's book of Romans, we read, "For the wrath of God is revealed from heaven against all ungodliness and unrighteousness of men, who hold the truth in unrighteousness" (Romans 1:18). While believers often experience God's loving chastening for our correction and we often endure the consequences of our sins and the sinful decisions of others, the Scriptures clearly reveal that the wrath of God is reserved for unrepentant sinners.

In Paul's first letter to the church at Thessalonica, he wrote about the different character and final spiritual destiny of the saints, "the children of light," in contrast to the unrepentant sinners, "the children of darkness." Paul affirmed Christ's absolute promise to His followers of supernatural deliverance from the coming wrath of God, "For God hath not appointed us to wrath, but to obtain salvation by our Lord Jesus Christ" (1 Thessalonians 5:9). In this passage, it is very clear that the destiny of "the children of light" (Christians) is "to obtain salvation by our Lord Jesus Christ." However, the destiny of "the children of darkness" (those who rebelliously reject Christ's offer of salvation) is to endure the eternal wrath of God.

In another passage, Paul specifically declared that Christ's Second Coming will protect His Church from "the wrath to come." The apostle encouraged Christians "to wait for his Son from heaven, whom he raised from the dead, even Jesus, which delivered us from the wrath to come" (1 Thessalonians 1:10). Note that this verse specifically outlines the precise chronological order of prophetic events: First, Christians are to expectantly wait for the imminent return of His Son from heaven. Second, Jesus will come from heaven for His Church. Third, Christ's coming for His followers will deliver "us from the wrath to come." In this one definitive verse we have the clearest possible expression that the resurrection of the saints will precede the Tribulation when "the wrath to come" will be unleashed from heaven upon the unrepentant sinners who will worship Satan rather than God.

Some scholars suggest that Christians must experience the Tribulation to somehow spiritually purify them in preparation for heaven before they will be raptured. However, this argument fails for two reasons. First, the majority of all the followers of Christ who compose the Church that will be present at the Rapture include hundreds of millions of departed Christian saints who died during the last two thousand years. Since these Christian souls are already in heaven without suffering the persecution of the future Tribulation, it does not make sense that believers living in the last days would be required to experience the persecution of the Tribulation to spiritually prepare them for the coming resurrection. Second, there is no need for believers in the last days to experience the Tribulation to purify them spiritually before they reach heaven—all believers in every generation are purified solely by the atoning power of Christ's blood shed for us at Calvary. Christ's atonement, by His perfect sacrifice on the Cross, is the only thing that can justify us and fully pay the price for our sins.

The Importance of Teaching the Pre-Tribulation Rapture

Why is it important to teach the doctrine of the pre-Tribulation Rapture? The apostle Peter warned that many people would challenge our Lord's promise of His Second Coming in the last days: "Knowing this first; that there shall come in the last days scoffers, walking after their own lusts, and saying, Where is the promise of his coming?" (2 Peter 3:3–4).

What does the Bible teach us about the proper attitude of a Christian with respect to the subject of Christ's return? In 1 Corinthians 1:7, Paul tells us, "So that ye come behind in no gift; waiting for the coming of our Lord Jesus Christ." Paul also commands Christians to demonstrate a constant expectation of the Rapture in Philippians 3:20: "For our conversation is in heaven; from whence also we look for the Saviour, the Lord Jesus Christ."

The great reformers of the Church encouraged believers in their constant hope of the Second Coming. John Calvin wrote, "It ought to be the chief concern of believers to fix their minds fully on His Second Advent." Martin Luther, in his *Sermon of Consolation*, declared that the hope of Christ's return is an absolute necessity for a Christian:

> If thou be not filled with a desire after the Coming of
> this day, thou canst never pray the Lord's prayer, nor

canst thou repeat from thy heart the creed of faith. For with what conscience canst thou say, 'I believe in the resurrection of the body and the life everlasting,' if thou dost not in thy heart desire the same? If thou didst believe it, thou must, of necessity, desire it from thy heart, and long for that day to come; which, if thou doest not desire, thou art not yet a Christian, nor canst thou boast of thy faith.

The New Testament contains numerous exhortations to hold on to the hope of our Lord's soon return as the focus of our spiritual life. The "blessed hope" of the Rapture should be a cornerstone of every Christian's spiritual life, for many reasons.

- Expecting Christ's soon return calls all believers to constant spiritual watchfulness. "But ye, brethren, are not in darkness, that that day should overtake you as a thief. Ye are all the children of light, and the children of the day: we are not of the night, nor of darkness. Therefore let us not sleep, as do others; but let us watch and be sober" (1 Thessalonians 5:4–6).

- This hope motivates us to witness to unbelievers in light of His imminent coming. "I must work the works of him that sent me, while it is day: the night cometh, when no man can work" (John 9:4).

- It reminds us to walk daily in holiness in an immoral world while we await His soon return. "And every man that hath this hope in him purifieth himself, even as he is pure" (1 John 3:3).

- His return comforts the saints by reminding them of their eternal destiny with Christ. "Let not your heart be troubled: ye believe in God, believe also in me. In my Father's house are many mansions: if it were not so, I would have told you. I go to prepare a place for you. And if I go and prepare a place for you, I will come again, and receive you unto myself; that where I am, there ye may be also" (John 14:1–3).

- God promises a crown for those who long for the Second Coming. "Henceforth there is laid up for me a crown of righteousness, which the Lord, the righteous judge, shall give me at that day: and not to me only, but unto all them also that love his appearing" (2 Timothy 4: 8).

- Finally, the approaching return of Christ encourages sinners to repent and accept the Lord while they still have time. "Repent ye therefore, and be converted, that your sins may be blotted out, when the times of refreshing shall come from the presence of the Lord; And he shall send Jesus Christ, which before was preached unto you: Whom the heaven must receive until the times of restitution of all things, which God hath spoken by the mouth of all his holy prophets since the world began" (Acts 3:19–21).

Unfortunately, some peoples' enthusiasm regarding the Rapture has led them to unwisely propose specific dates for Christ's return. The Scriptures specifically warn that no one but God will know the time of His return. The Gospel of Matthew declares, "Watch therefore, for ye know neither the day nor the hour wherein the Son of man cometh" (Matthew 25:13). For example, Harold Camping's book, *1994*, claimed that Christ would return on September 17, 1994.[8] Millions of readers of this book and other similar speculative writings were deeply disappointed when these unscriptural predictions proved false.

Christians must not abandon our hope for an imminent Rapture of Jesus because others have foolishly been misled. We must simply be obedient to Christ's scriptural command: "When these things begin come to pass, then look up, and lift up your heads, for your redemption draweth nigh" (Luke 21:28). John Wesley De La Fletchere wrote a compelling letter to Charles Wesley in 1755 that expressed the proper attitude all Christians should adopt concerning the Lord's return: "I know that many have been grossly mistaken as to the year of His return, but, because they were rash, shall we be stupid? Because they say 'Today!'; shall we say, 'Never!' and cry 'Peace, Peace,' when we should look about us with eyes full of expectation?"[9]

Christians live in a dynamic spiritual tension where we walk in daily expectation for our Lord's return while we obediently complete the Great Commission to "Go ye into all the world, and preach the gospel to every creature" (Mark 16:15). On the one hand, since the Lord might return at any moment, we need to watch expectantly for His coming. However, the Lord also commands us to "occupy till He comes," which reminds us to be faithful servants building churches and orphanages, support evangelical and medical missions, and witness to those around us until He returns.

If we are to be obedient to the command of Jesus Christ, we must live in daily holiness and constant expectation of our Lord's Second Coming; Christ could return at any moment. No other generation has ever witnessed so many prophecies fulfilled in its lifetime as we have witnessed since the rebirth of Israel in 1948. The following chapters will examine a number of fascinating prophecies fulfilled in our generation that point to the nearness of the Lord's return. "Blessed are those servants, whom the lord, when he cometh shall find watching. . . . Be ye therefore ready also: for the Son of man cometh at an hour ye think not" (Luke 12:37, 40). The apostle Peter warned, "Ye therefore, beloved, seeing ye know these things before, beware lest ye also, being led away with the error of the wicked, fall from your own stedfastness" (2 Peter 3:17). While we are commanded to live each day in holiness and urgently witness as though He will return before the dawn, we are also called to plan and work to fulfill the Great Commission as if He will tarry for another hundred years.

Notes

1. Dave MacPherson, *The Incredible Cover-Up* (Plainfield: Logos International, 1975).

2. John Bray, *The Origin of the Pre-Tribulation Rapture Teaching* (1980).

3. Paul J. Alexander, *The Byzantine Apocalyptic Tradition* (London: University of California Press, 1985).

4. Wilhelm Bousset, *The Antichrist Legend*, trans. A. H. Keane (London: Hutchinson and Co., 1896).

5. Andrew R. Anderson, *Alexander's Gate: Gog and Magog and the Enclosed Nations* (Cambridge: Medieval Academy of America, 1932) 16–18.

6. C. P. Caspari, *Briefe, Abhandlungen und Predigten aus den letzten zwei Jahrhunderten des kirchliche Alterthums und dem Anfang des Mittelalters* (Christiana, 1890) 208–220, 429–72.

7. "Teachings of the Twelve Apostles," *Ante-Nicene Fathers*, 10 vols. (Grand Rapids: Wm. B. Eerdmans Publishing Co., 1987).

8. Harold Camping, *1994* (New York: Vantage Publishing, 1992).

9. Melvill Horne, *Posthumous Pieces of the Late Rev. John William De La Fletchere* (Dublin: 1802).

8

The Imminent Return of Christ for His Church

"If any man love not the Lord Jesus Christ, let him be Anathema, Maranatha" (1 Corinthians 16:22).

The word *Maranatha* was a very popular greeting used by the Christians of the early Church when meeting fellow believers. It demonstrated their ever-present hope for the imminent return of Jesus Christ to resurrect His faithful followers.

Maranatha is formed from three Aramaic words: *Mar* means "Lord," *ana* means "our," and *tha* means "come." In Aramaic, Maranatha literally means "our Lord, come." In English, it translates, "The Lord comes!" The widespread use of the Maranatha greeting demonstrates the universal expectation of the early Church that Christ would return at some point in time to resurrect the saints and then, to defeat the Antichrist at the end of the Tribulation and establish His kingdom on earth.

I believe that the clear teaching of the New Testament demonstrates that the Holy Spirit taught His Church that Christ's return for the saints to resurrect their mortal bodies was imminent then and will remain imminent until the moment He returns. The widespread use of the Maranatha greeting only makes sense if these early Christians understood the teaching of the apostolic Church to include the imminent coming of Christ.

What Do We Mean By His Imminent Return?

The word "imminent" means simply that an event is certain to occur at some point in the future, that it could occur the next moment, but that its precise timing is unknown. It also conveys the assumption that no intervening event *must* occur before the event takes place. While another event could occur before the prophesied event, there is no requirement that it does. The *Webster's Ninth New Collegiate Dictionary* defines "imminent" as "ready to take place; *esp.*: hanging threateningly over one's head." As my colleague Renald Showers noted in his book *Maranatha Our Lord, Come!*, "Other things may happen before the imminent event, but nothing else must take place before it happens. If something else must take place before an event can happen, that event is not imminent."[1]

It is therefore obvious that no one can possibly know with certainty when an imminent event will actually occur. Therefore, no one can count upon a certain amount of time—days, weeks, months, or years—transpiring before the prophesied imminent event finally occurs. In recognition of this fact, we should always be ready for the occurrence of an imminent event, such as the Second Coming, to happen without warning at any moment.

An excellent definition of "imminence" appears in the writings of Arthur T. Pierson: "Imminence is the combination of two conditions, viz.,: certainty and uncertainty. By an imminent event we mean one which is certain to occur at some time, uncertain at what time."[2] An example of a current imminent event would be the promise of a traveler to return to his family at any time between Thanksgiving and Christmas. Once Thanksgiving occurs, his return is imminent. The traveler will return at any moment after Thanksgiving but he promises that he will definitely return before Christmas. No other event must occur before his appearance in fulfillment of his promise.

Christians who are obedient to Christ's command are watching for Him to come in the air and resurrect their body. "For the Lord himself shall descend from heaven with a shout, with the voice of the archangel, and with the trump of God: and the dead in Christ shall rise first: Then we which are alive and remain shall be caught up together with them in the clouds, to meet the Lord in the air: and so shall we ever be with the Lord" (1 Thessalonians 4:16–17). If the New Testament's prophecies teach the imminent coming of Christ to resurrect His saints at any moment, then the Rapture must precede the Tribulation. If the prophecies reveal the coming resurrection of the saints is imminent, then logically it cannot be delayed until some point during the prophesied events of the coming Tribulation (mid-Tribulation, pre-wrath toward the end of the tribulation, or post-Tribulation at Armageddon).

Scriptures Demonstrate the Imminence of His Return

The evidence presented in this chapter will demonstrate that the New Testament Scriptures declare repeatedly that the resurrection is an imminent event that can occur without the need for any intervening prophetic warning events or signs. The scriptural teaching of imminence is such a powerful argument in favor of the pre-Tribulation timing of the resurrection that the opponents of the pre-Tribulation resurrection vigorously deny that the coming of Christ for His Church is imminent.

Are there New Testament passages that clearly teach the truth of His imminent return? There are many verses that state that Jesus Christ might return at any moment, without any warning. Other passages instruct Christ's followers to watch and wait expectantly for the Lord's coming. Let us examine the evidence from Scripture to determine the truth regarding this vital doctrine of imminence.

* "Blessed are those servants, whom the lord when he cometh shall find watching: verily I say unto you, that he shall gird himself, and make them to sit down to meat, and will come forth and serve them" (Luke 12:37).

- "Be ye therefore ready also: for the Son of man cometh at an hour when ye think not" (Luke 12:40).
- "Watch ye therefore, and pray always, that ye may be accounted worthy to escape all these things that shall come to pass, and to stand before the Son of man" (Luke 21:36).
- "And not only they, but ourselves also, which have the firstfruits of the Spirit, even we ourselves groan within ourselves, waiting for the adoption, to wit, the redemption of our body" (Romans 8:23).
- "So that ye come behind in no gift; waiting for the coming of our Lord Jesus Christ" (l Corinthians 1:7).
- "Behold, I shew you a mystery; We shall not all sleep, but we shall all be changed, in a moment, in the twinkling of an eye, at the last trump: for the trumpet shall sound, and the dead shall be raised incorruptible, and we shall be changed" (l Corinthians 15:51).
- "Maranatha" (1 Corinthians 16:22).
- "For our conversation is in heaven; from whence also we look for the Savior, the Lord Jesus Christ" (Philippians 3:20).
- "Let your moderation be known unto all men. The Lord is at hand" (Philippians 4:5).
- "When Christ, who is our life, shall appear, then shall ye also appear with him in glory" (Colossians 3:4).
- "And to wait for his Son from heaven, whom he raised from the dead, even Jesus, which delivered us from the wrath to come" (1 Thessalonians 1:10).
- "Therefore let us not sleep, as do others; but let us watch and be sober" (1 Thessalonians 5:6).
- "And the Lord direct your hearts into the love of God, and into the patient waiting for Christ" (2 Thessalonians 3:5).
- "That thou keep this commandment without spot, unrebuke-able, until the appearing of our Lord Jesus Christ" (1 Timothy 6:14).
- "Looking for that blessed hope, and the glorious appearing of the great God and our Savior Jesus Christ" (Titus 2:13).
- "So Christ was once offered to bear the sins of many; and

unto them that look for him shall he appear the second time without sin unto salvation" (Hebrews 9:28).

- "For yet a little while, and he that shall come will come, and will not tarry" (Hebrews 10:37).
- "Be patient therefore, brethren, unto the coming of the Lord. Behold, the husbandman waiteth for the precious fruit of the earth, and hath long patience for it, until he receive the early and latter rain. Be ye also patient; establish your hearts: for the coming of the Lord draweth nigh. Grudge not one against another, brethren, lest ye be condemned: behold, the judge standeth before the door" (James 5:7–9).
- "Gird up the loins of your mind, be sober, and hope to the end for the grace that is to be brought unto you at the revelation of Jesus Christ" (1 Peter 1:13).
- "There shall come in the last days scoffers, . . . saying, Where is the promise of his coming? For since the fathers fell asleep, all things continue as they were from the beginning of the creation. For this they willingly are ignorant of, that by the word of God the heavens were of old, and the earth standing out of the water and in the water" (2 Peter 3:3–5).
- "We, according to his purpose, look for the new heavens and a new earth, wherein dwelleth righteousness. Wherefore, beloved, seeing that ye look for such things, be diligent that ye may be found of him in peace, without spot, and blameless" (2 Peter 3:13–14).
- "And now, little children, abide in him; that, when he shall appear, we may have confidence, and not be ashamed before him at his coming" (l John 2:28).
- "And every man that hath this hope in him purifieth himself, even as he is pure" (l John 3:3).
- "Keep yourselves in the love of God, looking for the mercy of our Lord Jesus Christ unto eternal life" (Jude 21).
- "Remember therefore how thou hast received and heard, and hold fast, and repent. If therefore thou shalt not watch, I will come on thee as a thief, and thou shalt not know what hour I will come upon thee" (Revelation 3:3).
- "Behold, I come quickly: hold that fast which thou hast, that no man take thy crown" (Revelation 3:11).

- "Behold, I come quickly: blessed is he that keepeth the sayings of the prophecy of this book" (Revelation 22:7).
- "And, behold, I come quickly; and my reward is with me, to give every man according as his work shall be" (Revelation 22:12).
- "He which testifieth these things saith, Surely I come quickly. Amen. Even so, come, Lord Jesus" (Revelation 22:20).

As these numerous passages attest, Christ's return for His saints is truly imminent. The Holy Spirit commands believers to look expectantly for our Lord's return at any moment and to continue living in holiness awaiting the glorious redemption of our body. The doctrine of the pre-Tribulation rapture accepts the full and literal implications to the promise of an any-moment resurrection event. Dr. John Walvoord, the acknowledged dean of prophecy teachers, wrote: "The exhortation to look for 'the glorious appearing' of Christ to His own (Titus 2:13) loses its significance if the Tribulation must intervene first. Believers in that case should look for signs."[3]

The Gentile and Jewish tribulation saints who become followers of Christ after the Rapture will experience the catastrophic events of the seven-year tribulation period described in the book of Revelation. These tribulation saints will observe the fulfillment of John's prophecies as signs of the final approach of Armageddon and Christ's coming defeat of Antichrist. However, those saints who belong to the Bride of Christ, the present Church of Jesus Christ, do not need to look for preliminary prophecies as preconditions to the imminent resurrection. They will obey the command of our Lord to watch expectantly for His return: "Be ye therefore ready also: for the Son of man cometh at an hour when ye think not" (Luke 12:40). Rather than waiting fearfully for the enduring of the seven years of the wrath of God during the Tribulation, Christians who belong to the Lord are commanded by God "to wait for his Son from heaven, whom he raised from the dead, even Jesus, which delivered us from the wrath to come" (1 Thessalonians 1:10).

Historic Teaching of the Imminent Return

A reader might reasonably ask whether any historical evidence exists to demonstrate whether any Christian leaders who lived before the 1800s taught that the coming of Jesus Christ to resurrect His saints was imminent. The answer is yes. As shown in earlier chapters, early Church leaders from Papias onward looked for an imminent return of Christ. For example, Cyprian (200–258) wrote enthusiastically about the imminent coming of Christ: "We who see that terrible things have begun, and know that still more terrible things are imminent, may regard it as the greatest advantage to depart from it as quickly as possible." Cyprian also declared, "Let us greet the day which assigns each of us to his own home, which snatches us hence, and sets us free from the snares of the world, and restores us to paradise and the kingdom."[4] Clement of Rome taught, "Let us every hour expect the Kingdom of God." Reverend Albert Barnes acknowledged in his commentary on 1 Corinthians 1:7 that there was a widespread longing for Christ's return within the early Church. "The earnest expectation of the Lord Jesus became one of the marks of early Christian piety."[5]

Though the imminence of the Second Coming fell out of favor in the teaching of the Church during the medieval period, it reappeared when the Reformers encouraged people to interpret the Scriptures for themselves. Martin Luther looked for the speedy and imminent return of Christ in the air to take His saints home to heaven. In his comment on the resurrection as prophesied by Daniel 12, Luther wrote: "I ever keep it before me, and I am satisfied that the last day must be before the door; for the signs predicted by Christ and the Apostles Peter and Paul have all now been fulfilled, the trees put forth, the Scriptures are green and flourishing. That we cannot know the day matters not; some one else may point it out; things are certainly near their end." Luther added, "We certainly have nothing now to wait for but the end of all things."[6]

The question that must appear in the mind of every thoughtful reader is this: Since the Scriptures teach that the Second Coming of Christ for His Church is imminent, why has the Lord delayed His return for almost two thousand years? Fortunately, the Scriptures provide the answer. "The Lord is not slack concerning his promise, as some men count slackness; but is longsuffering to us-ward, not willing that any should perish, but that all should come to repentance" (2 Peter 3:9). The reason Christ has delayed His return is to allow the Church time to fulfill the Great Commission: "Go ye therefore, and teach all nations, baptizing them in the name of the Father, and of the Son, and of the Holy Ghost" (Matthew 28:19). The growth of the Church in this last generation is witnessing up to 85,000 new converts to Christ every day according to some mission estimates. Christ's mercy toward sinners has apparently motivated Him to delay His return to provide an opportunity for the Church to reach the world's population with the Gospel in these last days. However, as the next chapter will demonstrate, after two thousand years the prophetic signs in our generation should awaken every Christian to His soon coming.

The Second Coming of Christ
The Rapture of the Saints and the Revelation of Christ

The Second Coming of Christ involves two major events separated by at least seven years—first, the Rapture of the resurrected saints, and second, the Revelation when Christ will return to earth with His army of saints to set up His kingdom. The numerous passages throughout the Bible that prophesy about the Second Coming deal with either the Rapture or the Resurrection. Some have suggested that the Second Coming cannot involve two separate events occurring at two different times. However, the First Coming of Christ involved hundreds of separate historical events (Jesus' birth, ministry, trial, death, and His resurrection) that took place over a period of thirty-three years. All of these diverse events are included in His First Coming. Therefore there is nothing illogical in considering both the Rapture and the Revelation to be included in His Second Coming.

Unfortunately, many have misunderstood the nature of these two key events in our future. If we wish to understand the truth about the Second Coming, we need to examine the biblical prophecies which describe these two critical and separate prophetic events.

The Difference Between the Rapture and the Revelation

The Rapture and the Revelation are totally different in purpose, character, participants, place, and timing.

The Rapture

For if we believe that Jesus died and rose again, even so them also which sleep in Jesus will God bring with him. For this we say unto you by the word of the Lord, that we which are alive and remain unto the coming of the Lord shall not prevent them which are asleep. For the Lord himself shall descend from heaven with a shout, with the voice of the archangel, and with the trump of God: and the dead in Christ shall rise first: Then we which are alive and remain shall be caught up together with them in the clouds, to meet the Lord in the air: and so shall we ever be with the Lord. (1 Thessalonians 4:14–17)

The Revelation

And I saw heaven opened, and behold a white horse; and he that sat upon him was called Faithful and True, and in righteousness he doth judge and make war. His eyes were as a flame of fire, and on his head were many crowns; and he had a name written, that no man knew, but he himself. And he was clothed with a vesture dipped in blood: and his name is called The Word of God. And the armies which were in heaven followed him upon white horses, clothed in fine linen, white and clean. And out of his mouth goeth a sharp sword, that with it he should smite the nations: and he shall rule them with a rod of iron: and he treadeth the winepress of the fierceness and wrath of Almighty God. And he hath on his vesture and on his thigh a name written, King of Kings, and Lord of Lords. (Revelation 19:11–16)

The differences between the Rapture and the Revelation when Christ appears at Armageddon are enormous as the following analysis reveals. The purpose of the Rapture is to resurrect the bodies of all Christians, both the departed saints in heaven and the believers living, at the time Christ comes in the air for His Bride. He will supernaturally transform the bodies of all of the saints into immortal, and incorruptible bodies fit for eternity. The purpose of the Revelation is to defeat Satan's forces and usher in the kingdom when Christ returns with His Bride (the saints). The Rapture will occur when Christ descends in the air to call all of the saints home to heaven. The Revelation will witness Christ's return to earth at Armageddon with His army of saints. As detailed in the previous chapter the Rapture will occur before the seven year Tribulation period, while the Revelation clearly occurs at the conclusion of the Battle of Armageddon which ends the Tribulation. At the Rapture Christ will withdraw all Christians as His ambassadors just before the seven year war erupts between Satan and God. At the Revelation Jesus Christ will return as conquering King of Kings together with His ambassadors to rule and reign throughout the Millennium.

The prophetic message of the Rapture is one of great comfort and hope to the Church as the righteous saints receive their glorious new immortal bodies. However, the prophecies about the approaching Revelation convey a message of terror to the unrepentant rebels who will then face defeat and judgment by the Lord. The Scriptures prophesy that the voice of an archangel will announce the Rapture. At the Revelation an army of angels will descend triumphantly from heaven with Christ and His resurrected saints to defeat Antichrist and establish His millennial kingdom. At the Rapture both the living and the departed saints will be resurrected and return to heaven with Jesus Christ. In contrast the Revelation will be a public event witnessed by every one of the Jews and Gentiles throughout the world.

The Revelation—
The Glorious Second Coming of Christ

The Revelation of Christ at the end of the Battle of Armageddon will transform life on earth for humanity forever. It is important for us to understand the nature of His Second Coming in light of the large number of scriptural passages that describe His return.

How Will Christ Return at the Revelation?

A. Jesus' Second Coming will be literal: The return of Christ is a literal event that will occur when Jesus physically returns in His resurrection body from heaven to earth at the end of the Battle of Armageddon. The angels told His disciples, "Ye men of Galilee, why stand ye gazing up into heaven? This same Jesus, which is taken up from you into heaven, shall so come in like manner as ye have seen him go into heaven" (Acts 1:11).

B. Everyone on earth will be aware of His triumphant return: "Behold, he cometh with clouds; and every eye shall see him, and they also which pierced him: and all kindreds of the earth shall wail because of him. Even so, Amen" (Revelation 1:7).

C. Christ will destroy the armies of the Antichrist: "And I saw the beast, and the kings of the earth, and their armies, gathered together to make war against him that sat on the horse, and against his army. And the beast was taken, and with him the false prophet that wrought miracles before him, with which he deceived them that had received the mark of the beast, and them that worshipped his image. These both were cast alive into a lake of fire burning with brimstone" (Revelation 19:19–20).

D. Christ will descend to earth: "Then shall the Lord go forth, and fight against those nations, as when he fought in the day of battle. And his feet shall stand in that day upon the mount of Olives, which is before Jerusalem on the east ..." (Zechariah 14:3–4).

E. Jesus will return with His resurrected saints: "And Enoch also, the seventh from Adam, prophesied of these, saying, Behold, the Lord cometh with ten thousands of his saints" (Jude 14).

F. *The Lord will return with His angelic army in judgment*: "And to you who are troubled rest with us, when the Lord Jesus shall be revealed from heaven with his mighty angels, In flaming fire taking vengeance on them that know not God, and that obey not the gospel of our Lord Jesus Christ" (2 Thessalonians 1:7–8).

The Time Relationship Between the Rapture and the Revelation

The diagram below illustrates the time relationships between the future events as predicted by the biblical prophets. Hopefully, the time line below will assist the reader to understand the sequence of events that will culminate in the return of Christ to establish His kingdom on earth.

Second Coming Time Line
Showing the Rapture and the Revelation

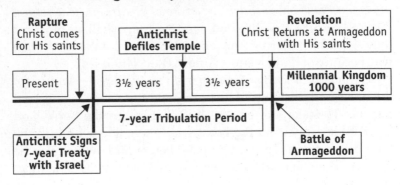

Rapture Christ comes for His saints		**Antichrist Defiles Temple**		**Revelation** Christ Returns at Armageddon with His saints
Present	3½ years		3½ years	**Millennial Kingdom 1000 years**
Antichrist Signs 7-year Treaty with Israel		7-year Tribulation Period		**Battle of Armageddon**

Notes

1. Renald Showers, *Maranatha Our Lord, Come!* (Bellmawr: The Friends of Israel Gospel Ministry, Inc., 1995).

2. Arthur T. Pierson, *Our Lord's Second Coming as a Motive to World-Wide Evangelism*, as cited in Renald Showers, *Maranatha Our Lord, Come!* (Bellmawr: The Friends of Israel Gospel Ministry, Inc., 1995) 127.

3. John F. Walvoord, *The Rapture Question: Revised and Enlarged Edition* (Grand Rapids: Zondervan, 1979) 273.

4. Cyprian, "Treatise of Cyprian," *Ante-Nicene Fathers,* 10 vols. (Edinburgh: T & T Clark, 1986) 5: 475.

5. Albert Barnes, *Barnes' Notes* (Grand Rapids: Baker House, 1897).

6. Joseph Seiss, *Last Times* (Baltimore: T. Newton Kurtz, 1856) 255.

9

The General Prophetic Signs of Christ's Return

And there shall be signs in the sun, and in the moon, and in the stars; and upon the earth distress of nations, with perplexity; the sea and the waves roaring; men's hearts failing them for fear, and for looking after those things which are coming on the earth: for the powers of heaven shall be shaken. And then shall they see the Son of man coming in a cloud with power and great glory. And when these things begin to come to pass, then look up, and lift up your heads; for your redemption draweth nigh. (Luke 21:25–28)

Some commentators think of prophecy as only "doom and gloom." They think of the Second Coming of Christ as the end of history. However, a biblically balanced view of the prophecies enables us to understand that the prophets present the most incredibly positive message we could ever hope to receive from God. The return of Jesus Christ will usher in the greatest period in human history. It is not the end of history; rather, Christ's return will be the opening event in the greatest adventure in the history of mankind.

As mentioned in the previous chapter, during the first few centuries following the ascension of Jesus into heaven, millions of Christians greeted each other by saying, "Maranatha," meaning "the Lord comes." The early Christians rejoiced in their confidence that Jesus would fulfill His prophecy that He would return in the last days to establish His eternal kingdom on earth.

The greatest single theme in Scripture is the Second Coming. While there are approximately three hundred prophetic passages in the Old Testament that foretold the first coming of Christ, there are more than eight times as many verses that describe the Second Coming and His triumphant rule. More than 2,400 verses throughout the Old and New Testaments reveal God's promises about the return of Christ. The remarkable number of prophetic passages about the Second Advent emphasizes the vital importance of this event in God's plan of redemption for humanity. In light of the recent evidence of the fulfillment of these key prophetic signs, we need to live in daily expectation of Christ's return.

It is significant that the Bible's very first and last prophecies refer to the Second Coming. The first prophecy, which the Lord addressed to Satan following the rebellion of Adam and Eve, predicted Christ's ultimate defeat of Satan at Christ's return at Armageddon. In reference to the final encounter between Christ and Antichrist, the Lord declared, "And I will put enmity between thee and the woman, and between thy seed and her seed; it shall bruise thy head, and thou shalt bruise his heel" (Genesis 3:15). The phrase, "it shall bruise thy head" prophesied that Christ ("her seed"—the seed of the woman) will finally defeat the Antichrist ("thy seed"—the seed of Satan).

One of the earliest prophecies concerning the Second Advent is surprisingly recorded in one of the final books of the New Testament, the book of Jude. The brother of Jesus, Jude, made reference to the righteous patriarch Enoch, who was raptured to heaven in the generations before the Flood. Jude revealed that Enoch prophesied the Second Coming: "Enoch, also, the seventh from Adam, prophesied of these, saying, Behold, the Lord cometh with ten thousands of his saints, to execute judgment upon all" (Jude 14–15).

The last prophecy in the Bible was recorded by the prophet John in the final verses of the book of Revelation. This prophecy declares, "And, behold, I come quickly; and my reward is with me, to give every man according as his work shall be" (Revelation 22:12). Christ's final message to His Church concludes with these words, "He which testifieth these things saith, Surely, I come quickly. Amen. Even so, come, Lord Jesus" (Revelation 22:20).

In every generation for the last two thousand years, there have been Christian scholars of the ancient prophecies who have wondered whether Christ will return to redeem the earth in their lifetime. Believers in every generation have naturally longed for the soon return of Jesus Christ. Skeptics correctly point out that these hopes have never yet been realized. These skeptics ask, "Why should we believe that our generation is the one that will witness the return of Christ when other generations were disappointed in their equally sincere hopes?" This is a legitimate question and deserves a serious answer. The truth is that no previous generation has ever witnessed the fulfillment of even a fraction of the prophecies that we have seen since the mid-twentieth century.

Will we witness the return of Jesus Christ? The answer to this question has profound implications for our motivation to win souls and is an encouragement to walk in holiness in the midst of an immoral world. After thirty-eight years of careful study of the prophecies and a detailed analysis of current world events, I am more convinced than ever that there is overwhelming prophetic evidence indicating the return of Jesus Christ in our lifetime. However, we must always realize that God is sovereign and can delay His coming if He chooses to.

As we analyze the evidence about these prophecies, we should note that there are two types of predictions. There are a number of broad prophecies that indicate general conditions that will exist when Christ will return. These general prophecies include such predictions as false Christs, false prophets, wars and rumors of wars, famines, earthquakes, and pestilence (Matthew 24:5-8). While there is ample evidence to demonstrate that these conditions now exist, the general nature of these predictions presents a certain degree of ambiguity. The evidence exists to demonstrate that the number of wars, famines, and pestilences has genuinely increased in recent years; yet, someone could legitimately argue that the number of wars, famines, and pestilences may continue to increase even more rapidly in future generations. Therefore, while these general prophetic signs provide confirmation that the times we live in may truly be "the last days," we must carefully examine the evidence detailed in the following chapter that reveals scriptural predictions that are unique to discover compelling evidence that we are truly living in "the end times."

Deception Concerning the Rise of False Christs

"And Jesus answered and said unto them, Take heed that no man deceive you. For many shall come in my name, saying, I am Christ; and shall deceive many" (Matthew 24:4–5). It is fascinating that Christ's very first prophecy warned about spiritual deception concerning the rise of both false messiahs and false prophets in the last days. Significantly, there are no historical references to any false messiahs before the life of Jesus of Nazareth. In fact, the first appearance of a false messiah occurred after the resurrection of Jesus. The Jewish scholar C. G. Montefiore wrote, "Of false Messiahs, we know of none among the Jews until Bar Cochba in 131 C.E."[1] The genuine always precedes the appearance of the counterfeit. Throughout history, a false messiah has appeared approximately once every century since the days of Christ. However, a veritable explosion of false messiahs has appeared in our generation. The false messiahs in our day include David Koresh, Sun Myung Moon, Charles Manson, Jim Jones, L. Ron Hubbard, Lord Maitreya, and numerous others. The rising number of false messiahs in our generation is preparing our society for the spirit of Antichrist worship that will manifest itself in the worship of the prophesied Antichrist in the last days.

Wars and Rumors of Wars

Jesus Christ said, "And ye shall hear of wars and rumours of wars: see that ye be not troubled: for all these things must come to pass, but the end is not yet. For nation shall rise against nation, and kingdom against kingdom" (Matthew 24:6–7). Twenty-five centuries ago, the prophet Joel was given a divine vision concerning our last days generation and prophesied as follows: "Proclaim ye this among the Gentiles; Prepare war, wake up the mighty men, let all the men of war draw near; let them come up: Beat your plowshares into swords, and your pruninghooks into spears: let the weak say, I am strong" (Joel 3:9–10).

Since the close of World War II, the number of wars throughout the world has increased tremendously. In 1981 Michael Kidron and Dan Smith wrote a military study, *The War Atlas*, that concluded the world has not known a single day without some nation waging a war or conflict somewhere on earth from the end of World War II until 1982. Dozens of new nations demanded independence and old empires disintegrated, and "there have been about three hundred wars since 1945. There has been no single day free of war and few islands of tranquility."[2] From 1982 until 1991, there were another forty-two wars according to *The New State of War and Peace* by Michael Kidron and Dan Smith.[3] The last decade has continued this trend of growing warfare.

Despite thousands of peace treaties, the last one hundred years truly became "the century of war." The standing armies and the reserves of the world's nations now contain hundreds of millions of soldiers. The major powers today could mobilize hundreds of millions of troops if needed for global war. An international think tank, the Club of Rome, issued the *Reshaping International Order Report*, which revealed that almost 50 percent (over one half million) of the world's scientists are now involved in weapons research.[4] The continued arms buildup in Russia, China, the West, the Middle East, and the Third World is setting the stage for the cataclysmic Battle of Armageddon.

The U.S. Arms Control and Disarmament Agency estimates

that global military spending by all nations now exceeds one trillion dollars annually. It is difficult to comprehend the true magnitude of the trillions of dollars spent in preparation for war. According to *The War Atlas*, the cost of a single French Exocet air-to-ship missile exceeds the combined annual income of more than ten thousand people in many Third World countries such as Bhutan.[5] At the present rate of military expenditure, every citizen will be forced to contribute over three years of his annual income in accumulated taxes to pay his or her portion of this staggering arms bill. The $3 billion spent on a single Trident nuclear submarine would pay for 16 million children to attend school for one year in the developing nations. The money spent on one advanced fighter plane would provide the funds to establish 40,000 village pharmacies in poor nations. Over 100 million people throughout the world are now employed by the military or defense industries.[6]

I am not arguing for unilateral disarmament. We must realistically acknowledge that we live in a dangerous world filled with totalitarian dictatorships that represent a serious military threat to our freedom and our physical survival. However, the awesome new scientific discoveries and massive military budgets have combined to produce devastating weapons of mass destruction that have the potential to destroy a large part of the human race. Although literally thousands of disarmament treaties have been signed in the last century, the weapons labs and military industrial complexes in virtually every nation are producing devastating nuclear, chemical, biological, electromagnetic, and conventional weapons in preparation for future battles.

The nation of Israel faces implacable hatred from twenty-one surrounding Arab states with a combined population of two hundred million and a territory that is five hundred times larger than the Jewish state. The Arab states possess virtually unlimited military budgets based on their staggering wealth derived from their enormous oil reserves. The total Arab conventional military forces facing the five million Jews are greater than the total conventional military force (armies, tanks, artillery, planes) of the European NATO armies. In response to this incredible military imbalance, Israel has developed over three hundred advanced nuclear weapons, including sophisticated neutron bombs that devastate their targets with powerful nuclear radiation that destroys biological life without creating a large explosion. In addition, intelligence sources indicate that Israel now possesses a remarkable electromagnetic weapon that can hide their planes from enemy radar systems as well as give Israeli commanders the ability to destroy enemy missiles and planes in the air at great distances from their territory. My sources reveal that a remarkable electromagnetic weapon was invented by a Jewish inventor in Toronto in 1969. The brilliant Sid Hurwich created a device that disables complex and simple weapons at a distance. A variation of this invention was used by the Israeli Air Force to block radar screens during the astonishing 1973 Entebbe rescue of Jewish hostages. In 1983 Israel blocked the radar of five Arab nations when its jet bombers destroyed Iraq's nuclear reactor to protect the Jewish state (*Weekend Magazine*, Dec. 19, 1977).

Famines

Christ warned that there would be famines that would be widespread and devastating, leading up to the final conflict of Armageddon (Matthew 24:7). John's Apocalypse also describes terrible famine in the last days. "And I beheld, and lo a black horse; and he that sat on him had a pair of balances in his hand. And I heard a voice in the midst of the four beasts say, A measure of wheat for a penny, and three measures of barley for a penny; and see thou hurt not the oil and the wine" (Revelation 6:5–6). The prophet John foresaw a future worldwide famine so devastating that a man's entire day's wages ("a penny" was a laborer's daily wage in ancient Rome) would only buy enough wheat to supply the needs of himself, with nothing left over to feed his family.

We face drought and famine conditions throughout significant portions of Africa, India, and Southeast Asia. Millions are at risk of famine: North Korea, Sudan, and China are currently unable to properly feed their populations. According to a recent *Annual Study of the UN Population Fund*, the amount of agricultural land worldwide is decreasing rapidly. Deserts are growing at the rate of 14.8 million acres every year. Over 26 billion tons of precious topsoil are lost each year, and the valuable tropical rain forests that contribute significant amounts of our planet's oxygen are shrinking every year by millions of acres.

The deadly combination of population growth and diminished food resources is already producing serious famine threats in Asia and Africa. The specter of widespread famine is here; the "black horseman" of the book of Revelation, representing the coming famine, is about to begin his deadly ride. The world population is growing at the rate of more than 210,000 people every single day.[7] According to the Environmental News Network article entitled *World Population Continues to Grow* issued on April 5, 1999, "The population of our planet will increase to 8 billion by the end of 2026, according to the census brief *World Population Profile: 1998*, and will reach 9.3 billion by 2050. The world population has already passed the 6 billion mark. While the rate of increase is slowing, according to the report, the global population increase is equivalent to adding a new Israel, Egypt, Jordan, West Bank and Gaza to the existing world population total every year. This is equivalent to adding an additional medium-sized city to the globe's population every twenty-four hours."[8]

Population growth and soil erosion are producing another dangerous problem. The average rate of population increase worldwide is approximately two percent, although it is much higher in the Third World countries that can least afford their hungry children. A rich country like Austria, with an extremely low rate of population growth, will take almost three thousand years to double its population. Meanwhile, a poor but populous nation like Nigeria is experiencing such a high population growth rate that it will double its already huge population in less than a dozen years. Ninety percent of the 150 new babies born every minute throughout the world will grow up in the Third World, where both food supplies and clean water are in short supply.

It is virtually impossible to increase food production in the

Third World quickly enough to prevent widespread famine. At the present rate of population growth, we are adding a billion new mouths to be fed every twenty years. While it took the time from the creation of man until World War I to produce a global population of two billion people, it is remarkable that another two billion people will be added to our current global population during the next forty years. The world's population now exceeds six billion people, and Africa, South America, and Asia constitute 85 percent of that total. The population explosion and its resulting famine was created because scientists solved the "death rate" problem with DDT pesticides, antibiotics, and improved sanitation before introducing effective fertility control measures to solve the "birth rate" problem. The resulting imbalance between rising birth rates and falling death rates has produced a nightmare of starvation in those countries that we thought we were helping.

Meteorologists are now predicting devastating global climatic changes that may lead to drastic reductions in the food-growing capacity in North America, Russia, and France. Yet, there are only four nations throughout the world—Canada, the United States, France, and Argentina—that can produce the vital food-surplus reserves beyond the needs of their own population to enable them to supply food to other nations. Large-scale flooding and massive crop failures in North Korea have produced unprecedented famine conditions.

We have destroyed more than 4.5 billion acres of topsoil since 1945. This tragic loss of agriculturally fertile land represents an area of land larger than the nations of China and India combined. So far, eleven percent of the world's precious topsoil has been eroded. This tragic loss has doomed the hopes for self-sufficiency for many Third World countries. The Sahara Desert is expanding relentlessly southward, destroying both the topsoil and the agricultural nomadic lifestyle of the Africans who have lived there for thousands of years.

Recently, the World Resources Institute in Washington, D.C. released a sobering study of the world's soil conditions. One of the areas most devastated is located in North America in the center of the Canadian prairies and the Midwestern American states. This relatively small area, only 5.3 percent of the world's agricultural land, has been the "world's breadbasket" for the last century. However, the study documents that over 235 million acres are now considered "degraded."[9]

Modern fertilizers and land-management techniques could restore a small portion of the North American soil loss, but at an enormous cost. However, the vast majority (over two billion acres) of global soil erosion has occurred in the poorest countries of Asia and Africa. There is little money in the budgets of Third World nations to begin the costly soil-reclamation projects. Over 20 percent of the agricultural soils of Europe, Asia, Africa, and Central America have been "degraded."

Pestilences

Jesus Christ warned that there would be devastating pestilence in the last days (Matthew 24:7). Tragically, pestilence and plague relentlessly follow famine and war, compounding their devastation. Jesus warned that worldwide pestilence would be a sign that we were living in the generation when He would finally return. The prophet John was given a terrifying vision of the coming holocaust during the seven-year tribulation, when God will unleash the terrible plagues that will decimate one-quarter of the world's population. "And I looked, and behold a pale horse: and his name that sat on him was Death, and Hell followed with him. And power was given unto them over the fourth part of the earth, to kill with sword, and with hunger, and with death, and with the beasts of the earth" (Revelation 6:8).

In April 1997, the World Health Organization (WHO) issued a frightening report that "at least 30 new infectious diseases with no known treatment, cure, or vaccine have emerged in the past 20 years." Their report, published on the Internet, stated: "New infectious diseases can emerge from genetic changes in existing organisms and appear suddenly in new populations. At least 30 new disease agents have been identified over the past two decades, and new agents are being added with disquieting regularity."[10] This modern explosion of infectious disease is a direct result of the increase in air travel, growing urbanization, and poor sanitation. Many diseases of the past, including bubonic plague, are re-emerging as deadly threats to humanity. The WHO recently reported that diseases such as malaria, smallpox, diphtheria, and yellow fever are also making devastating comebacks. Unfortunately, many of these diseases are becoming drug-resistant superbugs. The American Association for the Advancement of Science declared that "overuse of antibiotics is leading to a world in which the drugs are no longer effective."[11] A new form of malaria that causes paralysis and death has infected over 300 million victims worldwide and the disease no longer responds to the traditional treatment, quinine. The health authorities' decision to eliminate the use of DDT, the most effective pesticide against the mosquitoes that carry malaria, has allowed malaria to once again claim hundreds of millions of lives in the Third World.

Public health doctors are fighting a losing battle against the new scourge of fifty-three sexually transmitted diseases (STDs). The new epidemic of STDs is a modern form of pestilence that is a direct result of the widespread sexual immorality and perversion of this generation. Public health doctors estimate that as many as 40 percent of all single, sexually active adults in North America are now infected with a sexually transmitted disease.

The Tragic AIDS Plague

The deadly AIDS virus is the most dangerous plague in history. As individuals have sown the wind of immorality and lust, they have begun to reap sexually transmitted disease, sterility, and death. The worst of all these sexually transmitted diseases is the deadly virus known as AIDS, now the number-one killer disease worldwide, ahead of malaria and tuberculosis. In 1990, the CIA began a detailed global investigation of the growing AIDS threat to the national security interests of the United States. Once completed, this report, entitled Interagency Intelligence Memorandum 91:10005, was given to President George Bush in 1991. Selected portions of this report were released to the State Department under the title *The Global AIDS Disaster* and described the AIDS crisis as one of the most deadly calamities in human history. The 1991 report projected that up to 45 million people would be fatally infected by the year 2000. Incredibly, this early estimate of 45 million—though greater than the combined toll of soldiers killed in World War I, World War II, and the Korean War—proved to be an underestimate.

As of December 1, 2000, the United Nations/World Health Organization reported that more than 22 million had already died of AIDS and that another 36.1 million were currently infected with this fatal disease. The vast majority (25.3 million, or 70 percent) of those currently infected live in sub-Saharan Africa.[12] The latest updated death toll reveals that AIDS is the worst epidemic in human history, exceeding the Black Plague of the fourteenth century and the 20 million killed by the Spanish Flu in 1918–19.

Dr. Peter Piot, the Executive Director of the Joint United Nations Programme on HIV/AIDS, also warned about the inexorable rising death toll of AIDS in other nations: "What we had predicted and feared is now happening, and that's an explosion of HIV." Reports from Eastern Europe and the former Soviet Union reveal approximately 700,000 cases of HIV—a frightening 60 percent rise in only one year. A sobering report from the Russian Ministry of Health now estimates that within five years as many as 10 percent of the Russian population (a staggering 14 million citizens) may be infected by AIDS.[13]

AIDS is now exploding throughout the billions living in Asia. Experts from the Thai Red Cross estimate that more than five hundred people are infected with the deadly disease every single night in Thailand. Health workers estimate that up to 90 percent of the prostitutes in Thailand are now infected. Studies in India suggest that 3.7 million have AIDS. Meanwhile, 5.8 million are infected in South as well as Southeast Asia.[14]

The Growth of Pestilence and Plagues

Over 11 million people worldwide die from tuberculosis (TB) every year. This is aggravated by a new deadly drug-resistant TB strain. The Laboratory Center for Disease Control in Ottawa, Canada, reported that tens of thousands of North Americans have already become infected with a new drug-resistant form of TB that kills over 70 percent of its victims.[15]

Since the 1950s, a number of powerful antibiotics were developed that weaken or destroy the various bacteria that cause so many diseases. These antibiotics have saved hundreds of millions of lives throughout the world over the last five decades. However, our society has abused and overprescribed antibiotics to the point that many people can no longer derive full benefit from them. An article by science reporter Joseph Hall in the *Toronto Star* revealed that researchers recently warned the American Association for the Advancement of Science that "overuse of antibiotics is leading to a world in which the drugs are no longer effective."[16] University of Washington biologist Marilyn Roberts warned an international science conference that "tons of antibiotics are being used as farm additives on plants and animals, doctors are over-prescribing them and they are being misused in developing countries."[17]

The shortage of antibiotics, and their expense, has often led patients in poor countries to stop taking the drug after their symptoms have initially dissipated, yet before the strongest strains of the bacteria are fully destroyed. This common occurrence often facilitates the development of stronger drug-resistant bacteria that will no longer respond to traditional antibiotics. Professor Roberts ominously predicted that "if we don't change the way we use these medications, they will lose their effectiveness to fight diseases." It takes decades to research, create, and gain approval for a new antibiotic. There are fewer than a dozen effective antibiotics and many are becoming ineffective.

Massive pollution and ecological problems now appear to be almost insolvable. Since 1960, over 70,000 new chemicals were introduced into the earth's biosphere. Only 10,000 of these 70,000 new chemicals were even tested for their possible side effects on humans. When we add to this deadly chemical concoction thousands of new, environmentally untested chemicals created in laboratories every year, we may be creating problems and diseases for which there is no cure. The Toxic Substances Strategy Committee reported in 1980 that up to 90 percent of cancers were caused by exposure to hazardous substances in our environment.[18] The continued heavy usage of pesticides has aided in the production of new strains of germs, known as superbugs, that have developed resistance to pesticides and other chemicals. Environmental studies reveal that children living in homes that use garden pesticides have a 600 percent greater risk of developing leukemia.

Even if a new chemical is harmless by itself, it may become deadly when combined with other chemicals. The California Public Interest Group has calculated that over 250 billion pounds of synthetic chemicals are now produced every year in the United States. One report revealed that "45,000 [chemicals] are in commercial distribution, and it takes a team of scientists, 300 mice, two to three years, and about $300,000 to determine whether one single suspect chemical causes cancer."[19] Our continued lifelong exposure to harmful chemicals is causing 15 percent of U.S. citizens to develop supersensitivity to harmful chemicals in their environment. These supersensitive patients develop symptoms of allergies, depression, headaches, and irritability.

Scientists are discovering hazardous waste dumps hidden in many communities, leeching out their toxic elements into our water supply. The problem of disposal of radioactive waste from nuclear reactors remains unresolved, yet we continue to produce radioactive materials in the vain hope that someday we will find a solution.

The Gospel of the Kingdom Preached in All the World

"And this gospel of the kingdom will be preached in all the world as a witness to all the nations, and then the end will come" (Matthew 24:14).

In the last fifty years, the growth of evangelism throughout the world has been breathtaking. In the Muslim nation of Indonesia, more than 20 percent of the population has recently accepted Christ. Despite decades of dedicated missionary efforts, by 1900 only 3 percent of Africans had become followers of Jesus Christ. However, by 2000, over 45 percent of the five hundred million people living in Africa have accepted

Christ. While Christianity was almost unknown before World War II, up to 40 percent of the South Korean population now follows Christ.

A 1991 study by the National Council of Churches concluded that church membership is growing at twice the speed of growth of the world population, with the greatest growth in Evangelical churches. The Lausanne Statistics Task Force concluded that the number of born-again Christians has grown three times faster than the world's population during the seventeen years from 1980 to 1997.

- In 1430, one person in **99** of the world's population was a Christian.
- In 1790, one person in **49** of the world's population was a Christian.
- In 1940, one person in **32** of the world's population was a Christian.
- In 1970, one person in **19** of the world's population was a Christian.
- In 1980, one person in **16** of the world's population was a Christian.
- In 1983, one person in **13** of the world's population was a Christian.
- In 1986, one person in **11** of the world's population was a Christian.
- In 1997, one person in **10** of the world's population was a Christian.

Lausanne Statistics Task Force on Evangelism

In only sixty years, the number of Christians throughout the world has grown by 1,300 percent. The evangelical Church has grown from only 40 million in 1934 to 540 million today. Meanwhile, the world's population has grown by only 400 percent.

Christian radio broadcasts are now reaching almost half of the world's 360 mega-languages, covering 78 percent of the earth's population. The Church is rapidly fulfilling the Great Commission. There were fewer than one million Chinese Christians at the time of the communist takeover in mainland

China in 1949. However, the lowest estimates suggest there are more than 100 million followers of Christ in the underground church in Communist China today. As many as 25,000 people accept Christ in China every day. Every year, more than 300 million Bibles, New Testaments, and Scripture selections are distributed throughout the world.

The Apostle Paul's Warning Signs of the Last Days

This know also, that in the last days perilous times shall come. For men shall be lovers of their own selves, covetous, boasters, proud, blasphemers, disobedient to parents, unthankful, unholy, without natural affection, trucebreakers, false accusers, incontinent, fierce, despisers of those that are good, traitors, heady, highminded, lovers of pleasure more than lovers of God; having a form of godliness, but denying the power thereof: from such turn away. (2 Timothy 3:1-5)

The apostle Paul wrote to Timothy and prophetically warned him of these spiritual conditions that would characterize the people living in the generation when Jesus Christ would return to establish His kingdom. This prophecy so accurately depicts today's world that it could have been written by any columnist in this morning's newspaper. Paul's prophetic list of the symptoms of our disintegrating North American and European society reveals that our world is standing at a spiritual crossroads as the astonishing scriptural prophecies of the last days are beginning to unfold in our generation.

Notes

1. C. G. Montefiore, *Rabbinic Literature and Gospel Teachings* (New York: Ktav Publishing House, Inc., 1970).

2. Michael Kidron and Dan Smith, *The War Atlas* (London: Pan Books, 1983) 1.

3. Michael Kidron and Dan Smith, *The New State of War and Peace* (London: Harper Collins Publishers, 1991).

4. Jan Tinbergen, *Reshaping the International Order, A Report to the Club of Rome* (New York: E. P. Dutton & Co., Inc., 1976).

5. Michael Kidron and Dan Smith, *The War Atlas* (London: Pan Books, 1983).

6. Ruth Leger Sivard, *World Military and Social Expenditures* (Leesburg: World Priorities, 1980).

7. "National Wildlife Federation," http://www.nwf.org/population/quickhistory.html.

8. http://www.enn.com/enn-news archive/1999/04/040599/population_2496.asp.

9. "Topsoil Loss–Causes, Effects, and Implications–A Global Perspective," http://www.alltel.net/~bsundquist1/seo.html.

10. http://www.aawhworldhealth.org/wheal97.html.

11. *Toronto Star* 18 Feb. 1997.

12. "Report—On the Global HIV/AIDS Epidemic" 1 Dec. 2000.

13. Chris Talbot, internet, 4 Dec. 2000, WSWSW.

14. "Report—On the Global HIV/AIDS Epidemic" 1 Dec. 2000.

15. *Toronto Star* 22 Nov. 1995.

16. Joseph Hall, *Toronto Star* 18 Feb. 1997.

17. Joseph Hall, *Toronto Star* 18 Feb. 1997.

18. http://www.feelhealthy.com/nontoxichome.html.

19. Debra L. Dadd, *Non-Toxic, Natural and Earthwise: How to Protect Yourself and your Family from Harmful Products and Live in Harmony with the Earth* (Los Angeles: Jeremy P. Tarcher, 1990).

10

Unique Signs Pointing to the Second Coming

We will now examine a number of unique biblical prophecies that point to the soon return of Jesus Christ in our generation. Every one of these significant prophecies is unique in that history reveals that none of these predictions was ever fulfilled in any previous generation. The unusual nature of these unique predictions suggests that it is almost impossible that they could be fulfilled again in a following generation. Jesus Christ encouraged His followers in these inspired words, "And when these things begin to come to pass, then look up, and lift up your heads; for your redemption draweth nigh" (Luke 21:28).

Let's examine several of these unique predictions that suggest our generation will witness the return of Christ in glory.

The Rebirth of Israel in 1948

Throughout the Old Testament—from Genesis to Malachi—hundreds of specific prophecies declare that God gave the ancient land of Canaan to the Jewish people as their Promised Land to enjoy forever. Jerusalem was their sacred capital. In Genesis, we discover that God made an eternal covenant with Abraham and his descendants that they would enjoy possession of the Holy Land forever under the rule of His Messiah. The Lord God declared to Abraham: "Lift up now thine eyes, and look from the place where thou art northward, and southward, and eastward, and westward: For all the land which thou seest, to thee will I give it, and to thy seed for ever" (Genesis 13:14–15).

Abraham's son Isaac and his grandson Jacob, the forefathers of the Jews and the "seed of promise," received repeated promises that their Jewish seed would have sovereignty over the Promised Land. However, we need to remember that Ishmael, the other son of Abraham, was also included in this divine promise; his Arab descendants would also live in the land forever. The Arabs now inhabit twenty-one nations throughout the Middle East, occupying vast oil-rich territories covering an area that is five hundred times larger than the tiny Jewish state of Israel (8,000 square miles). The Arab population now exceeds two hundred million people, more than forty times larger than Israel's five million Jews. And yet, the Arabs demand that the Jews surrender their precious ancient homeland to the Arabs to achieve peace. The truth is that there will be no true peace until the Messiah returns to create peace in the hearts of both the Arabs and the Jews.

The prophet Ezekiel described in his great vision of "the valley of dry bones" (Ezekiel 37) Israel's final, miraculous return from the "valley of dry bones" in the last days leading to the return of their long awaited Messiah.

> Then he said unto me, Son of man, these bones are the whole house of Israel: behold, they say, Our bones are dried, and our hope is lost: we are cut off for our parts. Therefore prophesy and say unto them, Thus saith the Lord God; Behold, O my people, I will open your graves, and cause you to come up out of your graves, and bring you into the land of Israel. And ye shall know that I

am the Lord, when I have opened your graves, O my people, and brought you up out of your graves, and shall put my spirit in you, and ye shall live, and I shall place you in your own land: then shall ye know that I the Lord have spoken it, and performed it, saith the Lord. (Ezekiel 37:11–14)

No other ancient people has lost its historic homeland for many centuries and then recovered its territory to resume its national existence once again. Yet Israel defied astronomical odds to take its place as a Jewish nation in 1948, after almost two thousand years of persecution and exile among the Gentile nations.

Without a doubt, the rebirth of the nation Israel on May 15, 1948, is one of the most extraordinary of all the prophecies in the ancient Scriptures. It is not only historically unprecedented, but the prophecy of the rebirth of Israel is also unique in that it cannot easily be fulfilled again in any generation. If the restoration of Israel in 1948 is not the fulfillment of Ezekiel 37 and Matthew 24, then the Jews must be exiled from Israel for centuries and return once more to become a nation. This is so unlikely that we can eliminate it as a possibility. The restoration of Israel was foreseen by many of the Old Testament prophets, and these prophecies motivated the Jews during their many centuries of exile in foreign lands to maintain their age-old longing to travel to the Promised Land in anticipation of their coming Messiah.

During the last century, millions of Jews from more than seventy Gentile nations as diverse as Russia, Morocco, and Ethiopia abandoned their ancient homes, possessions, and neighbors to undertake an arduous journey toward the fulfillment of their age-old Passover dream: "Next year in Jerusalem." Against staggering odds and rampant persecution, these Jews gathered their extended families together and began their dangerous personal journey toward the Promised Land. Following the rebirth of the nation on May 15, 1948, over 600,000 Jews who had lived for several thousand years in every nation throughout the Muslim world—from Morocco in North Africa to Iran—left their homes to return to the new Jewish state. In an attempt to save their lives and gain religious freedom most of these Jewish exiles were forced to leave behind their homes, personal property, bank accounts, and businesses with little or no compensation.

Throughout history, most nations evolved gradually over the centuries until they became recognized nation-states, such as Egypt, England, and France. The prophet Isaiah predicted the rebirth of Israel in these words: "Who hath heard such a thing? who hath seen such things? Shall the earth be made to bring forth in one day? or shall a nation be born at once? for as soon as Zion travailed, she brought forth her children" (Isaiah 66:8). From the time the ancient prophets first announced their prophecies about the rebirth of Israel until recent times, no one had ever witnessed a nation being created "in one day." Yet that is precisely what happened.

During hearings before the British Royal Commission on Palestine, David Ben Gurion, as chairman of the Jewish Agency, announced, "The Bible is our only mandate. The mandate of the League [of Nations] is only a recognition of this right and does not establish new things." Remarkably, when the British Mandate over Palestine, authorized by the League of Nations, ended at midnight on May 15, 1948, Israel's first prime minister, David Ben Gurion, declared publicly that Israel was once again a nation and now took its rightful place on the stage of world history. Ben Gurion announced, "The Land of Israel was the birthplace of the Jewish people. . . . Here they wrote and gave the Bible to the world. . . . Impelled by this historic association, Jews strove throughout the centuries to go back to the land of their fathers and regain their statehood."[1]

The Miraculous Restoration of Hebrew

Twenty-five hundred years ago, the prophet Zephaniah predicted that the Jewish state would restore its ancient Hebrew language to be spoken in Israel during the last days. This prediction of the restoration of Hebrew was as unlikely and impossible in normal historical terms as the prophecy regarding the rebirth of Israel. The Hebrew language had ceased to be the common spoken language of the Jews long before the days of Jesus Christ. After the exile of the Israelite captives from the ten tribes of northern Israel to Assyria in 721 B.C. and the exile of the Jewish captives from the tribes of Judah and Benjamin in 606 B.C., there were relatively few Jews still surviving in ancient Israel. Following the seventy years of captivity in Babylon, the fifty thousand Jews who returned to Canaan in 536 B.C. and the vast majority of Jewish exiles who remained in Babylon had adopted the Babylonian Aramaic language and lost the normal use of Hebrew as their daily language. The priests who served in the second Temple in Jerusalem after 516 B.C. were the only Jews who still used the ancient Hebrew language. Most of the Jews living in Israel in the first century spoke Greek, Aramaic (the ancient Babylonian language), or Latin (if they dealt with the Roman government).

However, in 520 B.C., God foretold through His prophet Zephaniah that in the end times He would cause the returned exiles to restore the ancient language of Hebrew: "For then will I turn to the people a pure language, that they may all call upon the name of the Lord, to serve him with one consent" (Zephaniah 3:9). A study of historical records confirms that no other nation throughout the history of the nations has ever lost its natural language and later recovered it as a living language after a period of centuries. For example, there are no cultures in the Middle East still speaking the ancient Egyptian, Sumerian, or Chaldean languages from ancient times.

Eliazar ben Yehuda, a Jewish Hebrew language scholar living in Palestine in the early decades of the last century, received a distinct vision that God was calling him to restore the ancient Hebrew "tongue of the prophets." Eliazar was the first man in history who personally restored a lost language from the ancient world virtually single-handedly. Using these Hebrew words from both the Bible and the Talmud as a foundation, Eliazar created thousands of new Hebrew words to describe modern objects such as "fountain pen," "airplane," et cetera, based on the ancient Hebrew root words and the grammatical rules of biblical Hebrew to guide his efforts. He persevered in his remarkable project, despite powerful opposition from his neighbors in Jerusalem and the Orthodox religious authorities who were scandalized at his radical concept of using the sacred Hebrew "tongue of the prophets" in ordinary conversation. Eliazar and his supporter ultimately created a sixteen-volume Hebrew language dictionary that was only published after his death in 1922.[2]

Palestine was ruled by England under the League of Nations' sanctioned British Mandate until it expired on May 15, 1948. After almost two thousand years, the Jewish exiles began to return to the Promised Land from seventy different nations. The new Israeli government and military wisely used compulsory Hebrew language classes run by the army to bring together these widely divergent Jewish exiles into a united Israeli people by teaching them the revived Hebrew language as their common language in their restored homeland. The inhabitants of Israel can now truly join in one Hebrew voice to call "upon the name of the Lord, to serve him with one consent." The restoration of the ancient tongue of the prophets certainly qualifies as one of the most extraordinary miracles and unique biblical predictions ever fulfilled.

Arab-Israeli Conflict

Three thousand years ago, King David prophetically listed the ancient enemy tribes that would ultimately form the modern-day nations that will join in a military alliance opposing the return of the Jews to their homeland in the final conflict during the years before the return of the Messiah:

> For, lo, thine enemies make a tumult: and they that hate thee have lifted up the head. They have taken crafty counsel against thy people, and consulted against thy hidden ones. They have said, Come, and let us cut them off from being a nation; that the name of Israel may be no more in remembrance. For they have consulted together with one consent: they are confederate against thee: The tabernacles of Edom, and the Ishmaelites; of Moab, and the Hagarenes; Gebal, and Ammon, and Amalek; the Philistines with the inhabitants of Tyre; Assur also

is joined with them: they have holpen the children of Lot. (Psalms 83:2–8)

The nations in the current Arab League of Nations who violently oppose the existence of present-day Israel are also found in King David's ancient prophecy. The ancient names of the tribes and nations that opposed the existence of Israel during the Exodus and the following centuries while King David and Solomon developed the Jewish state were listed in the prophecy in the book of Psalms as an extraordinary preview of the future Arab confederacy of the last days that will seek to destroy the Chosen People. The following list details the ancient tribal name and its corresponding equivalent nation in the Middle East today.

Ancient Tribe	Modern National Name
Edom, descended from Esau, brother of Jacob	Jordan
Ishmaelites, descended from Ishmael, son of Hagar	Arabs
Moab, son of Lot	Jordan, east of Dead Sea
Hagarenes, from one of Hagar's sons	Jordan and northwest Saudi Arabia
Gebal, ancient Byblus	Lebanon north of Beirut
Ammon, son of Lot	Ammon, capital of Jordan
Amalek, descended from Esau	Southern Jordan
Philistines, from Ham	Palestine and Syria
Tyre, a Phoenician city	Lebanon
Assur, founded Assyria	Iraq, Syria, and Iran
Children of Lot, Moab and Ammon	Jordan

It is remarkable that thousands of years ago the ancient biblical prophets received a vision regarding the profound hatred that the surrounding Arab nations had toward the rebirth of Israel in the last days. The Lord inspired King David to foretell that the Jews' return to the Promised Land would trigger a bitter interracial blood feud. David prophesied that the surrounding nations of Lebanon, Syria, Iraq, Jordan, Saudi Arabia, and Egypt would gather their military forces in a final attempt to eliminate the Jewish state of Israel from the Middle East forever.

The hatred of the Arabs for the Jewish people was first predicted four thousand years ago through God's prophetic command to Hagar, Abraham's concubine. The Lord commanded that she should call her son Ishmael "because the Lord hath heard thy affliction. And he will be a wild man; his hand will be against every man, and every man's hand against him; and he shall dwell in the presence of all his brethren" (Genesis 16:11–12). This prophecy was tragically fulfilled; there has been hatred for thousands of years between the descendants of Abraham. The Arabs descended from his son Ishmael and the Jews descended from his son Isaac. As the descendants of Ishmael, the Arab people traveled for forty centuries as nomads throughout the Middle East.

Population in Jerusalem and Palestine

Many modern Middle East media commentators and most North Americans have been led to believe that the Arab Muslims formed the majority of the population of Palestine and Jerusalem until the waves of Jewish immigration from Europe and Russia beginning in the 1800s and 1900s overwhelmed them. The PLO has often declared in their propaganda that the Palestinian Arabs formed a majority of the population in the land of Canaan until the Jewish immigrants came from Europe and took over their properties. However, the official historical documents of both the Muslim Turkish and anti-Jewish British authorities that ruled the territory of Palestine provide authoritative and compelling evidence that the Jewish inhabitants have formed a majority of the population in Jerusalem and throughout Palestine for the last one hundred and fifty years.

The consistent evidence from historical sources is that the Promised Land was quite desolate with a very small population from ancient times until the last century. In 1788, Count Constantine F. Volney wrote about his extensive visits to the Holy Land in his *Travels through Syria and Egypt in the Years 1783, 1784, 1785*. Volney claimed that the whole population of Jerusalem contained less than 14,000; the city of Hebron had

900 men and the town of Bethlehem had only 600 adult men.[3] The British Consul James Finn wrote in 1858 to his superior, the Earl of Clarendon, about the population of Jerusalem. Consul Finn wrote, "The Mohammedans of Jerusalem are less fanatical than in many other places owing to the circumstances of their numbers scarcely exceeding one quarter of the whole population—and of their being surpassed in wealth, in trade and manufactures by both Jews and Christians."

The British consul of Jerusalem wrote in his *Report of the Commerce of Jerusalem During the Year 1863* that the "population of the City of Jerusalem is computed at 15,000, of whom about 4,500 [are] Moslem, 8,000 Jews and the rest Christians of various denominations."[4] An indication of the static population in Jerusalem until God motivated the Jews to begin returning from exile in the 1880s is found in the fact that the total population of Jerusalem increased by only one thousand people during the seventy-eight years from the census figures for 1785 until 1863.

The evidence that the Jews formed the majority of the population of Palestine as well as Jerusalem is found in examining the historical records (Turkish Census, 1844; Calendar of Palestine 1895–96; 1922 Census by British Mandate; Jerusalem—The Old City—1962; Israel Central Bureau Of Statistics; Jerusalem Municipality Report).[5]

Official Population Statistics for Jerusalem
from 1844 to 1996

Year	Jews	Muslims	Christians
1844	7,120	5,000	3,390
1863	8,000	4,500	2,500
1896	28,112	8,560	8,748
1922	33,971	13,413	14,699
1948	100,000	40,000	25,000
1967	195,700	54,963	12,646
1983	300,000	105,000	15,000
1996	421,000	166,000	15,000

The Islamic Koran Declares that
Israel Belongs to the Jews

There have been numerous statements in recent years from Muslim authorities that have asserted that the Jews have no right to live in the Middle East, no right to live in Jerusalem, and no historical or religious right to visit the Temple Mount. In fact, many Muslim authorities now deny that the Jewish Temple ever existed on the Haram Es Sharif (Temple Mount).

However, it is fascinating to note that there are a number of passages (known as *Surahs*) in the key Islamic religious text, the Koran, written by Mohammed that relate to the children of Israel and her legitimate possession of her ancient homeland, the land of Israel. I am indebted to Dr. Michel Calvo's internet article, *Sovereignty to G-d* and Jerusalem Ministries International, which recently published several excerpts from his article.[6] I examined the Koran to verify these intriguing passages.

These ancient passages in the Koran clearly acknowledge and affirm the right of the Jews to possess the land of Israel. This declaration by the Muslim prophet Mohammed directly contradicts the repeated statements of modern Islamic spokesmen who deny the Jewish people have any right to live at peace in their ancient homeland. However, the Koran declares that the Jews had the right to enter and possess the Promised Land and that Allah "had not given to any other among the nations":

> And when Musa [Moses] said to his people [Israel]: O my people! remember the favor of Allah upon you when He raised prophets among you and made you kings and gave you what He had not given to any other among the nations. O my people! enter the holy land which Allah has prescribed for you and turn not on your backs for then you will turn back losers. (*Surah* 5:20–21)

This key passage, *Surah* 5:20–21, actually declares that the Jews were to "enter the holy land" that was given to Israel and was not given by Allah to any other people except the Jewish people. The Koran affirms to the Jews of Israel that Allah "made you kings and gave you what He had not given to any other among the nations." This remarkable statement is reinforced and confirmed in several other Koranic passages, including *Surah* 7:137–138 and *Surah* 17:104:

> And We made the people who were deemed weak to inherit the eastern lands and the western ones which We had blessed; and the good word of your Lord was fulfilled in the children of Israel because they bore up (sufferings) patiently; and We utterly destroyed what Firon and his people had wrought and what they built. And We made the children of Israel to pass the sea; then they came upon a people who kept to the worship of their idols They said: O Musa! make for us a god as they have (their) gods He said: Surely you are a people acting ignorantly. (*Surah* 7:137–138)

> And We said to the Israelites after him: Dwell in the land: and when the promise of the next life shall come to pass, we will bring you both together in judgment. (*Surah* 17:104) [the word *Musa* refers to Moses]

It is fascinating that the Koran clearly declares that Allah chose and blessed the Jewish people ("above the nations") and gave them the Torah ("the communications wherein was clear blessing"). The Koran states: "And certainly We chose them, having knowledge, above the nations. And We gave them of the communications wherein was clear blessing" (*Surah* 44:32–33). In an extraordinary statement in *Surah* 45:16, we find these words endorsing the biblical Torah and even a declaration that God created Israel to "excel the nations" (*Surah* 45:16). "And certainly We gave the Book and the wisdom and the prophecy to the children of Israel, and We gave them of the goodly things, and We made them excel the nations" (*Surah* 45:16).

The remarkable fact is that the Muslim's most holy book, the Koran, actually declares that Allah affirmed the right of the Jewish people ("and no other") to possess the Land of Israel. This declaration is extraordinary. If this statement from the Koran was publicly acknowledged and clearly taught throughout the

Islamic world, it might create a real possibility of negotiating a true peace between Israel and the Palestinians as well as with her surrounding Arab Islamic neighbors.

The Return of the Ethiopian Jews

Zephaniah prophesied that the Ethiopian Jews would finally return from thousands of years of exile to come home to the land of Israel. Approximately three thousand years ago, during the days of King Solomon, a group of Jews including representatives from each of the twelve tribes immigrated to Ethiopia with Prince Menelik, the son of King Solomon, and his mother, the Queen of Sheba. (For more on this subject, see my book *Armageddon—Appointment with Destiny*.) The prophet Zephaniah foretold the return of these Jews to their Israeli homeland in the last days: "From beyond the rivers of Ethiopia my suppliants, even the daughter of my dispersed, shall bring mine offering" (Zephaniah 3:10).

The prophet Isaiah confirms the prediction of Zephaniah: "I will say to the north, Give up; and to the south, Keep not back: bring my sons from far, and my daughters from the ends of the earth" (Isaiah 43:6); the "north" refers to Russia and the "south" refers to Ethiopia. In another passage, Isaiah prophesied about the land of Ethiopia and the coming Millennial "rest" or Sabbath.

> Woe to the land shadowing with wings, which is beyond the rivers of Ethiopia: That sendeth ambassadors by the sea, even in vessels of bulrushes upon the waters, saying, Go, ye swift messengers, to a nation scattered and peeled, to a people terrible from their beginning hitherto; a nation meted out and trodden down, whose land the rivers have spoiled! All ye inhabitants of the world, and dwellers on the earth, see ye, when he lifteth up an ensign on the mountains; and when he bloweth a trumpet, hear ye. For so the Lord said unto me, I will take my rest, and I will consider in my dwelling place like a clear heat upon herbs, and like a cloud of dew in the heat of harvest. . . . In that time shall the present be brought

unto the Lord of hosts of a people scattered and peeled, and from a people terrible from their beginning hitherto; a nation meted out and trodden under foot, whose land the rivers have spoiled, to the place of the name of the Lord of hosts, the mount Zion." (Isaiah 18:1–4, 7)

Remarkably, during the period from 1989 to 1991 following the end of the Ethiopian civil war, tens of thousands of black Ethiopian Jews known as Falashas were flown home to Israel in fulfillment of the ancient prophecy of Zephaniah. Although they followed many of the Jewish rituals of worship and feasts such as Passover, they had no knowledge of the Feast of Purim or Hanukkah because these festivals were instituted in the centuries after they were separated from their race.

The Astonishing Fertility of Israel

The prophet Isaiah also predicted that Israel would become fertile in the last days. "He shall cause them that come of Jacob to take root: Israel shall blossom and bud, and fill the face of the world with fruit" (Isaiah 27:6). In the light of the history of utter desolation in agriculture and deforestation throughout Palestine for almost two thousand years since the time of Christ, it is remarkable that the Bible prophesies that the land of ancient Canaan will become fertile and abundant in the last days. The Roman legions stripped the land of its trees and burned its orchards as part of its scorched earth policy in A.D. 70. The Turkish absentee landlords displayed no genuine concern for the land and allowed the removal of almost all trees for firewood for centuries. In Mark Twain's book *The Innocents,* he comments about his 1867 tour of the Holy Land: "There was hardly a tree or shrub anywhere. Even the olive and the cactus, those fast friends of a worthless soul, had almost deserted the country."[7]

However, the returning Jews have transformed the Promised Land, previously deserted and desolate, into the most agriculturally efficient land on earth according to the United Nations. The value of the agricultural crops produced annually exceeds $2 billion.[8] Today, Israel supplies over 90 percent of the citrus fruit consumed by almost five hundred million

Europeans and has annual agricultural exports to Western Europe exceeding $802 million.

The astonishing fertility of Israel in the last days is verified by these yields:

- Peak yields of tomatoes reach 202 tons per acre.
- 1.2 million roses are grown in greenhouses per acre per season.
- Annual milk yields per cow reach an average of 2,640 gallons.
- In the Negev Desert, peak yields of citrus reach 32 tons per acre.[9]

The terribly dry environment forced the Jews to innovate and develop remarkable new drip-irrigation techniques that ensure every drop of water is delivered directly through to the plant's roots. Utilization of the pure fertilizer provided from the minerals found in the Dead Sea has allowed Israel's farmers to turn the deserts into lush gardens growing bananas, mangos, and grapes.

The rainfall in Palestine increased dramatically during the last century, as compared to earlier centuries. The returning Jewish exiles planted two hundred million trees, transforming the complete environment of the Promised Land. The prophet Joel declared that the desert nation of Israel would experience tremendous increases of rain during the last days. "Be glad then, ye children of Zion, and rejoice in the Lord your God: for he hath given you the former rain moderately, and he will cause to come down for you the rain, the former rain, and the latter rain in the first month" (Joel 2:23). Isaiah, too, prophesied about increased fertility: "And the parched ground shall become a pool, and the thirsty land springs of water: in the habitation of dragons, where each lay, shall be grass with reeds and rushes" (Isaiah 35:7). As a result of this unprecedented reforestation, Israel's climate is beginning to return to the original conditions of the ancient past when Israel was called "a land of milk and honey."

The Rebuilding of Jerusalem

One of the most fascinating and little-known end-time prophecies is the twenty-five-century-old prediction by the prophet Jeremiah that the city of Jerusalem will be precisely "rebuilt for the Lord" in the last days in a very particular sequence.

> Behold, the days come, saith the Lord, that the city shall be built to the Lord from the tower of Hananeel unto the gate of the corner. And the measuring line shall yet go forth over against it upon the hill Gareb, and shall compass about to Goath. And the whole valley of the dead bodies, and of the ashes, and all the fields unto the brook of Kidron, unto the corner of the horse gate toward the east, shall be holy unto the Lord; it shall not be plucked up, nor thrown down any more for ever. (Jeremiah 31:38–40)

The order and the modern equivalents, in brackets, are as follows: "The city shall be built to the Lord from the tower of Hananeel [northwest corner of Temple Mount] unto the gate of the corner [Jaffa Gate]. And the measuring line shall yet go forth over against it upon the hill Gareb [northeast of the corner gate on the ancient wall], and shall compass about to Goath [Schneller's Orphanage]. And the whole valley of the dead bodies, and of the ashes [ancient cemetery], and all the fields unto the brook of Kidron [follows the ancient Brook Kidron], unto the corner of the horse gate toward the east [an ancient walled up gate near the sealed Eastern Gate] shall be holy unto the Lord; it shall not be plucked up, nor thrown down any more for ever" (Jeremiah 31:38–40).

This unusual prophecy has been fulfilled with astonishing precision in the last generation as the Jewish exiles have returned from seventy nations throughout the globe to rebuild their ancient capital as documented in the following pages.

G. Olaf Matson wrote a tourist's travel guide booklet entitled *The American Colony Palestine Guide* early in the last century that presented information to help English-speaking tourists to make their way around Jerusalem and Palestine. The phrase

"American Colony" refers to the section of Jerusalem that housed many of the American diplomats, expatriates, and tourists coming to the Holy City. Matson's interesting analysis of the city building developments reveal fascinating parallels with the prophecy of Jeremiah 31:38–40. Another book, *Fulfilled Prophecy That Prove the Bible* by George T. B. Davis, detailed how the expansion of the modern city has precisely followed the ancient prophecy.[10]

After very careful analysis of Jeremiah's prophecy and detailed examination of the precise stages of the expansion of the modern city of Jerusalem, Professor Peter Stoner concluded in his book *Science Speaks: An Evaluation of Certain Christian Evidences* that the odds against the rebuilding of the Holy City fulfilling this precise prediction by random chance were only one in 80 billion. Professor Stoner explained his calculation of the mathematical probabilities of Jeremiah correctly guessing the precise directions and sequence of the rebuilding of this ancient city as follows:

> It is rather easy to find the number of ways in which the city of Jerusalem might have grown in its first nine steps. There are six definite corners to the old city. Certainly the growth might have started from any one of these corners, to say nothing of the sides. Let us say then, that the first development could have come at any of these six corners. Having built at point number 1 it could have next built at any of the old corners, or gone on in any one of these directions from number 1; thus, the second expansion could have come as any of 8 places. Continuing this on for the nine points and multiplying the results together, we find that the probability of Jeremiah writing this prophecy, from human knowledge, and having come true would be about 1 in 8×10^{10}.[11]

Two fascinating prophecies correctly foretold that Jerusalem would be an "unwalled city" in the last days. The prophet Ezekiel predicted an invasion by Russia and the Arab nations in the last days: "And thou shalt say, I will go up to the land of unwalled villages; I will go to them that are at rest, that dwell safely, all of them dwelling without walls, and having neither bars nor gates" (Ezekiel 38:11). Zechariah repeated this unusual detail in his prophecy: "And said unto him, Run, speak to this young man, saying, Jerusalem shall be inhabited as towns without walls for the multitude of men and cattle therein" (Zechariah 2:4).

The reason this prediction was so unusual is that defensive walls surrounded virtually every single village, town, or city in the ancient world. However, the development of long-range weapons of destruction—including artillery, aerial bombs, and missiles—have made defensive walls useless, even for Israeli military bases surrounded by Palestinian territory. Since everyone was familiar with the many prophecies that describe Israel as surrounded by enemies in the last days, it was nothing less than extraordinary for Ezekiel and Zechariah to predict that Israel and Jerusalem would not have defensive walls at the time of the end.

Another unusual prophetic reference regarding the last days relates to the unprecedented and unusual love of archeology and the deep attachment to the ancient walled city of Jerusalem that characterizes the Jews of Israel. King David prophesied, "Thou shalt arise, and have mercy upon Zion: for the time to favour her, yea, the set time, is come. For thy servants take pleasure in her stones, and favour the dust thereof. So the heathen shall fear the name of the Lord, and all the kings of the earth thy glory. When the Lord shall build up Zion, he shall appear in his glory" (Psalms 102:13–16).

The Jews in the Promised Land have a profound love of their ancient capital and often visit its Western Wall and numerous other historical and religious sites within its walls. Almost every Israeli citizen I have visited collects objects such as ancient pottery and coins of archeological interest. Unlike their Arab neighbors, who usually display little interest in the historical ruins that surround them, many of the Jews have a deep interest in the archeological objects and discoveries that demonstrate their historic connection with their ancestors and their ancient homeland.

Israel's Plans to Rebuild the Temple

Isaiah wrote, "And it shall come to pass in the last days, that the mountain of the Lord's house shall be established in the top of the mountains, and shall be exalted above the hills; and all nations shall flow unto it" (Isaiah 2:2). The prophet John prophesied that the angel transported him forward through time into the last days to measure the future third Temple that will exist during the final seven-year Tribulation period. "And there was given me a reed like unto a rod: and the angel stood, saying, Rise, and measure the temple of God, and the altar, and them that worship therein. But the court which is without the temple leave out, and measure it not; for it is given unto the Gentiles: and the holy city shall they tread under foot forty and two months" (Revelation 11:1–2). Numerous prophecies describe the rebuilding of the Temple in the last days. The apostle Paul confirmed that the Antichrist will occupy the future Temple. "Let no man deceive you by any means: for that day shall not come, except there come a falling away first, and that man of sin be revealed, the son of perdition; who opposeth and exalteth himself above all that is called God, or that is worshiped; so that he as God sitteth in the temple of God, shewing himself that he is God" (2 Thessalonians 2:3–4). Daniel described the final cleansing of the third Temple (defiled by the Antichrist during the Tribulation) by the Messiah: "Then shall the sanctuary be cleansed" (Daniel 8:14).

The prophet Ezekiel described his vision of the final and fourth Temple of the coming Messiah that will be cleansed and cared for by ministering Levites and priests worshiping God in the millennial kingdom (Ezekiel 41:1).

Oil of Anointing

One of the most unusual aspects of the ancient Tabernacle and Temple worship service was the sacred "oil of anointing" that disappeared almost two thousand years ago. This sacred oil was prepared by the priests using five specific ingredients to anoint the Temple, the ark of the covenant, and the high priest. The kings of Israel, including King David and Solomon, were anointed with this oil. Moses initially described God's sacred commandment to Israel as follows: "And thou shalt make it an oil of holy ointment, an ointment compound after the art of the apothecary: it shall be an holy anointing oil. And thou shalt anoint the tabernacle of the congregation therewith, and the ark of the testimony" (Exodus 30:25–26). The rare and precious plant known as *afars'mon* was one of the five ingredients mentioned in the book of Exodus that was required to prepare the sacred oil for the Tabernacle or Temple service. This valuable ingredient was lost, seemingly forever, almost two thousand years ago when Jerusalem was destroyed. When the Roman legions destroyed the Jewish Temple, the escaping Jewish rebels burned the only two surviving groves in Jericho and Ein Gedi where these very rare *afars'mon* trees grew. The Jewish sages taught that the Jews could never reinstitute the Temple services without this special oil of anointing because they had lost forever the missing ingredient of *afars'mon.*

One of Daniel's most significant prophecies was that the coming Messiah would be anointed with this special oil of anointing. It is significant that the title "Messiah" and "Christ" mean "anointed." Daniel wrote: "Seventy weeks are determined upon thy people and upon thy holy city, to finish the transgression, and to make an end of sins, and to make reconciliation for iniquity, and to bring in everlasting righteousness, and to seal up the vision and prophecy, and to anoint the most Holy" (Daniel 9:24). While Jesus was never anointed with this sacred oil during His First Coming, He will finally be anointed when He returns as Israel's acknowledged King at His Second Coming.

The official ancient Jewish tradition tells us that the Temple treasures including the "oil of anointing" were lost forever. How could these sacred prophecies about the rebuilding of the Temple and the anointing of the Messiah be fulfilled when some of the key ingredients were missing?

The ancient Copper Scroll, part of the Dead Sea Scrolls, discovered in 1995, actually describes over sixty separate locations where the ancient Temple priests and Essenes hid the precious treasures of the second Temple before the Roman legions burned the sacred building to the ground. Following a careful search based upon the detailed descriptions in the Copper Scroll regarding one particular burial place, a group of Christian researchers found an ancient clay flask. Incredibly, archeologists associated with the Israel Museum in Jerusalem declared that this ancient clay flask buried near the Dead Sea caves was actually filled with the ancient oil of anointing. Chinese scholars who specialized in the chemical composition of ancient oils verified the age of the oil and its composition based on Carbon 14 dating techniques. Scientists confirmed that the oil in the flask was approximately two thousand years old and is composed of the five precise ingredients described in Exodus 30:25–26. It is remarkable that the Jews now have the oil of anointing they would need to purify the third Temple and resume worship there. In addition, the oil of anointing is now available to anoint "the most Holy," the Messiah Jesus when He returns as King of kings and "God's Anointed."

Implements Required For Temple Worship

The Temple Institute in the Old City of Jerusalem has recently prepared over eighty-five sacred Temple worship objects described in the Torah, including sacred vessels and linen priestly garments for the Kohanim priests that will be required for future Temple services. Several Orthodox yeshivas (Jewish Bible colleges) in Jerusalem have trained more than five hundred young Jewish men, descended from the tribe of Levi, to fulfill their future duties of Temple worship services. Many of these Kohanim have already been trained in the Temple worship rituals and have learned to play the restored biblical musical instruments including the lyre and harp. An Israeli radio news report on September 28, 1999, by Yosef Zalmanson, a reporter for *Arut-7*, revealed that the Temple Institute recently completed a golden seven-branch candelabra—a menorah—according to the strict divine instructions found in the biblical book of Exodus. Rabbi Yisrael Ariel, the leader of the Temple Institute, stated that the menorah was constructed "for the sake of the commandment." The menorah is six and a half feet high and was cast with ninety-two pounds of pure gold costing over $400,000.

Rabbi Ariel stated, "It, or other menorahs, will be consecrated when the Temple is rebuilt."[12]

The Red Heifer Sacrifice

An important part of the purification ritual is the sacrifice of the red heifer. God said through Ezekiel: "Then will I sprinkle clean water upon you, and ye shall be clean: from all your filthiness, and from all your idols, will I cleanse you" (Ezekiel 36:25). The red heifer sacrifice is necessary to produce the waters of purification, as described in Numbers 19. The waters of purification are required to cleanse the Temple objects and even the ancient stones on the Temple Mount that were spiritually defiled through numerous bloody conquests. This ritual cleansing is necessary to prepare for resumption of animal sacrifices in the Third Temple according to Jewish religious law.

It is interesting to note that the Jewish groups in Israel that are preparing for the rebuilding of the Temple are raising a breed of pure red cattle that they hope will eventually produce in a pure red heifer. When one is found that meets the strict qualifications of Numbers 19, it will be sacrificed on the Mount of Olives directly opposite the sealed Eastern Gate. Several years ago the Jews thought they had the perfect animal, and it was certified as such by Rabbi Reichman of the Temple Institute. However, as often occurs with cattle, the heifer developed some white hairs in a place where it had been bruised and was therefore disqualified. The Temple Institute is raising cattle on a ranch near Mount Carmel in northern Israel, hoping that they will eventually find a perfect red heifer without any white or black hair, "without spot, wherein there is no blemish, and upon which never came yoke" (Numbers 19:2).

The Roman Empire Will Be Revived

The Roman Empire was the most powerful and militarily successful empire in history. The Scriptures repeatedly foretold that the Roman Empire would rise again during the last days, leading to the final crisis known as the Tribulation and the Battle of Armageddon, which will usher in the millennial kingdom. Both Daniel and the book of Revelation predicted that the powerful empire that dominated the world in the days of Christ would be revived during the years leading to the return of the Messiah.

Daniel received an interpretation of King Nebuchadnezzar's remarkable prophetic dream about a gigantic metallic statue. This statue represented the four great world empires that would rule the world from the time of Daniel until the last days when Jesus Christ would supernaturally destroy the last Gentile world empire and establish His righteous millennial kingdom on earth. The first three Gentile world empires—Babylon, "the head of gold," Medo-Persia, "the chest of silver," and Greece, "the thighs of brass"—succeeded each other in turn exactly as God had revealed to the king through Daniel's interpretation. The fourth Gentile world empire, Rome, "the legs of iron," which succeeded the Grecian Empire of Alexander the Great and his generals, was prophesied to split into two portions, as symbolized by the two legs. This prediction was fulfilled when the Roman Empire was severed into a western empire under Rome and an eastern empire under Constantinople.

> And the fourth kingdom shall be strong as iron: forasmuch as iron breaketh in pieces and subdueth all things: and as iron that breaketh all these, shall it break in pieces and bruise. And whereas thou sawest the feet and toes, part of potter's clay, and part of iron, the kingdom shall be divided; but there shall be in it of the strength of the iron, forasmuch as thou sawest the iron mixed with miry clay. And as the toes of the feet were part of iron, and part of clay, so the kingdom shall be partly strong, and partly broken. And whereas thou sawest iron mixed with miry clay, they shall mingle themselves with the seed of men: but they shall not cleave one to another, even as iron is not mixed with clay. And in the days of these kings shall the God of heaven set up a kingdom, which shall never be destroyed: and the kingdom shall not be left to other people, but it shall break in pieces

and consume all these kingdoms, and it shall stand for ever. (Daniel 2:40–44)

The Lord gave Daniel divine understanding to interpret the king's vision that revealed the fourth empire, Rome, would be revived in the last days in the form of a ten-nation confederacy or superstate. The vision revealed that the ten "toes of the feet were part of iron, and part of clay, so the kingdom shall be partly strong, and partly broken." This correctly describes the nations of modern Europe that would include both powerful and weak member states. Significantly, these ten future nations will unite into this ten-nation superstate and give their power to an evil dictator, the Antichrist, for a period of time until God destroys it as revealed in Daniel 7:8–9:

> I considered the horns, and, behold, there came up among them another little horn, before whom there were three of the first horns plucked up by the roots: and, behold, in this horn were eyes like the eyes of man, and a mouth speaking great things. I beheld till the thrones were cast down, and the Ancient of days did sit, whose garment was white as snow.

The final portion of Daniel's vision of the metallic statue confirmed that this confederacy will be destroyed suddenly at the return of Jesus Christ when He establishes His own eternal kingdom.

> And in the days of these kings shall the God of heaven set up a kingdom, which shall never be destroyed: and the kingdom shall not be left to other people, but it shall break in pieces and consume all these kingdoms, and it shall stand for ever. Forasmuch as thou sawest that the stone was cut out of the mountain without hands, and that it brake in pieces the iron, the brass, the clay, the silver, and the gold. (Daniel 2:44–45)

An additional fascinating prophecy is revealed in Daniel's last sentence that Christ's return will supernaturally and suddenly destroy, not only the "iron and clay" (the revived

Roman Empire), but also "the brass" (the revived Grecian Empire), "the silver" (the revived Medo-Persian Empire), and "the gold" (the revived Babylonian Empire). Therefore, students of prophecy should closely watch the political, economic, and military activities of the European Union, Turkey, Syria, Iran, and Iraq. All four of these ancient empires will play crucial prophetic roles in the dramatic strategic events of the last days in the final crisis of the Tribulation.

In 1991, the leaders of Europe signed the Maastricht Treaty, which consolidated the fifteen nations of the European Union into the world's first true superstate. Both the prophecy of Daniel (Daniel 7) and John's predictions (Revelation 13 and 17) confirm that the Roman Empire would be revived in the final days. In 1957, after two devastating world wars and the death of fifty million people, the political leaders of Europe held a conference to plan an unprecedented European superstate, creating a unique confederation between the major nations of Western Europe for the first time since the Roman emperors. Initially six European countries signed the 1957 Treaty of Rome and laid the foundation for the future United States of Europe. A powerful European statesman, Henri Spaak, the former secretary-general of NATO, admitted during a BBC documentary on the European Union: "We felt like Romans on that day. . . . We were consciously re-creating the Roman Empire once more." Now fifteen nations comprise the EU: Austria, Belgium, Denmark, Finland, France, Germany, Greece, Ireland, Italy, Luxembourg, the Netherlands, Spain, Portugal, Sweden, and the United Kingdom.

The European Union has evolved into an economic, political, and potentially, a powerful military colossus that will dominate world events in the near future. The emerging European superstate is ruled by the appointed president of the European Commission together with the twenty-one non-elected members who create the rules and taxes that administer the EU from the thirteenth floor of the Berlaymont, an enormous government building in Brussels, Belgium. The directly elected European Parliament has 626 members and has gradually increased its executive powers over laws and taxation since the Treaty of

Amsterdam (May 1, 1999). The 1991 Maastricht Treaty (Treaty of the European Union) solidified the unification of the nations occupying the territory of the ancient Roman Empire through its creation of the Economic and Monetary Union (EMU). The Maastricht Treaty provided for the creation of the world's first international currency, the Euro, as well as for the European Central Bank and the Common Foreign and Security Policy. The political consolidation of the EU has produced a common European citizenship and passport, a single High Court, a European Central Bank and currency, with a common foreign policy defended by a European army. Joint European political, economic, and military control has produced the first unified power in Europe since the days of ancient Rome.

It is significant to note that former German Chancellor Helmut Kohl revealed a plan by the major powers of the European Union (France, Germany, Belgium, Italy, and Spain) to unite politically, economically, and militarily, as well as to surrender their individual sovereignty. This plan suggests that this inner circle of five powers will be surrounded by the other European Union members who will unite economically but retain some political sovereignty—at least initially. Then, the plan envisions another five key members of the superstate eventually submerging their national sovereignty as they join in a ten-nation confederation. The outer circle of additional nations of the European Union will retain some of their political autonomy during the transition period.

The Western European Union (WEU) was created in 1954 as another key European organization responsible for coordination of European military strategy. The WEU originally had six members—Great Britain, France, Germany, Belgium, the Netherlands, and Luxembourg—and now includes Spain, Portugal, Italy, and Greece. There is a powerful move within the European Union to have the WEU replace NATO and provide for joint European defense themselves. To further this project, Britain and France have created a 100,000-man rapid reaction military force that provides an important initial step toward the creation of a powerful European military force that can act independently from the Unites States and NATO.

Preparations for the Battle of Armageddon

The Scriptures record three unique predictions regarding the future Battle of Armageddon that could never be fulfilled in any previous generation in history. The first prediction regarding an army of 200 million soldiers of the kings of the East implies that there must be significant increase in the population of males in Asia. Second, the Scriptures indicate that the kings of the East will prepare a military highway across Asia to facilitate the marching of that huge army toward Israel. Third, the prophecies about the final Battle of Armageddon describe an event when the Euphrates River will suddenly dry up to allow the army of the kings of the East to cross it and march west toward Israel. Then the vast army of the "kings of the East" will confront the western armies of the Antichrist to determine whether the West or the East will rule the earth. The following paragraphs will document evidence that these unique prophecies are being fulfilled in our generation for the first time in history.

An Unprecedented Increase in the Male Population in Asia

The apostle John foretold the final Battle of Armageddon: "And he gathered them together into a place called in the Hebrew tongue Armageddon" (Revelation 16:16). The name Armageddon is derived from the Greek phrase that means "mount of Megiddo," the small mountain that overlooks the ancient ruins of the biblical city of Megiddo. From the mountain you can look out over the enormous Valley of Jezreel that extends from northern Israel far to the south toward Jerusalem. Numerous strategic battles have been fought at Armageddon including the triumphant victory recorded in Judges 5:19 and the devastating Egyptian victory over the forces of the righteous King Josiah. The last great battle at Megiddo occurred when Lord Allenby and his Allied Expeditionary Force defeated the armies of Turkey in 1918 and set the stage for the rebirth of Israel.

The prophecy indicated that the army of the Oriental alliance from the nations of the kings of the East will consist of an astonishing army of two hundred million soldiers:

"And the number of the army of the horsemen were two hundred thousand thousand: and I heard the number of them" (Revelation 9:16). This statement was remarkable when you realize that the entire population of the ancient Roman Empire in the first century was only approximately 200 million people. Some students of prophecy mistakenly assumed that the Bible referred to 200 million horsemen. However, there are only approximately 35 million horses throughout the globe. A careful reading of the prophecy reveals that John's use of the word "horsemen" in Revelation 9:16 actually refers to "the four horsemen of the Apocalypse" described by John under the symbols of the first four seal judgments (Revelation 6:1–8). The best interpretation is that the prophecy reveals that the army of the four horsemen of the Apocalypse that represents God's wrath will include 200 million soldiers.

Many have wondered if this number could actually be literal. Yet, the population of Asia is growing so quickly that the nations of the East could field an army in the next few years that would contain 200 million soldiers. The Chinese government instituted an unprecedented One Child Policy in 1979 in an attempt to reduce the massive population growth that threatened their ability to feed their rapidly growing billion-plus population. Under this policy, each couple can only have one child during their lifetime and each woman must obtain an authorized birth coupon prior to conceiving a child. Incredibly, this horrendously intrusive population policy requires that fertile women's menstrual cycles be publicly monitored and that they undergo mandated pelvic examinations if suspected pregnant. An official circular of the Party Central Committee and the State Council in November 1982 required mandatory sterilization of all couples who have had two or more children. The official policy requires that all unauthorized pregnancies must be aborted whenever detected, regardless of the stage of pregnancy. Government population control doctors use forceps to crush the unborn baby's skull, or inject pure formaldehyde into the soft cap of baby's head either before birth or during the actual delivery of fully developed babies in the ninth month. Fines equal to one year's income are imposed on couples who have an unauthorized birth. An article in the *New York Times* in April 1993 reported that punishments also included the confiscation of property, the destruction of their houses, and severe physical beatings. This was also confirmed by an Internet article. [13] As a result of the Communist government's cruelty, Chinese couples who become pregnant frequently abort babies if an ultrasound test indicates the unborn child is a female. They often continue to abort female fetuses until the test reveals that the woman is carrying a male fetus. Then they allow the male child to be born. Since they can only have one child, many couples choose to have a son to continue their family name and to support them in their retirement.

In 1991, an article in a Shanghai, China, journal warned that the unbalanced ratio of boys to girls would eventually produce an army of young bachelors numbering some 70 million strong, without any prospect of marriage by the year 2000.[14] The *Toronto Star* newspaper reported in 1995 that Chinese officials admitted this unprecedented imbalance of boys and girls. Numerous reports by human rights organizations reveal that China, India, and North Korea are also involved in the selective abortion of female babies. In addition, many families in these nations admit to killing or abandoning their young female children. This unprecedented situation may set the stage for the fulfillment of the ancient biblical prophecy about an army of 200 million in the last days.

A Highway for the Kings of the East

The prophet John also prophesied in Revelation about the preparation of a military highway across Asia in the last days that will allow this massive Oriental army to march across the vast reaches of Asia toward the final Battle of Armageddon in northern Israel. John refers to the building of this highway in these curious words: "The way of the kings of the east might be prepared" (Revelation 16:12). The Chinese Communist government has recently spent extraordinary sums of money and expended hundreds of thousands of lives of construction workers to build an unprecedented military super-highway from mainland China across southern Asia, heading directly west toward the land of Israel. This new highway through the most rugged mountain terrain across the south of China and through Tibet, Afghanistan, and Pakistan has no obvious economic purpose, and no forcigners are allowed near it. The following (poorly translated) statement regarding this highway, from a January 1999 article by Oleg Limanov in *Marco Polo Magazine*, read: "Karakorum highway, connecting Afghanistan through Central Asia states and China to Pakistan with probable joining India would be very significant for all concerning parties, agreement on using of which was signed by China, Pakistan, Kazakhstan and Kyrgyzstan in July 1996."[15]

Another Internet article describes the land route from China towards the Middle East: "With Myanmar [Burma] support, the Indian government is creating a transportation corridor from South Asia through Myanmar to Southeast Asia. This corridor will compete with other grand trans-Eurasian projects, such as a land transportation link from China through Central Asia to Turkey and Europe."[16]

The Drying Up of the Euphrates River

Another prophecy of the apostle John in Revelation declares that the Euphrates River will dry up to allow this army to cross from Asia into the Middle East to invade Israel: "And the sixth angel poured out his vial upon the great river Euphrates; and the water thereof was dried up, that the way of the kings of the east might be prepared" (Revelation 16:12). Throughout history, the Euphrates River has been an almost impassable military barrier between East and West, often preventing large armies from crossing from one side to the other in their attempts to conquer the nations on the other side.

The former Turkish president Turgut Ozal built a series of twenty-two dams on the Tigris and Euphrates river systems during the 1980s and 1990s. The huge Ataturk Dam, the fifth-largest dam on earth, is part of the $32 billion Southeastern Anatolia Project, which was designed to produce electricity and to double the irrigation to approximately 30,000 square miles of semi-arid land. This series of dams is intended to allow Turkey to produce ample food for the growing population of the Middle

East. The Ataturk Dam is estimated to provide irrigation to over four million acres of land, enabling Turkish farmers to grow cotton, tobacco, sugarbeets, and soybeans.

What's most notable about the Ataturk Dam, one mile long and 600 feet high, is that it is capable of completely blocking the headwaters of the Euphrates River for the first time in history. The great Euphrates River can now be dried up exactly as prophesied to allow an Asian army to march toward Israel across the ancient battlefields of Mesopotamia, which have witnessed so many historically decisive battles throughout history. This is another example of a unique prophecy that can now be fulfilled in our generation.

Babylon Rises Again

The Bible's prophecy that the ancient city of Babylon will be rebuilt and will play a key role in end time events is so unusual that many scholars doubted that it could ever be literally fulfilled. Some have attempted to spiritualize this prophecy or treat it as an allegory. However, the prophet Isaiah revealed that the rebuilt city of Babylon will be destroyed by supernatural fire from heaven in a similar manner to the destruction of Sodom and Gomorrah. Although Babylon was repeatedly attacked and destroyed several times in ancient history, the specific supernatural nature of the destruction described by Isaiah has never occurred. Therefore, this prediction must refer to a future destruction in the last days. The name Babylon was derived from *Bab-ili*, meaning "Gate of God." Babylon was the most powerful kingdom of the ancient world during the rule of King Nebuchadnezzar II, the greatest of the Chaldean kings who ruled the Middle East from 605 to 562 B.C. The sands of the desert ultimately covered the city of Babylon for over a thousand years until it was rediscovered by archeologists, such as Sir William Ramsey and Austen Layard, in the early 1800s.

The Lord repeatedly commanded His people to "come out of her" and to "flee from the midst of Babylon, and each of you save his life" before He would ultimately destroy Babylon at the Great Day of the Lord (Isaiah 13:1, 6, 19; Revelation 18:4; Jeremiah 51:6). The context of these prophetic passages reveals that Babylon will be rebuilt as a literal city during the last days. John prophetically refers to the destruction of Babylon as a real "great city" (Revelation 18:10). He also predicts the utter annihilation of the rebuilt city at the end of the Tribulation:

> And a mighty angel took up a stone like a great millstone, and cast it into the sea, saying, Thus with violence shall that great city Babylon be thrown down, and shall be found no more at all. And the voice of harpers, and musicians, and of pipers, and trumpeters, shall be heard no more at all in thee; and no craftsman, of whatsoever craft he be, shall be found any more in thee; and the sound of a millstone shall be heard no more at all in thee; and the light of a candle shall shine no more at all in thee; and the voice of the bridegroom and of the bride shall be heard no more at all in thee: for thy merchants were the great men of the earth; for by thy sorceries were all nations deceived. (Revelation 18:21–23)

The prophet Isaiah foretold this future divine destruction as follows: "The burden of Babylon, which Isaiah the son of Amoz did see. . . . Howl ye; for the day of the Lord is at hand; it shall come as a destruction from the Almighty. . . . And Babylon, the glory of kingdoms, the beauty of the Chaldees' excellency, shall be as when God overthrew Sodom and Gomorrah" (Isaiah 13:1, 6, 19).

Obviously, this prophecy of future destruction requires that the ruined city of Babylon must be first rebuilt. The president of Iraq, Saddam Hussein, who has ruled the nation ruthlessly for almost three decades, has spent over $1.5 billion rebuilding the ancient city since 1978. The Iraqi government published a booklet entitled *Babylon*, which dealt with Hussein's plans to rebuild the ancient city. The back cover of the booklet reads: "Archaeological Survival of Babylon is a Patriotic, National, and International Duty." *L.A. Times* journalist Michael Ross wrote: "Babylon has assumed additional importance for the government since the war [with Iran] broke out in September, 1980. Keen on establishing a link between its current conflict with the Persians and the legendary battles of the past, the Iraqi government has speeded up the reconstruction in order to make Babylon a symbol of national pride."[17]

Hussein began rebuilding Babylon during the eight-year-long Iraq/Iran war to motivate the Iraqi people. He has manufactured over sixty million new clay bricks to rebuild the sixty miles of walls that surround the city. These new bricks are cemented into the wall above the original ancient bricks that are marked with Nebuchadnezzar's name. The new bricks are embossed with the following statement in Arabic that declares, "In the era of Saddam Hussein, protector of Iraq, who rebuilt the Royal Palace."

Saddam identifies powerfully with King Nebuchadnezzar, the ancient ruler who invaded Israel and took the Jewish population as captives back to Babylon. Incredibly, Hussein has stated that he believes that he is the reincarnation of Nebuchadnezzar and that he was given a supernatural vision to restore the great Babylonian empire and to conquer the territory of Saudi Arabia, Syria, Lebanon, Jordan, Kuwait, and Israel once again. He threatened to set Israel "on fire," demonstrating his implacable hatred for the Jewish people. The Arab News Internet site reported on January 18, 2001: "Iraq's President Saddam Hussein stressed that Iraq is ready to bombard Israel for six continuous months and this is in the first place to liberate the Arab lands, occupied by Israel in 1967."[18]

Hussein has announced that Babylon will become the center of a future revived Babylonian empire. The chief archaeologist of Babylon, Shafqa Mohammed Jaafar, declared, "Because Babylon was built in ancient times, and was a great city, it must be a great city again in the time of our new great leader, Saddam Hussein."[19]

Charles Dyer, the respected prophecy teacher and author of *The Rise of Babylon* described the International Babylon Festival in 1988, among the ruins of the ancient city of Babylon:

> It is a cloudless September night, and the moon casts its shining image on the banks of the gentle Euphrates River. Thousands of guests and dignitaries walk by torchlight to Babylon's Procession Street and enter the

city from the north. Instructed to line the streets along the massive walls, the guests obediently follow orders. When the audience is in place, the dark-eyed man in charge nods, and the procession begins. Rows and rows of soldiers parade in, dressed in Babylonian tunics and carrying swords, spears and shields. Interspersed among the ranks of soldiers are groups of musicians playing harps, horns and drums. Clusters of children carry palm branches, and runners bear bowls of incense. Then come soldiers and still more soldiers in a seemingly endless line of men and weapons. After the procession, the guests attend a ceremony paying tribute to Ishtar, the mother goddess of Babylon.[20]

For the last twelve years, the Iraqi government has celebrated a Babylonian Festival among the archeological ruins and new buildings of the rebuilt ancient city with invited guests from fifty Arab and many other nations. During the fall of 2000, the Arabic News organization reported:

"Artistic bands representing some 50 Arab and foreign states, took part in the activities of the festival which lasted for ten days, performed art shows on three stages in the city which is four thousand years old, and is 90 kilometers [60 miles] to the south of the capital Baghdad. On the sideline of the festival, musical, singing, and cultural activities were organized including an intellectual seminar on the Iraqi antiquities and photo exhibition and visits for the main archaeological sites.[21]

The prophet Daniel was given a very important prophetic vision about the last days recorded in Daniel 2:34–45 in which he witnessed the revival of the ancient empire of Rome. However, although most prophecy teachers have ignored this part of the prediction, Daniel's prophecy clearly predicts that there will also be a simultaneous revival of the empires of Babylon, Persia, and Greece in the days prior to the return of the Messiah. Therefore we should not be surprised to see the rise of Iraq as a powerful nation in our days together with Iran (ancient Persia), and Turkey–Syria (the ancient Grecian empire). While Saddam Hussein is a definite threat to his Arab neighbors, they admire him for his courage in standing up to the perceived military threat from Britain, America, and Israel. *L.A. Times* journalist David Lamb wrote: "Finally, for the first time since Egypt's Gamal Shawki Abdel Nasser, an Arab leader had been bold enough to stand up to the West and had said all the catchwords—Palestine, Islam, unity, sharing Arab oil—that reminded the Arabs how much should be right, and how much had gone wrong."[22]

It is important to note that Iraq possesses the second-largest oil reserves in the world, which almost equal those of her neighbor Saudi Arabia. This enormous oil wealth will allow Iraq to quickly rebuild its nation into a powerful economic and military regional power in only a few years once the decade-long UN oil and economic sanctions end. In addition, Saddam's armies and his rapid development of weapons of mass destruction will make it possible for Iraq to quickly dominate the surrounding nations including the militarily weak oil states of Saudi Arabia, the United Arab Emirates, and Kuwait.

Isaiah foretold that the wicked city will burn forever as an object lesson to humanity of God's ultimate judgment:

> For it is the day of the Lord's vengeance, and the year of recompenses for the controversy of Zion. And the streams thereof shall be turned into pitch, and the dust thereof into brimstone, and the land thereof shall become burning pitch. It shall not be quenched night nor day; the smoke thereof shall go up for ever: from generation to generation it shall lie waste; none shall pass through it for ever and ever. (Isaiah 34:8–10)

During the War in the Gulf, the final burning of Babylon was illustrated to the watching world through the cameras of CNN when Saddam Hussein set fire to hundreds of Kuwaiti oil wells, filling the desert with black smoke and fire that took months to extinguish.

Plans for Global Government

The prophets Daniel and John predicted that a global government would exist in the last days and will be dominated by the Antichrist (Daniel 7:14). "And it was given unto him to make war with the saints, and to overcome them: and power was given him over all kindreds, and tongues, and nations. And all that dwell upon the earth shall worship him" (Revelation 13:7–8). These prophecies reveal that the world will be under the totalitarian control of a global government, led by the Antichrist, in the final years leading to Christ's return. For the first time in history, the future Antichrist will have power "over all kindreds, and tongues, and nations." Despite the rise and fall of countless empires over the past several thousand years, a one-world government has never before been achieved in human history. The rising political, economic, and military power of the United Nations, World Bank, International Monetary Fund, World Trade Organization, International Court of Criminal Justice, and World Court are rapidly destroying national sovereignty and the independent powers of nations.

The United Nations Commission on Global Governance published a report in 1995 entitled *Our Global Neighborhood*, which encouraged world leaders to plan for a World Conference on Global Governance. The UN Commission on Global Governance has proposed a number of remarkable changes in international relations that would transform the relations between nations and erode their independent sovereignty. Although this was not an official organization of the UN, it was authorized by the UN secretary-general and funded jointly by the UN and several key global elite foundations including the Ford, Carnegie, and McArthur Foundations.[23] While denying that they are seeking a new world order, they call their goal "global governance," which is world government by another name.

These global governance proposals include:
- Establishing a new system of global taxation to enable the UN to raise its own revenues without dependence on dues from member states

- Creating a powerful standing UN army militarily capable of enforcing the will of the Security Council
- Setting up an International Court of Criminal Justice that would function independently of nation states
- Expanding the power and authority of the UN secretary-general
- Creating an Economic Security Council to coordinate global economic policies
- Establishing UN authority over the global commons including the oceans and the environmentally sensitive seacoasts of all nations
- Eliminating the veto power of permanent Security Council members
- Creating a new parliamentary body of "civil society" representatives based on present-day private groups called non-government organizations (NGOs).[24]

If anyone thinks that these proposals are not serious, they should carefully evaluate the significant international developments that have taken place during the last few years. The General Agreement on Trade and Tariffs (GATT) has created the World Trade Organization, which has eroded every nation's economic sovereignty. For example, as soon as President Clinton signed the GATT, both the European Union and Japan presented lists of hundreds of federal and state laws that they demanded must be rescinded immediately to comply with World Trade Organization rules.

A key goal of the global elite is the creation of a powerful United Nations standing army, including a rapid-reaction armored force that will allow the Security Council to enforce the will of the world body against any nation or group of nations that opposes its political agenda. In the last decade, the UN has engaged in more peacekeeping operations around the world than it did in its first four decades. The UN's peacekeeping budget has experienced massive increases in military and civilian personnel. During the last few years, the UN Security Council deployed peacekeeping troops in nineteen countries around the globe, at an annual cost of over $3 billion.

According to the authoritative study *The Military Balance*

2000/2001 published in October 2000 by the Institute of Strategic and International Studies, the United Nations has currently deployed 28,900 troops contributed from thirty-eight countries in fourteen UN peacekeeping operations around the world. During the 1993–95 period of peacekeeping operations, over 70,000 UN troops were deployed throughout the globe. International military expenditures throughout the globe amounted to $809 billion, with $53.4 billion in international arms sales by America, the United Kingdom, Europe, Russia, and China.[25]

The globalists have embarked on a worldwide socialist program to subvert and erode the sovereignty of nation-states, including America and Canada. The plans for an international court of criminal justice were brought to fruition in July 1998 when the nations met in Rome to create the International Criminal Court (ICC). President Clinton signed this treaty before leaving the White House. This global ICC now claims legal jurisdiction and binding verdict power over every nation and citizen on earth, including those who are citizens of nations that refuse to ratify the treaty. Now the ICC will be able to charge an American or Canadian peacekeeping soldier with war crimes anywhere on earth. Additionally, nations will have to turn to the International Monetary Fund (IMF) and World Bank for a financial bailout, but under the condition that borrowers abandon their historic national sovereignty to the UN.

The proposal to eliminate the veto power of the five superpowers in the UN Security Council would put the western democracies at the mercy of the majority votes of the 189 present member states in the UN General Assembly. We need to remember that the majority of these nations do not share our values concerning economic free enterprise, democracy, the rule of law, or religious freedom. The existing veto power in the UN Security Council is held by the United States, United Kingdom, France, Russia, and China. This veto power allows these superpowers to prevent any UN action against their fundamental national security interest. This power has prevented the potentially devastating problem of the UN coming into military conflict with a superpower with weapons of mass destruction. The elimination of the veto power could produce a very dangerous military confrontation in the future. In addition, proposals to greatly enhance the political power of the UN secretary-general would transform him from his present situation as an important diplomatic representative of the world body into a true global president—a potential world dictator as described in the ancient prophecies.

Henry Lamb, a researcher who has carefully studied global government, wrote:

> The foundation of global governance is a set of core values, a belief system, which contains ideas that are foreign to the American experience and ignores other values and ideas that are precious to the American experience. The values and ideas articulated in the Commission's report are not new. They have been tried, under different names, in other societies. Often, the consequences have been devastating.[26]

In 1994 the Ford Foundation created a United Nations study entitled *Renewing the United Nations System*, which recommended massive changes to streamline UN operations. Recommendations include that the United Nations General Assembly, Security Council, International Monetary Fund, World Health Organization, and International Labor Organization should be transferred to Bonn or New York to improve efficiency and centralize political control. The study suggested a radical new voting system for the International Monetary Fund to permit poor undeveloped nations to determine when and where loans would be made from wealthy nations to poor ones.[27]

These global governance proposals in *Renewing the United Nations System* are intended to set the stage for a coming one-world government. "While there is no question, *at present*, of the transformation of the UN system into a supranational authority, the organization is in a transitional phase, basically shaped and constrained by national sovereignty, but sometimes acting outside and beyond it" (emphasis added).[28] This important document repeatedly uses such expressions as "gradual limitation of sovereignty," "notable abridgements of national sovereignty," "chipping away at the edges of traditional sovereignty," as well as "small steps towards an eventual trans-sovereign society." The authors, Childers and Urqhart, enthusiastically describe the elite program to erode our nation's historic democratic sovereignty step-by-step. Significantly, the study suggests that this transition toward global government should proceed incrementally "until the world is ready for world government," to avoid a political backlash by the patriotic voters of the western nations who will ultimately be forced to surrender their political freedom and national sovereignty.

The study recommends that the United Nations should independently raise its own budget by assessing a global surcharge tax on all "arms sales," on "transnational movement of currencies," on "international trade," and "petroleum." They also suggest "a United Nations levy on international air and sea travel" as well as a "one day" income tax on all global citizens annually. These proposals provide compelling evidence that we are witnessing a well-planned transformation of the United Nations from an international consultative body into a global superstate. There are now calls for a "world people's assembly."[29]

Technology and the Mark of the Beast

John prophesied a cashless society during the last three and a half years of the rule of the Antichrist in the last days. Only those who possess a "mark" containing the digits "666" will be able to "buy or sell" and thus survive. The only way anyone can receive this "mark" is to worship the Antichrist as God and give him public allegiance. John wrote:

> And he causeth all, both small and great, rich and poor, free and bond, to receive a mark in their right hand, or in their foreheads: And that no man might buy or sell, save he that had the mark, or the name of the beast, or the number of his name. Here is wisdom. Let him that hath understanding count the number of the beast: for it

is the number of a man; and his number is Six hundred threescore and six. (Revelation 13:16–18)

This was an incomprehensible prophecy about the last days when John initially proclaimed it in the first century. It is only in the last few years that powerful advances in microchips have made such a personal identification and financial control system possible. John foretold the time when all currency, coin, and paper, will be replaced by something new—a cashless system that will be able to monitor every single financial transaction and thus reveal your purchases, your location, and your loyalty to the world dictator who will rule the coming global government during the Tribulation. The obvious advantages of credit and debit cards, smart cards, checks, electronic funds transfer, wire transfers, secure Internet transactions, and direct deposit have already replaced coins and paper currency for 97 percent of all financial transactions in North America and Europe Globally, less than five percent of the total money in our society still exists as paper currency or coins.

The book of Revelation foretold that the number 666 will be placed as a "mark" beneath the skin in the right hand or forehead in order to verify people's worship to the Antichrist and to monitor the activities of everyone living in the Antichrist's empire. High-technology industries are developing methods for miniature computer chips capable of holding your complete medical and financial records as well as your biometric identification beneath the skin. Recently, scientists developed a chip so powerful that it will hold between five and ten megabytes of information containing a person's complete financial, identification, and medical records in a chip the size of a grain of rice.

Implantable microchips can contain a miniature, passive radio-frequency transponder that requires no internal battery power to operate. These devices can store a permanent, unique identification number that can be read, but not modified, by a scanner. External scanners can be portable or they can be placed in doors and will activate the passive transponder chip by transmitting low frequency radio waves. The transponder chip, known as an implantable transponder or radio frequency identification device (RFID), will respond by sending the stored ID number to the scanning device. A variation on this involves an implantable microchip read-write device that allows the information in the chip to be changed from a distance through radio waves. Advanced implantable read-write microchips contain an internal power supply that emits an identification radio signal that enables you to be continuously tracked or monitored. Sophisticated data compression techniques allow this tiny chip to hold data equal to that contained in thirty complete sets of the *Encyclopedia Britannica.*

The latest generation of implantable microchips contain a miniature digital transceiver that is powered biologically for years through your natural bodily movements. The implanted devices are actually miniature computers that both receive and send data to remote sensors allowing continuous tracking through the global positioning system (GPS). An English professor at Reading University, Dr. Kevin Warwick, who has implanted a microcomputer in his body to enable him to monitor and control devices in his laboratory, stated, "The same computing power that once required an entire building to harness now can be inserted in your left arm."[30]

Business Week magazine reported on June 3, 1996 that MasterCard International is testing a new "smart card" computer chip that includes your fingerprint and other biological identification information that can be embedded in a credit/debit card. Card scanners in stores and banks will scan your fingerprint and compare it to the information on the card to verify your identity to prevent fraud or theft.

It is remarkable that the apostle John prophesied that the nations in the last days would operate their economies without cash. The cashless technology of these last days points directly to the prophecy of John about the Antichrist's Mark of the Beast as recorded in Revelation 13:16–18.

Instantaneous Global Television Communications

Incredibly, two thousand years ago, John described in Revelation 11 the phenomenon of worldwide instantaneous television communications. John foretold that during the future Tribulation, the Antichrist will kill God's two witnesses (Moses and Elijah). The Antichrist and the wicked population of earth will hate these witnesses of God who will stop the rain as well as unleash other supernatural judgments for three and a half years. John declared that the world will be delighted to witness the deaths of these two godly prophets, and will be able to observe their dead bodies lying unburied for three and a half days in the streets of Jerusalem. The book of Revelation declares that the population of the whole world will hold a party, exchanging gifts in their happy relief that their prophetic tormentors are finally dead. The New Testament prophesied that these wicked people will watch in astonishment as God will resurrect His two righteous witnesses to rise to heaven (Revelation 11:9–10).

This prophecy could never have been fulfilled during any past generation. Think about the details! How could the news that these two prophets were killed in Jerusalem by the Antichrist possibly travel around the globe in only three and a half days in any other generation than today? Only seventy years ago it would have taken a week for news to travel from Israel to Japan, New York, or San Francisco. Today, however, CNN and other global news organizations on television and the Internet immediately transmit photos, sound, and text about any important event throughout the globe instantaneously. For the first time in human history, this prophecy can be fulfilled literally.

Knowledge Shall Be Increased

Twenty-five centuries ago, Daniel predicted that there would be an explosion of knowledge paralleled by a huge increase in travel in the last days. Daniel wrote these words: "But thou, O Daniel, shut up the words, and seal the book, even to the time of the end: many shall run to and fro, and knowledge shall be increased" (Daniel 12:4).

Throughout thousands of years of history, the level of knowledge increased slowly and incrementally. In some centuries and nations, the level of general knowledge actually decreased for a time, such as during the thousand years known as the Dark Ages following the fall of Rome. Yet, since 1850 we have witnessed an explosion of knowledge in all fields beyond anything ever experienced in human history. There are more scientists alive today (500,000) than have lived in all of the rest of history. Recently it was calculated that the sum total of human knowledge is growing so quickly that it literally doubles every twenty-four months. This is intriguing in light of Daniel's ancient prediction that "knowledge shall be increased" at "the time of the end."

Daniel also referred to the fact that at "the time of the end: many shall run to and fro." This prediction appears to refer to the fact that the speed of travel will dramatically increase in the last days. From the dawn of history and throughout the thousands of years that followed, the highest speed attainable was approximately thirty-five miles an hour—the speed of a racing horse. During the middle of the 1800s the famous Pony Express developed a brilliantly conceived system involving twenty-four-hour relays of horses and riders that succeeded in transferring mail from St. Joseph, Missouri to Sacramento, California, in only nine days. However, in our generation, the speed of travel has accelerated to the point that astronauts can now travel at more than 18,000 miles an hour in the space shuttle.

An Earthquake Will Divide the Mount of Olives

The Bible foretells that, among the cataclysmic earthquakes and transformations that will occur during the upheavals of the Great Tribulation, a great earthquake will cause catastrophic damage at the very moment when Jesus Christ will return from heaven to descend to the summit of the Mount of Olives, the very place where He ascended in the clouds almost two thousand years ago. The two angels told His disciples as they stood on the top of the Mount of Olives, "This same Jesus, which is taken up from you into heaven, shall so come in like manner as ye have seen him go into heaven. Then returned they unto Jerusalem from the mount called Olivet, which is from Jerusalem a sabbath day's journey" (Acts 1:11–12).

The prophet Zechariah described this earthquake as follows: "And his feet shall stand in that day upon the mount of Olives, which is before Jerusalem on the east, and the mount of Olives shall cleave in the midst thereof toward the east and toward the west, and there shall be a very great valley; and half of the mountain shall remove toward the north, and half of it toward the south. And ye shall flee to the valley of the mountains; for the valley of the mountains shall reach unto Azal: yea, ye shall flee, like as ye fled from before the earthquake in the days of Uzziah king of Judah: and the Lord my God shall come, and all the saints with thee" (Zechariah 14:4–5).

Professor Bailey Willis of Leland Stanford University was an expert on earthquake activity. During a speech to the British Association of Science for the Advancement of Science, Dr. Willis discussed the recent geological research that revealed a significant earthquake fault line passed directly through the Holy City and the Mount of Olives. Professor Willis declared, "The region around Jerusalem is a region of potential earthquake danger. A 'fault line,' along which an earth slippage may occur at any time, passes directly through the Mount of Olives."[31]

The Generation That Will See the Lord's Return

The Scriptures teach that the final "last days" generation, the population who are living when Christ returns, will witness the fulfillment of numerous prophecies pointing to the soon return of the promised Messiah. Our generation of Christians has witnessed more fulfilled prophecies than any other generation in the two-thousand-year history of the Church. The visions of the Old Testament prophets, together with the New Testament's prophetic words of Jesus and His apostles, testify with one united voice that the generation that sees the fulfillment of these prophecies will also witness the triumphant victory of Jesus the Messiah over Satan. The establishment of the long-awaited Kingdom of God is at hand. In light of the incredible fulfillment of so many prophecies in our lifetime, we need to heed the prophetic words of Jesus Christ that speak especially to our generation: "And when these things begin to come to pass, then look up, and lift up your heads; for your redemption draweth nigh" (Luke 21:28).

The Lord has not left us in spiritual darkness concerning the approximate time of Christ's Second Coming. Although we are specifically warned that we cannot know "the day nor the hour wherein the Son of Man cometh" (Matthew 25:13), the fulfillment of dozens of specific prophecies in our generation strongly suggests that Jesus Christ's Second Coming will occur in our lifetime. Someday soon, without warning, the heavens will open "with a shout, with the voice of an archangel, and with the trumpet of God" (1 Thessalonians 4:16) announcing to all true Christians the awesome news that our years of anxiously waiting are finally over!

At that final moment of this age of God's grace, Jesus Christ will suddenly appear in the clouds to receive His Bride, His faithful Church composed of hundreds of millions of Christian saints, who will arise supernaturally in the air in their new resurrection bodies to meet their Lord and King and to ascend to their new home in heaven. Despite the dangers that lie ahead for humanity, those who truly love Jesus Christ as their personal Savior can rest secure in the knowledge that all these future climactic prophetical and historical events are totally in the Lord's hands. The apostle John concluded his great book of Revelation with the final promise of Jesus Christ. "He which testifieth these things saith, Surely I come quickly. Amen. Even so, come, Lord Jesus" (Revelation 22:20).

Notes

1. David Ben Gurion, *The Proclamation of the Rise of the State of Israel* (May 15, 1948).
2. Robert St. John, *Tongue of the Prophets* (Garden City, 1952).
3. Constantine F. Volney, *Travels Through Syria and Egypt in the Years 1783, 1784, 1785* (London: 1788) 2: 147.
4. *Report of the Commerce of Jerusalem During the Year 1863*, Foreign Office report (May, 1984)
5. "Demography of Jerusalem," http://www.jewishpeople.net/demofjer.html#Table 1.
6. Michel Calvo, *Sovereignty to G-d* (Everett: Jerusalem Ministries International, 2001).
7. Mark Twain, *The Innocents Abroad* (London: Chatto & Windus, 1881).
8. "Agritech Israel 99," http://www.israel.nl/ambassade/agritech/israel_agrcltr2.html.
9. "Agritech Israel 99," http://www.israel.nl/ambassade/agritech/israel_agrcltr2.html.
10. George T. B. Davis, *Fulfilled Prophecy That Proves the Bible* (Philadelphia: The Million Testaments Campaigns, 1931) 90.
11. Peter W. Stoner, *Science Speaks: An Evaluation of Certain Christian Evidences* (Chicago: Moody Press, 1963).
12. Yosef Zalmanson, *Arut-7* (September 28, 1999).
13. "One-Child Population Control Policy of Communist China," http://forerunner.com/lci/X0004_Population_Control_C.html, Life Control International.
14. "One-Child Population Control Policy of Communist China," http://forerunner.com/lci/X0004_Population_Control_C.html, Life Control International.
15. Oleg Limanov, "Central Asian strategy of China: political containment or economic involvement," *Marco Polo Magazine* Jan. 1999, http://www.google.com/search?q=cache:www.traceca.org/marco/mp17.pdf+Military+highway+across+asia+China+Pakistan&hl=en.

16. "New routes across Asia?" http://home.aigonline.com/content/0,1109,5753-649-ceo-,00.html, 2 Dec. 2000.

17. Michael Ross, *Los Angeles Times* 16 Jan. 1987.

18. http://www.arabicnews.com/ansub/Daily/Day/010118/2001011808.html.

19. http://hope-of-israel.org/saddam.html.

20. http://hope-of-israel.org/saddam.html.

21. "Babel's festival's participants call for lifting the embargo on Iraq," http://www.ArabicNews.com, 3 Oct. 2000.

22. David Lamb, "The Line in the Sand," *Los Angeles Times* 25 Nov. 1990.

23. Henry Lamb, *Report of the Commission on Global Governance: Our Global Neighborhood* (Jan/Feb, 1996).

24. Henry Lamb, *Report of the Commission on Global Governance: Our Global Neighborhood* (Jan/Feb, 1996).

25. *The Military Balance 2000/2001,* Institute of Strategic and International Studies (October 2000).

26. Henry Lamb, *Report of the Commission on Global Governance: Our Global Neighborhood* (Jan/Feb, 1996).

27. Erskine Childers and Brian Urqhart, *Renewing the United Nations System* (Motala: Motala Grafiska Ab,1994).

28. Erskine Childers and Brian Urqhart, *Renewing the United Nations System* (Motala: Motala Grafiska Ab, 1994) 19.

29. Erskine Childers and Brian Urqhart, *Renewing the United Nations System,* (Motala: Motala Grafiska Ab, 1994).

30. "Professor Warwick chips in," *Computerworld* 11 Jan. 1999.

31. George T.B. Davis, *Seeing Prophecy Fulfilled in Palestine* (Philadelphia: The Million Testaments Campaigns, 1937) 76.

11

How Should We Respond to the Coming Kingdom

Those who possess a strong faith in Christ's promise of His glorious Second Coming and the kingdom of God discover that their belief transforms their comprehension of the rest of the Scriptures as well. It is significant that Christians who enthusiastically accept the blessed hope of His imminent return strongly endorse the authority of the Word of God, affirm the deity of Christ, and are motivated to obey Jesus' command to "Go ye into all the world, and preach the gospel to every creature" (Mark 16:15). In my own experience, I have found that those who are animated by a deep love for the Lord's return are usually committed to a continuing study of the Scriptures and have great enthusiasm for evangelism and missions. When we fully accept the implications of the Second Advent, we find a compelling motivation to walk in holiness in the knowledge that we will someday soon give an account to our Lord for our daily walk before Him.

Effects of Belief in Imminent Second Coming

The belief in the imminent Second Coming and the literal kingdom of God expresses itself in numerous significant areas that support this as the true teaching of the Word of God.

Our Study of the Scriptures

Our belief in the reality of the return of the Lord and our expectation of His coming kingdom should motivate us to enter into a lifelong and serious study of the Word of God. Many of the great teachers of the Bible since the Reformation include those whom strongly uphold the literal kingdom of God and the Second Coming: Charles Ellicot, Frédéric Godet, Johann Lange, Robert Jamieson, Andrew Fausset, John Ryle, John Calvin, Huldrych Zwingle, Martin Luther, Philip Melanchthon, John Knox, John and Charles Wesley, John Bunyan, Hugh Latimer, Nicholas Ridley, Nathaniel West, Charles Spurgeon, Dwight L. Moody, William Blackstone, C. I. Scofield, George Peters, Dwight Pentecost, John Walvoord, Hal Lindsey, David Lewis, and Tim LaHaye. Over the last thirty-eight years, I have encountered thousands of Christians who have told me that their love of prophecy has motivated them to pursue an in-depth and lifelong study of the Bible.

Our Relationships with Others

Some critics who oppose the literal Second Coming and the reality of the kingdom of God raise a curious argument that suggests that belief in such will dissuade Christians from responsible caring for the earth or helping others in need. However, historical evidence supports that those who long for the Second Coming and His kingdom are usually found on the front lines of organizations for evangelism, world missions, as well as practical medical and social efforts. The financial support from these premillennial Christians formed a huge portion of those who supported world missions and evangelism during the last two centuries. Far from abandoning their concern for the world and its suffering humanity, those who love His soon return are motivated by their love for Christ to assist those in need.

Our Motivation to Walk in Holiness

The apostle John commands believers to live in holiness in light of Christ's return and His coming kingdom. "Beloved, now are we the sons of God, and it doth not yet appear what we shall be: but we know that, when he shall appear, we shall be like him; for we shall see him as he is. And every man that hath this hope in him purifieth himself, even as he is pure" (1 John 3:2–3). The primary motivation for the efforts of Christians lies in their expectation regarding their future. The Scriptures affirm the validity of this principle when the apostle Paul declared the importance of his expectations: "The time of my departure is at hand. I have fought a good fight, I have finished my course, I have kept the faith: Henceforth there is laid up for me a crown of righteousness, which the Lord, the righteous judge, shall give me at that day: and not to me only, but unto all them also that love his appearing" (2 Timothy 4:6–8).

Our Deepened Spiritual Life

Those who look daily for the return of the Lord from heaven to establish His kingdom on earth will naturally focus upon the eternal issues of holiness and withstand the fiery darts of Satan's temptations. The apostle Paul taught us that we need to rely upon the spiritual defenses that God has provided for us as detailed in this passage:

> Put on the whole armour of God, that ye may be able to stand against the wiles of the devil. For we wrestle not against flesh and blood, but against principalities, against powers, against the rulers of the darkness of this world, against spiritual wickedness in high places. Wherefore take unto you the whole armour of God, that ye may be able to withstand in the evil day, and having done all, to stand. Stand therefore, having your loins girt about with truth, and having on the breastplate of righteousness; and your feet shod with the preparation

of the gospel of peace; above all, taking the shield of faith, wherewith ye shall be able to quench all the fiery darts of the wicked. (Ephesians 6:11–16)

Surrendering Our Life to Christ

Those believers who truly accept the truth of the reality of the Second Coming will be motivated to abandon their earthly ambitions and follow Christ's command to seek righteousness. The apostle Paul wrote to his disciples and advised them to live in daily expectation of "the blessed hope":

> For the grace of God that bringeth salvation hath appeared to all men, teaching us that, denying ungodliness and worldly lusts, we should live soberly, righteously, and godly, in this present world; looking for that blessed hope, and the glorious appearing of the great God and our Saviour Jesus Christ. (Titus 2:11–13)

Our Repentance and Acceptance of Christ's Forgiveness

Paul wrote that God "now commandeth all men every where to repent: because he hath appointed a day, in the which he will judge the world in righteousness by that man whom he hath ordained; whereof he hath given assurance unto all men, in that he hath raised him from the dead" (Acts 17: 30–31).

In light of the precision of God's fulfillments of past and present prophecies concerning Israel and the nations, it is logical to conclude that the Lord will also fulfill Paul's prophecy about the final judgment of every one of us "because he hath appointed a day." Jesus warned His disciples, "When ye shall see all these things, know that it is near, even at the doors. Verily I say unto you, This generation shall not pass, till all these things be fulfilled" (Matthew 24:33–34). The preceding pages have focused on impending world events. As we turn to examine our personal future, we can see that these same incredibly accurate Scriptures prophesied that everyone will someday stand before God to give an account of how we have spent our lives and what we have done with the resources He placed at our disposal.

The book of Hebrews described our personal destiny: "It is appointed unto men once to die, but after this the judgment" (Hebrews 9:27).

Each of us has rebelled against God. The apostle Paul wrote, "For all have sinned, and come short of the glory of God" (Romans 3:23). Every one of us has rebelled and walked away from God, and we are therefore unfit to enter a holy heaven. God's Word declares, "For the wages of sin is death; but the gift of God is eternal life through Jesus Christ our Lord" (Romans 6:23). The Scriptures declare that our sin has alienated us from the holiness of God. Our continued sinful behavior and our rejection of Christ will prevent us from ever entering heaven until we repent and ask Christ to forgive us. Our genuine repentance and acceptance of the sacrificial death of Jesus Christ on the Cross is the only way we can find true peace in our hearts. The only way we can be filled with the grace of God is to ask Him to forgive us and accept Him as our Lord and Savior.

Jesus asked His disciples this vital question, "But whom say ye that I am?" His disciple Simon Peter answered and said, "Thou art the Christ, the Son of the living God" (Matthew 16:15–16). Every one of us must someday answer that same vital question. If the Bible truly is the Word of God, your answer to that question will determine your eternal spiritual destiny. Each of us must answer; we cannot evade it. If we refuse to answer, we have already chosen to reject Christ's claims to be our Lord and Savior. The Scriptures warn that the choices we make in this life will have eternal consequences in the world to come.

God declared, "For it is written, As I live, saith the Lord, every knee shall bow to me, and every tongue shall confess to God. So then every one of us shall give account of himself to God" (Romans 14:11–12). Therefore, all of us will someday bow our knee to Jesus Christ as King of Kings and acknowledge Him as Almighty God. The ultimate question is this: will you choose to repent of your sins now and bow your knee willingly to your Savior and Lord? Or, will you reject His offer of salvation now and be forced by His divine power to bow your knee before Jesus Christ as your final Judge when you are sent to an eternity in hell?

When we finally meet Jesus Christ at the end of our life, we must acknowledge whether we accepted or rejected His precious gift of salvation. When Jesus was crucified, He paid the full price for our sins. His final statement on the Cross was, "It is finished." As the sinless Lamb of God, Jesus allowed Himself to be offered as a perfect sacrifice to pay the price of our sins and to reconcile each of us to God. However, in a manner similar to a pardon offered to a prisoner awaiting execution, each of us must actually repent of our sins and personally accept Christ's pardon for His offer of salvation to become effective. The New Testament declares, "We shall all stand before the judgment seat of Christ" (Romans 14:10). The basis of God's judgment following our death will be our personal relationship with Jesus Christ—not whether we were better or worse than most other people—and this relationship alone will determine whether we will spend an eternity with God in heaven or an eternity without Him in hell.

Nicodemus, one of the righteous religious leaders of Israel, came to Jesus, and asked Him how he could be saved. Jesus answered, "Verily, verily, I say unto thee, Except a man be born again, he cannot see the kingdom of God" (John 3:3). It is not simply a matter of intellectually accepting the facts about Christ and salvation. To be born again, you must sincerely repent of your sinful life, ask Him to forgive you, and trust in Christ for the rest of your life. This decision will transform your life forever. God will give you a new purpose and meaning.

The Lord promises believers eternal life in heaven: "This is the will of him who sent me, that every one which seeth the Son, and believeth on him, may have everlasting life: and I will raise him up at the last day" (John 6:40). The moment a person commits his life to Christ, he receives God's promise of eternal life. Though your body will someday die, you will live forever with Christ in heaven. Jesus explained to Nicodemus, "For God so loved the world, that he gave his only begotten Son, that whosoever believeth in him should not perish, but have everlasting life" (John 3:16). Every sinner stands condemned by

God. Yet Jesus said, "He that believeth in him is not condemned: but he that believeth not is condemned already, because he hath not believed in the name of the only begotten Son of God" (John 3:18).

Jesus said, "I am the way, the truth, and the life: no man cometh unto the Father, but by me" (John 14:6). God has declared that there is no other path to salvation than accepting the "way, the truth, and the life" of Jesus Christ. Christ's sacrificial gift of His life paid the price for our sins. Every one of us, by accepting Jesus' pardon, can now stand before the judgment seat of God clothed in Christ's righteousness: "For he hath made him [Jesus] to be sin for us, who knew no sin; that we might be made the righteousness of God in him" (2 Corinthians 5:21).

This fact of Christ's atonement is perhaps the greatest mystery in creation. Jesus is the only one in history who, by His sinless life, was qualified to enter heaven. Yet He loved each one of us so much that He chose to die upon that Cross to purchase our salvation. In a marvelous act of God's mercy, the righteousness of Jesus will be placed to our account with God when we accept His offer of salvation. The apostle John wrote, "But as many as received him, to them gave he power to become sons of God, even to them that believe on his name" (John 1:12). Your decision to accept Christ as your personal Savior is the most important one you will ever make. It will change your eternal destiny, but it will also give you peace today as your guilt from sin will be removed forever.

However, this decision will cost you a great deal to live as a committed Christian. Many people will challenge your new faith in the Bible and in Christ. Your decision and commitment to Jesus Christ will change you in numerous ways including your relationships, goals, and activities. Your commitment to Christ will unleash His supernatural grace and power to transform your life into one of hope, joy, and peace beyond anything you have ever experienced. While the decision to follow Christ will cost you a lot, it will cost you far more if you do not accept Him as your Savior before you die. Jesus challenges us with these words, "For what shall it profit a man, if he shall gain the whole world, and lose his own soul?" (Mark 8:36).

All who have accepted Christ are called to be "witnesses" of Christ's message to our world. To be a faithful witness to Christ demands an active, not passive, involvement in the life of our Christian friends and relatives. It requires a willingness to pay the price of a personal commitment to our coming Messiah. Our belief in the imminent Second Coming should motivate us to witness to our unsaved brothers and sisters about His salvation.

The belief in the Second Coming will purify our walk before the Lord. John wrote: "And every man that hath this hope in him purifieth himself, even as he is pure" (1 John 3:3). If you are a Christian, I challenge you to share the evidence in this book to witness to your friends and family about your faith in Jesus Christ. As the prophetic clock ticks on toward the final midnight hour, the invitation of Christ remains open: "Behold, I stand at the door, and knock: if any man hear my voice, and open the door, I will come in to him, and will sup with him, and he with me" (Revelation 3:20). As the sixteenth-century writer Thomas Fuller once wrote, "You cannot repent too soon, because you do not know how soon it may be too late."

In the final chapter of his book of Revelation the prophet John recorded the angel's inspired encouragement to believers: "And he saith unto me, Seal not the sayings of the prophecy of this book: for the time is at hand" (Revelation 22:10). If the time of Christ's return was "at hand" nineteen hundred years ago, how much closer and more urgently "at hand" must His Second Coming be in our day? If the true followers of the Lord have watched, read the prophecies, and prayed for His return over so many centuries, how much more should we watch who live in this generation when so many of the prophetic signs are coming to pass before our very eyes? If it was time to awaken from spiritual sleep to hear the "Midnight Cry" of the coming Bridegroom then, surely it is our duty and calling in these last days to awaken each day with the thought "Perhaps today!"

The poetic writer Christina G. Rossetti wrote the following words in her book *The Face of the Deep*:
The night is far spent, the day is at hand:
Let us therefore cast off the works of darkness,
And let us put on the armour of light.
Night for the dead in their stiffness and starkness!
Day for the living who mount in their might
Out of their graves to the beautiful land.[1]

The ancient Scriptures warn us the generation of men living during the coming Tribulation will endure the greatest evil ever unleashed by Satan. The wrath of God will be poured out on unrepentant sinners during that unprecedented seven-year period. Satan himself will be unleashed by God to release his wrath against humanity. He will launch his relentless campaign to establish his satanic kingdom throughout the earth under the rule of his personal representative, the Antichrist. However, these same Scriptures assure us that Jesus Christ will return from heaven at the moment the earth faces its final crisis to defeat the armies of the Antichrist and save humanity from certain destruction. The prophets reveal that two-thirds of earth's population will die in horrific judgments, wars, famines, and plagues during this terrible seven-year period. Jesus Himself warned about the terrible global crisis that would occur just before He returns in glorious triumph. Matthew recorded His prophetic warning: "For then shall be great tribulation, such as was not since the beginning of the world to this time, no, nor ever shall be. And except those days should be shortened, there should no flesh be saved: but for the elect's sake those days shall be shortened" (Matthew 24:21–22).

However, this final trial of humanity in this age will end triumphantly with the glorious return of Jesus Christ from heaven with an army of powerful angels and the saints of all the ages. When Christ finally defeats the evil leaders of the world, He will establish His righteous government throughout the earth from His throne in Jerusalem. Ultimately, the sound of gunfire will be silenced forever, the terror of torture chambers will be destroyed, the horror of starvation and plague will be removed, and the fear of violence and abuse will be lifted from the hearts of men and women. Humanity will finally experience true peace under the kingdom of God ruled forever by the Messiah Jesus Christ. Christ's final promise is this:

> He which testifieth these things saith, Surely I come quickly. Amen. Even so, come Lord Jesus. (Revelation 22:20)

Notes

1. Christina G. Rossetti, *The Face of the Deep* (London: Society For Promoting Christian Knowledge, 1892).

Triumphant Return

Selected Bibliography

Alexander, Paul J. *The Byzantine Apocalyptic Tradition*. Berkley: University of California Press, 1985.

Anderson, Robert. *The Coming Prince*. London: Hodder & Stoughton, 1894.

Armstrong, Amzi. *Lectures on the Visions of the Revelation*. Morristown, PA: P. A. Johnson, 1815.

Atter, Gordon F. *Rethinking Bible Prophecy*. Peterborough, Ontario: College Press, 1967.

Barnes, Albert. *Notes on the Book of Daniel*. New York: Leavitt & Allen, 1855.

Barnes, Albert. *Notes on the Book of Revelation*. Edinburgh: Gall & Inglis, 1852.

Baylee, Joseph. *The Times of the Gentiles*. London: James Nisbet & Co., 1871.

Blackstone, Wm. E. *Jesus Is Coming*. London: Fleming H. Revell, 1908.

Blackstone, Wm. E. *The Millennium*. New York: Fleming H. Revell, 1888.

Bloomfield, Arthur, E. *A Survey of Bible Prophecy*. Minneapolis, Minn.: Bethany Fellowship, 1971.

Bloomfield, Arthur E. *The End of the Days*. Minneapolis: Bethany Fellowship, 1961.

Brooks, James H. *Maranatha*. Chicago: Fleming H. Revell, 1889.

Bullinger, E. W. *The Apocalypse*. London: Eyre & Spottiswoode, 1909.

Burnett, Bishop. *The Sacred Theory of the Earth*. London: 1816.

Butterfield, Herbert. *Christianity and History*. New York: Charles Scribner and Sons, 1949.

Chaldler, Bishop Edward. *A Defence of Christianity from the Prophecies of the Old Testament*. London: James and John Knapton, 1725.

Charles, R. H. *A Critical and Exigetical Commentary on the Revelation of St. John*. 2 vols. Edinburgh: T. and T. Clark, 1920.

Chilton, David. *The Days of Vengeance*. Tyler, TX: Dominion Press, 1987.

Coates, C. A. *An Outline of the Revelation*. London: Stow Hill Bible Depot and Publishing Office, 1985.

Culver, Robert Duncan. *Daniel and the Latter Days*. Chicago: Moody Press, 1977.

Cummings, John. *Lectures on the Book of Daniel*. Philadelphia: Lindsay and Blakiston, 1855.

Cummings, John. *Apocalyptic Sketches*. London: Hall, Virtue and Co., 1850.

Davidson, John. *Discourses on Prophecy*. London: John Murray & Co., 1825.

Dean, I. R. *The Coming Kingdom—The Goal of Prophecy*. Philadelphia: Philadelphia School of the Bible, 1928.

Edersheim, Alfred. *The Life and Times of Jesus the Messiah*. 2 vols. New York: Longmans, Green, and Co., 1896.

Edersheim, Alfred. *The Temple: Its Ministry and Services as They Were at the Time of Christ.* Grand Rapids: William B. Eerdmans Publishing Co., 1980.

Elliott, E. E. *Horae Apocalyptic.* London: Seeley, Burnside, & Seeley, 1846.

Eusebius. *Eusebius' Ecclesiastical History.* Oxford: The Clarendon Press, 1881.

Feinberg, Charles. *Premillennialism or Amillennialism?* Grand Rapids: Zondervan Publishing, 1936.

Fruchtenbaum, Arnold G. *The Footsteps of the Messiah.* Tustin: Ariel Press, 1982.

Gentry, Kenneth L. *Before Jerusalem Fell: Dating the Book of Revelation.* Fort Worth: Institute for Christian Economics, 1989.

Graham, Billy. *Approaching Hoofbeats: The Four Horsemen of the Apocalypse.* Waco: Word Publishing, 1983.

Guinness, H. Grattan. *The Approaching End of the Age.* London: Hodder & Stoughton, 1882.

Gundry, Robert H. *The Church and the Tribulation.* Grand Rapids: Zondervan Publishing, 1977.

Haldeman, I. M. *The Coming Of Christ.* New York: Chas. C. Cook, 1906.

Hallifax, Dr. Samuel. *Twelve Sermons on the Prophecies Concerning the Christian Church.* London: T. Cadell, 1776.

Harrison, William K. *Hope Triumphant: Studies on the Rapture.* Chicago: Moody Press, 1966.

Hawley, Charles A. *The Teaching of Apocrypha and Apocalypse.* New York: Association Press, 1925.

Ironside, H. A. *Lectures on the Book of Revelation.* New York: Loizeaux Brothers, 1930.

Jarvis, Rev. Samuel F. *The Church of the Redeemed.* Boston: 1950.

Josephus, Flavius. *The Jewish War*. Edited by Gaalya Cornfeld. Grand Rapids: Zondervan Publishing House, 1982.

Jones, Alexander, ed. *The Jerusalem Bible*. Garden City, N.Y.: Doubleday, 1968.

Keith, Rev. Alexander. *The Signs of the Times*. Edinburgh: William White & Co., 1832.

Kellogg, Dr. Samuel. *The Jews or Prediction and Fulfillment*. New York: Anson D. F. Randolf & Co., 1883.

Kidron, Michael and Dan Smith. *The War Atlas*. London: Pan Books, 1983.

Ladd, George. *The Blessed Hope*. Grand Rapids, Mich.: Wm. B. Eerdmans, 1956.

LaHaye, Tim. *No Fear of the Storm*. Sisters, OR: Multnomah Press, 1992.

LaHaye, Tim. *The Beginning of the End*. Wheaton, IL: Tyndale, 1976.

Larkin, Clarence. *Rightly Dividing The Word*. Philadelphia: Erwin W. Moyer Co., 1943.

Larkin, Clarence. *The Book of Daniel*. Philadelphia: Clarence Larkin, 1949.

Lindsay, Hal. *The Late Great Planet Earth*. Grand Rapids, MI: Zondervan Publishing, 1970.

Litch, Josiah. *Messiah's Throne and Millennial Glory*. Philadelphia: Joshua V. Himes, 1855.

Litt, Charles, R. H. *Studies In The Apocalypse*. Edinburgh: T. & T. Clark, 1913.

Lockyer, Herbert. *All The Messianic Prophecies Of The Bible*. Grand Rapids: Zondervan Publishing, 1973.

Ludwigson, R. *A Survey of Bible Prophecy*. Grand Rapids: Zondervan Publishing, 1951.

Marsh, John. *An Epitome of General Ecclesiastical History*. New York: J. Tilden & Co., 1843.

McGinn, Bernard. *Visions of the End*. New York: Columbia University Press, 1979.

Mesorah Publications. *Daniel: A New Commentary Anthologized From Talmudic, Midrashic and Rabbinical Sources*. Brooklyn, NY: Mesorah Publications, 1980.

Newton, Bishop Thomas. *Dissertations on the Prophecies*. 2 vols. London: R & R Gilbert, 1817.

Patrides, C. A. and Joseph Wittreich. *The Apocalypse in English Literature*. Ithaca, NY: Cornell University Press, 1984.

Payne, J. Barton. *Encyclopedia of Biblical Prophecy*. Grand Rapids: Baker Book House, 1980.

Pentecost, Dwight. *Things to Come*. Grand Rapids, MI: Dunham, 1958.

Peters, George. *The Theocratic Kingdom*. 3 vols. Grand Rapids: Kregel Publications, 1957.

Pusey, E. B. *Daniel the Prophet*. Plymouth, UK: The Devonport Society, 1864.

Riley, William B. *The Evolution of the Kingdom*. New York: Chas. C. Cook, 1913.

Rossetti, Christina. *The Face of the Deep*. London: Society for Promoting Christian Knowledge, 1895.

Russell, J. Stuart. *The Parousia*. Grand Rapids: Baker Book House, 1983.

Seiss, Joseph. *The Apocalypse*. Philadelphia: Approved Books, 1865.

Showers, Renald. *Maranatha Our Lord, Come!* Bellmawr, NJ: The Friends of Israel Gospel Ministry, 1995.

Smith, Chuck. *The Tribulation & the Church*. Costa Mesa, Cal.: The Word for Today, 1980.

Stuart, Moses. *Commentary of the Apocalypse*. 2 vols. Andover, MI: Allen, Morrill and Wardwell, 1845.

Taylor, G. F. *The Second Coming Of Jesus*. Franklin Springs, GA: The Publishing House, 1950.

Thompson, J. L. *That Glorious Future*. London: Morgan and Scott, 1887.

The Ante-Nicene Fathers. 10 vols. Grand Rapids: Eerdmans Publishing Co., 1986.

Tinbergen, Jan. *Reshaping The International Order: A Report to the Club of Rome*. Scarborough, Ontario: The New American Library of Canada, 1976.

Tristram, H. B. *The Seven Golden Candlesticks*. London: The Religious Tract Society, 1872.

Walvoord, John F. Daniel, *The Key to Prophetic Revelations. A Commentary*. Chicago: Moody Press, 1971.

Walvoord, John F. *The Rapture Question*. Findlay: Dunham Publishing Co., 1957.

Weber, Timothy P. *Living in the Shadow of the Second Coming*. New York: Oxford University Press, 1979.

West, Nathaniel. *Second Coming of Christ—Premillennial Essays*. Chicago: Fleming H. Revell, 1879.